Exploring ELF

THE CAMBRIDGE APPLIED LINGUISTICS SERIES

The authority on cutting-edge Applied Linguistics research

Series Editors 2007–present: Carol A. Chapelle and Susan Hunston
1988–2007: Michael H. Long and Jack C. Richards

For a complete list of titles please visit: www.cambridge.org/elt/cal

Recent titles in this series:

Genres across the Disciplines
Student Writing in Higher Education
Hilary Nesi and Sheena Gardner

Disciplinary Identities
Individuality and Community in Academic Discourse
Ken Hyland

Replication Research in Applied Linguistics
Edited by Graeme Porte

The Language of Business Meetings
Michael Handford

Reading in a Second Language
Moving from Theory to Practice
William Grabe

Modelling and Assessing Vocabulary Knowledge
Edited by Helmut Daller, James Milton and Jeanine Treffers-Daller

Practice in a Second Language
Perspectives from Applied Linguistics and Cognitive Psychology
Edited by Robert M. DeKeyser

Feedback in Second Language Writing
Contexts and Issues
Edited by Ken Hyland and Fiona Hyland

Task-Based Language Education
From Theory to Practice
Edited by Kris van den Branden

Second Language Needs Analysis
Edited by Michael H. Long

Insights into Second Language Reading
A Cross-Linguistic Approach
Keiko Koda

Research Genres
Explorations and Applications
John M. Swales

Critical Pedagogies and Language Learning
Edited by Bonny Norton and Kelleen Toohey

Exploring the Dynamics of Second Language Writing
Edited by Barbara Kroll

Understanding Expertise in Teaching
Case Studies of Second Language Teachers
Amy B. M. Tsui

Criterion-Referenced Language Testing
James Dean Brown and Thom Hudson

Corpora in Applied Linguistics
Susan Hunston

Pragmatics in Language Teaching
Edited by Kenneth R. Rose and Gabriele Kasper

Cognition and Second Language Instruction
Edited by Peter Robinson

Learning Vocabulary in Another Language
I. S. P. Nation

Research Perspectives on English for Academic Purposes
Edited by John Flowerdew and Matthew Peacock

Computer Applications in Second Language Acquisition
Foundations for Teaching, Testing and Research
Carol A. Chapelle

Exploring ELF

Academic English shaped by non-native speakers

Anna Mauranen

University of Helsinki

CAMBRIDGE UNIVERSITY PRESS
Cambridge, New York, Melbourne, Madrid, Cape Town,
Singapore, São Paulo, Delhi, Mexico City

Cambridge University Press
The Edinburgh Building, Cambridge CB2 8RU, UK

Published in the United States of America by Cambridge University Press, New York

www.cambridge.org
Information on this title: www.cambridge.org/9780521177528

First published 2012

Printed and Bound in Great Britain by the MPG Books Group

A catalogue record for this publication is available from the British Library

Library of Congress Cataloging in Publication Data

Mauranen, Anna.
Exploring ELF : academic English shaped by non-native speakers/Anna Mauranen.
p. cm. – (Cambridge applied linguistics series)
Includes bibliographical references and index.
ISBN 978-0-521-17752-8 (pbk.) – ISBN 978-1-107-00395-8 (hardback)
1. English language–Study and teaching–Foreign speakers. I. Title.

PE1128.A2M373 2012
420.71–dc23
2012009994

ISBN 978-0-521-17752-8 Paperback
ISBN 978-1-107-00395-8 Hardback

Contents

Series editors' preface

For many years now, the majority of users of English worldwide have been people for whom it is a second (or third, or fourth) language. Increasingly, English is used as a shared common language (a lingua franca) between people with different language backgrounds. This has led to an expansion in the communities of people who have ownership of English. English is not solely the preserve of people who use it in all areas of their lives; those who have English as part of a repertoire of languages, and who use it in only some contexts, have a right also to determine how it is used. Professor Mauranen's timely study of English as a lingua franca (ELF) is set against this background. She focuses on communities of academics working in northern Europe, all of whom use English in their working lives, and who, specifically, use English as the common language of communication among groups comprising various nationalities. She seeks to establish what is distinctive about ELF, in lexis, grammar, and discourse, using a corpus of spoken academic lingua franca English (ELFA) as the main resource for her study.

This book sets out a framework for studies of this kind, considering large-scale sociolinguistic issues, but also more localised interpersonal issues and, turning to the individual, the cognitive consequences of using a lingua franca. It raises intriguing questions such as how research into language proficiency should be carried out when there is no agreed standard language against which the language use is compared. And it contains a wealth of information and examples about how speakers of ELF negotiate norms of usage and discourse rules.

Professor Mauranen is careful to distinguish between a user of ELF and learners of English. At the same time, everything she says is of relevance to teachers of English worldwide, whose students increasingly need the language as a global lingua franca. In the final chapter of the book, she considers in detail some issues of language teaching and testing raised by her research.

Although this book is about a specific language, English, and a particular set of situations summarised as 'academic', it addresses larger themes too. English is an example of a language that is changing as it 'goes global', and Professor Mauranen uses the evidence from her corpus to propose models of what happens to a language in this situation.

The existence of ELF presents challenges to language researchers and language teachers. For thousands of individuals, however, it is not an issue, a question, or a problem but simply a way in which daily communication gets done. Professor Mauranen's book reflects, describes, and theorises this situation. It is a welcome addition to the series.

Carol A. Chapelle and Susan Hunston

Acknowledgements

I have been meaning to write a book about academic ELF since we made the first recordings that ended up in the ELFA corpus some ten years ago. When ELFA was finally completed in 2008, I started to work on the corpus. Until then, only parts of it had been usable. In late 2009 I drafted the first chapters, and found the data and writing about it just as inspiring as I had imagined. A selection of my explorations are presented in this book.

Compiling a corpus is a shared enterprise that requires a great deal of teamwork. The wonderful research teams I have had at Helsinki and, before that, Tampere have been crucial not only for the compilation of the corpus, but for the pleasure of discovery and discussion. We have shared our work, organized events together, written and edited publications, and I have benefited from everyone's contributions. I thank Niina Hynninen, Elina Ranta, Maria Metsä-Ketelä, Jaana Suviniitty, Diane Pilkinton-Pihko, Svetlana Vetchinnikova, Henrik Hakala, Ray Carey, and Anna Solin for sharing their research and ideas and for their delightful company. Many other students and research assistants have worked with and contributed to the corpus; even though I cannot mention them all, I would like to single out Mari Sihvonen for her invaluable work with recordings and transcription.

In the early days when English as a lingua franca was not as popular as it has become over the last five years or so, it was marvellous to find like-minded colleagues with whom to share the conviction that there is something in ELF, and that it is worth the effort to gather data about it. Barbara Seidlhofer, Jennifer Jenkins, and Henry Widdowson deserve my warmest thanks for all the joint events that we participated in, the discussions we've had over the years, and all the fun. Their research teams and doctoral students have also been important in taking the field forward and to me personally.

Over the years, I have also benefited from discussions with many colleagues who have shared their ideas with me. First and foremost I am grateful to John Sinclair, who inspired me to think of language in new ways. On research into academic discourse, I have enjoyed a shared interest and many great discussions with John Swales, Susan Hunston, Tony Dudley-Evans, and Marina Bondi among many others.

I owe a debt of gratitude to all those people who gave permission to be recorded, and whose names I do not even know. Research into natural language would not be possible without their unprejudiced willingness to participate and cooperate.

This work would not have been possible without the Academy of Finland's support for the ELFA project, the support of the University of Helsinki for the SELF project and that of the Copenhagen Business School, which hosted me during a peaceful and pleasant five-month period of research and writing in 2010.

1 *Introduction*

What happens to a language when it goes global? We do not really know. It may look like any other language, only bigger. Or scale may do something new to it. What we do know is that when languages get very small, below a certain level they disappear fast, because there is no community to sustain them. When they get very large, they tend to spread themselves thinly and start diversifying. When they get enormous, and a lion's share of the use is as a lingua franca – this is uncharted territory.

This book addresses English as a lingua franca (ELF) – its characteristics, processes of use, and the linguistic consequences of its unprecedented spread. Clearly, this is a vast area of study, and one book can but scratch the surface. What I have chosen to do is to put one territory into special focus, and criss-cross that area with a few paths so as to get an overview of the landscape and what more there might be to be discovered. My province is academia, and in this domain I analyse samples and endeavour to see what they might tell us about the wider scene of which they form a part.

Academia is a good choice for exploration because it is inherently international, its domain spans the globe, and it has settled on English as its common language. The academy relies on verbal communication, exchanging concepts and ideas that are abstract, novel, and complex; academic discussion makes sophisticated demands on verbal skills. How speakers manage in a lingua franca in such circumstances tells a very different story from studies describing the spontaneous development of pidgins or lingua francas between speakers or groups to cope with rudimentary communicative needs. The growing global higher education market brings a vast proportion and a typologically diverse selection of the world's languages into contact with English. This gives us a rare opportunity to investigate the intricacies of language contact of unforeseen complexity.

The exploration of ELF has potential for uncovering general, perhaps universal, features of language use – processing, change, and language in interaction. In this lies its theoretical contribution. It helps gauge phenomena that are similar in language use across the board, whether speakers and environments are monolingual or multilingual, what aspects may be shared by second language use and language contact, and what might be specific to lingua francas, or just to ELF itself.

Among the general theoretical and descriptive issues are matters of processes: how do speakers go about dealing with the contingencies of communicating in a non-native language? We can pose questions about multilingual processing as a cognitive phenomenon, taking into account the contingencies of online processing, or we can look at it in terms of communicative strategies, such as discourse reflexivity. Both are taken on board in this book, with the focus distinctly on language and discourse.

A wider perspective of language change as a consequence of language contact presents questions arising from today's increased geographic and social mobility: although it is known that language change accelerates in periods of mobility, there are also centripetal forces counteracting change, seeking commonalities across uses and users, in order to secure a sufficient level of comprehensibility. Language change may also be affected by numbers of speakers. As Croft (2000: 204) points out, a possible scenario where native speakers accept and adopt non-native features is when native speakers are outnumbered by non-natives. Like many sociolinguists discussing language contact, he speaks of 'shifting' speakers, which does not directly apply to ELF: lingua francas are used by speakers who maintain their first languages. Thus, even though speakers who use English as an additional language outnumber native speakers (speakers of English as a native language, ENL), their influence is even harder to predict than the direction of language change in general. The question of numbers is nevertheless important, as are the shifting parameters of prestige. Standard English is the unquestioned prestige variety at the moment, but since the status of languages and varieties normally follows that of their speakers, alterations in social and political power on the international scene may well affect the balance between different Englishes as well.

ELF is, then, also specifically about English. As we go about describing characteristics of ELF, the questions that arise are particularly interesting for probing variability and regularity: how do they relate to other Englishes? English has diversified as it has spread around the world, giving rise to a large number of indigenised varieties. Over the last couple of decades, World Englishes have attracted lively research (Kachru 1990; Kortmann et al. 2004; Schneider 2006; Mesthrie & Bhatt 2008; papers in Kirkpatrick 2010, to name but a few). Even though it is out of reach of the present book to make comparisons beyond some sporadic observations, developments in second-language varieties (Mukherjee & Hundt 2011) are significant to ELF and changing English. Similarities and parallels with present or past developments in native English (such as the recent increase in *-ing* form, see Smith 2005; Mair 2006; Ranta 2006) raise further issues about changes in language and the constraints that a given matrix language imposes. Features of lexis, grammar, and phraseology are likely to be affected, as is pragmatic usage. The consequences of the massive volume of ELF to English taken as a whole, as the aggregate use of the language, is essentially a descriptive issue: what new features of English are emerging and taking hold?

The timescale of language change is variable, with some changes occurring rapidly and others slowly, and in many cases old forms will linger on alongside innovations. Some strata or systems of language are more susceptible to change than others, and lexis has usually been found to be the site of rapid spread of influences, in contrast to structure, which is more resistant. Fast changes may nevertheless be more ephemeral, and it seems that the robustness of linguistic elements is in part dependent on the timescale that we adopt in assessing it. It is not an easy task to set an appropriate timescale for assessing change triggered by the use of ELF, or to give definitive answers concerning the features that have changed or will change. We can observe features that are common to ELF in different contexts, but their possible influence on English as a whole takes longer to observe. This issue is taken up in Chapter 2, and discussed further in connection with empirical analyses in later chapters. What seems clear at this point is that the worldwide spread of English, carefully described in several recent treatises (e.g. Crystal 1997; Brutt-Griffler 2002; Jenkins 2009), has continued from the early seventeenth century through different phases and under different circumstances, but that the most recent, explosive expansion could perhaps most reasonably be timed to coincide with the rise of the Internet. This took place in the mid-1990s and had an enormous effect on global communication in ELF: on this count, we are living the first generation of ELF.

English must have been used as a lingua franca from very early days (as far back as we can speak of 'English'), most likely long before any written records survive. However, as a phenomenon of a global scale, ELF is relatively new. Its nature and position is only gradually making its way to common awareness, where well-entrenched conceptualisations operate in terms of native speakers and language learners.

A question that often arises when discussing ELF with people who are new to it, or have only vaguely heard about it, is: how is ELF different from learner language? This topic is not very prominent in the rest of this book, although comparisons to learner language come up here and there. Therefore, to clarify the difference and at the same time to illustrate certain basic issues about ELF, I draw some distinctions between learner language and lingua francas at this point. The discussion is also intended to illuminate the approach to ELF adopted in this book, namely a three-level view on lingua francas: a macrosocial, a cognitive, and a microsocial or interactive perspective.

Using a lingua franca means being a user of a second language (L2) but not a learner. We can draw a line between second language use (SLU) and second language acquisition (SLA), with important implications. They have of course much in common: fundamental bilingual processes must be essentially very similar whenever the simultaneous use of more than one language is being dealt with. Learners, translators, and other bilingual users such as early bilinguals, initial monolinguals with their later languages, or plurilinguals with their complex mixture of language resources can be assumed to share some processing mechanisms. It is also a reasonable guess that a speaker's later languages are less well entrenched than their first. Similarities found across bilingual language use are therefore not surprising. All speakers probably have common processes in their first, second, and *n*th languages, such as memory storage and retrieval in terms of neural pathway formation, information chunking, or simultaneous processing and monitoring. One would nevertheless expect that things like ease and speed of retrieval, access to alternative expressions, or mapping linguistic and social repertoires routinely onto each other operate differently in a speaker's first and other languages. By and large, processes that diverge from monolingual first language use are likely to have much in common among all bi- or multilinguals, and therefore research on any group is of interest to the study of all the others. Together they deepen our understanding of the fascinating multifariousness of human languages in use: monolingualism is neither the typical condition nor the gold standard.

Much of what separates learners and users boils down to the peculiar social environment of the classroom. A classroom is a social environment of its own kind which imposes particular social positions on learners that do not hold outside its confines. The learner position outweighs any other social parameters in a classroom setting, whereas outside the classroom other social parameters override learner status. Educational and classroom goals are relevant from a learner position, and they regulate the norms of interaction in every respect. This is particularly obvious in giving and receiving instructions or feedback, providing and following models of behaviour, and in practices of assessing performance. Some pedagogical genres are entirely confined to educational environments, such as particular kinds of question–

answer sequences, fill-in exercises, essays, or 'composition'. Out of the bounds of educational settings, interactional parameters do not follow classroom rules. While it is possible to negotiate and transcend such borderlines at times, this does not often happen; even when a non-native speaker is assuming a learner position relative to a native-speaker interlocutor, native speakers tend to orient to them as speakers, attending to the contents of what is being said, not correcting their language (see Kurhila 2003, 2006).

It is often pointed out that people can alternate in these roles – in the classroom they are learners, but as soon as they get outside they may turn into users of the same language. Thus, the argument goes, the identities are inseparable because the people are the same. However, identities are not simple and constant, but assumed situationally. Different identities and their elements are foregrounded, backgrounded, and drawn on in response to the social environment. When people enter an educational context as learners, their position shifts from that of a user.

A learner identity can also be seen as reductive and limiting, as has been pointed out by Firth and Wagner (1997) who criticise the SLA research paradigm for precisely that: seeing learners as deficient communicators who struggle with difficulties. Firth and Wagner called for a broader basis of SLA studies that would embrace the everyday use of a second language outside classroom settings and include L2–L2 communication. Lingua franca research is one way of broadening the horizon for SLA in this way, expanding it to include SLU.

Sociocultural corollaries of the classroom vs. lingua franca difference include cultural assumptions and the relationship with 'target culture'. ELF speakers do not share a cultural background or a first language, whereas in a vast number of classrooms around the world one or both are shared. Much pedagogical effort rests on the assumption that learners of the same native language will have similar problems with a target language and are therefore offered similar remedies. In an environment of shared linguistic and cultural assumptions, orientation to the new language is also shared, and along with it, cultural identities and expectations relative to target language speakers. English-speaking countries, or more precisely in Kachru's (e.g. 1985, 1990) terminology, the 'inner circle', constitute 'target cultures' which learners are to view against their own cultural background for comparison, contrast, and models of target appropriateness. In contrast, a lingua franca is chosen as a matter of convenience or necessity, and interlocutors may know little of each other's cultural backgrounds or be unfamiliar with Anglo-American cultures. Conventions of English-speaking cultures may be quite inappropriate when communicative effectiveness hinges upon dealing with cultural mixes of different kinds. A definable, let alone national, target culture for norms of appropriateness or politeness is irrelevant and unreliable as a repertoire of shared assumptions.

A sociolinguistic question of a more macrosocial kind is the relationship to Standard English. It is perhaps useful to distinguish standards, as 'imposed norms', from natural, or spontaneous, norms. Norms can be imposed from outside, and standard languages have been a typical case of such societal regulation, particularly pronounced in nineteenth-century Europe with the development of the nation-state. Such imposed standards are different from the natural norms that arise in groups and communities primarily in face-to-face interaction to regulate interaction in the interests of mutual intelligibility and smooth communicative progress. Natural norms arise from what a speech community adopts, tolerates, or rejects. 'Norms' can thus refer either to those imposed in standard languages or to the much more variable norms of language communities, which include non-standard varieties and variant forms. The distinction is not always clearly maintained in discussions where 'native-speaker norms' are confusingly referred to in either meaning. The issue is perhaps further blurred in corpus-based language teaching, where the preferred usage as manifest in native-speaker data is taken as a model. This is obviously a more accurate reflection of natural speech community norms than prescriptive reference works, including as it does some variability. However, reference corpora are not compiled with wide sociolinguistic representation in mind; they are biased towards standard language and 'good usage'.

It is standard language that guides learners and teachers. Learner language cannot influence the target language by definition, because learners are committed to acquiring proficiency in terms of given standards. Learners get corrected for their errors, and accept the correction because it is in line with the goals of the whole enterprise of learning – and the target language remains intact. ELF does not have a 'target language' because it is a vehicular language itself, an instrument for achieving communication. Although ELF is typically associated with fleeting encounters between strangers, it is also the working language of more long-lasting communities, for example business, trade, or academia. Spontaneous norms arise in communities of these kinds; they can thus become endonormative for their own duration and purposes. In the absence of linguistic authority other than communicative efficiency, group norms are negotiated internally. Communities of practice can share members, individuals in them change and move across communities; in this way these mobile individuals become agents of spreading the practices of one community to the next. In brief, the diffusion of usages initiated in ELF communities resembles the mechanisms of diffusion of innovations or dialect features in ENL communities. Communities of this kind, with some duration, are likely sites for innovations that may spread to the language beyond their own boundaries, as will be discussed in Chapter 2.

In cognitive terms, lingua franca speech orients to achieving mutual comprehension. Many ELF scholars have noted a strong orientation to content over form in ELF discourse (e.g. Karhukorpi 2006; Ehrenreich 2009), in line with researchers working on L1–L2 interaction in real-life conversations (Kurhila 2006). In contrast, learners' cognitive orientation is far more towards language form. This is a consequence of the pedagogical setting, where learning things like grammar or phonology are necessarily in focus. Feedback and evaluation are based on mastering elements of the language, and it is hard to imagine an educational setting where this would not be so. Although long-term objectives of SLA curricula are often defined in real-life communicative terms, those objectives remain outside the classroom. They can only be simulated in class, but not performed there. Real-life communication cannot be assessed in class for success or effectiveness outside it. Communicative simulations may be pedagogically useful, as Widdowson has often pointed out (e.g. 2000), even realistic and meaningful, but not authentic in its basic sense of being real (cf. Mauranen 2004a). Success in SLA and SLU contexts thus depends on different criteria, and the situated cognitive orientation in SLA and SLU consequently diverge.

The cognitive load in ELF is unusually heavy on account of the variety and unpredictability of language parameters: interlocutors' accents, transfer features, and proficiency levels. Even in multilingual classrooms such variability is more confined, and speakers adapt to their classmates' speech fairly soon on account of regular contact (cf. Smit 2010).

At the interface of the wider social context and an individual's cognitive determinants of processing is social interaction, by means of which speakers go about negotiating language and the norms of interaction itself. ELF speakers typically find themselves in situations where discourse norms are not clear or given: group norms are negotiated within ELF groups by participants, none of whom can claim the status of a linguistic model. Even if ENL speakers are present, they can decline the role of language expert (Hynninen forthcoming). ELF speakers engage in various interactive strategies to achieve mutual comprehensibility; they seem to be prepared for the possibility of misunderstanding and take steps to pre-empt that, which in effect results in misunderstandings being rare (Mauranen 2006a; Kaur 2009). In co-constructing comprehension, any solutions that serve the purpose may be adopted by common consent – the best solutions need not be the most standard-like or native-like (see Hülmbauer 2009). Practices ruled out in L2 classrooms, like language mixing, can be effective strategies in ELF communication (e.g. Klimpfinger 2009). In mediating norms, speakers may even deliberately appeal to practices that are international although not in accordance with British or American norms (Hynninen 2011). For learners the appropriate discourse conventions are those of the target culture, just like lexicogrammatical standards. Native-speaker authority and superior expertise are axiomatic for foreign-language learners, and native preferences at all levels of language use are to be emulated for improved proficiency. Clearly, classroom tasks can require learners to attend to comprehensibility. The difference here is one of emphasis: for users it is a constant determiner of behaviour, for learners it may be desirable but not vital, since the classroom safety net will prevent major disasters ensuing from communication breakdown.

The consequences of these differences are reflected in appropriately different research design and data compilation principles for learner and ELF studies, as will be discussed further in Chapter 3. Here it is enough to point out that the two fundamental differences relate to speaker proficiency and participants' native language. SLA data rests on controlling for learner proficiency as carefully as possible, whereas for an ELF study this would be an untenable solution, because it is in the nature of lingua franca communication that speakers' proficiencies are variable. For learner research, first-language backgrounds are also usually kept separate, and each represented in comparable proportions. In contrast, realistic data for lingua franca research should include first languages in different mixes.

Learners are primarily identified by reference to their role in the education system. ELF speakers must be identified with respect to a definition of a lingua franca. This book adopts a general definition compatible with the traditional concept of a lingua franca as a vehicular language used by speakers who do not share a first language. This is a situation-based definition, and speakers may take on the identity of a lingua franca speaker in response to situational demands, irrespectively of whether in other situations they approach the same language as a target language to be learned. However, on a more stable basis, the prototypical ELF speaker is one who uses English habitually without either being a native speaker or a learner.

Our definition excludes contexts where English is the object of study, therefore English courses and CLIL (Content and Language Integrated Learning) are ruled out. What about the native speaker? Can we speak of ELF with ENL speakers present? Since ENL speakers do not share a first language with those who speak English as an additional language, they fit the definition.[1] However, in interactions where native speakers are the majority in a group situation, language use tends to be determined in ENL terms. Although there is no principled theoretical basis for rejecting such instances, they are of marginal interest in investigating ELF. Native-/non-native dyadic interaction is the limiting case: it is a linguistically special, asymmetric situation, where the interlocutors have a different relationship to the language. It has been studied extensively in SLA, even if not much in authentic environments, and its special features render it relatively uninteresting as ELF interaction. Prototypical cases are more important than borderline instances for charting a new research domain.

ELF was contrasted to learners along three dimensions: the macrosocial, the microsocial, and the cognitive. This three-way perspective is adopted as the general approach in this book. The rationale for adopting a three-pronged framework is to contextualise ELF in the field of language study. A research domain that is primarily defined by its object of study necessarily touches upon many traditions. Any one of them can be taken as the point of departure, but the need to integrate more than one is perhaps strongest when a new territory is being explored. The perspectives chosen here have different relations to the data at hand, as will be discussed more thoroughly in Chapter 2. The macrosocial view provides a general backdrop to the whole and takes note of the tendencies in the overall quantitative findings, the cognitive perspective can be inferred from close observation of some of the data, and the interactional viewpoint is involved in the analyses of samples of discourse.

Research on ELF is still in its early stages. A few general introductions to English in the world mention it (e.g. Graddoll 1997, 2006; Kirkpatrick 2007) but do not go into detail. Change in research activity has been fast over the last few years, and a dramatic difference is seen between the time of writing this and the turn of the millennium, when ELF could boast only a handful of mainly small-scale exploratory studies (e.g. Knapp 1987; Firth 1996; Firth & Wagner 1997; Meierkord 1998, 2000). A landmark of change was Jenkins's (2000) extensive study of phonology in ELF. This book inspired more research into ELF, along with fuelling the ongoing debates around the ownership of English and English Language Teaching (ELT). The debate was much shaped by disputes between Quirk (1985) and Kachru (1985), as well as an influential paper by Widdowson (1994), which stated the case for international users of English and the need to consider their English as not merely an imperfect form of ENL but language use in its own right. For the most part, the still ongoing argument around teaching and ELF generates yet more debate rather than serious research.

This has not prevented major empirical research taking off, resulting in monographs investigating attitudes and ideologies (Jenkins 2007), general processes in ELF (Seidlhofer 2011), ELF in Asia (Kirkpatrick 2011), English in education (Smit 2010), in 'outer circle' and 'expanding circle' contacts (Guido 2008), and collections of research papers (e.g. Knapp & Meierkord 2002; Mauranen & Metsä-Ketelä 2006; Mauranen & Ranta 2009; Mauranen & Hynninen 2010), as well as a large number of individual articles in journals and collected volumes. Many new PhD studies have also been completed in different countries within the last few years (e.g. Lesznyák 2004; Dewey 2006; Cogo 2007; Björkman 2010; Mortensen 2010; Dröschler 2011; Pitzl 2011), and more are in progress. The doctoral studies have focused on pragmatic, interactional, and morphosyntactic features of ELF, laying a good foundation for an emerging field.

ELF studies have predominantly been concerned with spoken language. This is an interesting reversal of the usual order in linguistic research, where written modes have been analysed before spoken. It is undoubtedly speech that more readily adapts to change than written text, especially in its published form. Writing is more oriented to standard language and more conservative, and publications tend to go through editing cycles, which lose some of the original voice of the author. Things are changing fast on this front, though, even in the academy, where a wealth of online academic publishing, science blogging, and other new forms of reporting and discussing findings materialises almost by the day (see e.g. Myers 2010). Editing, traditionally performed by native speakers, is losing its hold on academic publication as a consequence. Web-based forms of study make further inroads to ELF in academia, and discussion groups as part of university courses with international students offer interesting ELF data (Karhukorpi 2006). The relations between spoken and written modes are thus changing, presumably manifesting themselves in writing above all, since writing is quite flexible in incorporating spoken features, while speaking seems to be more similar across registers (Biber 2009), as it is subject to conditions of real-time processing that determine its shape. Online discussion groups, chatting, etc. mix features of speech and writing. This hybrid mode has been much investigated, and while it is interesting as ELF, most of it falls outside the scope of this book.

One of the approaches used in ELF research over the last few years has been corpus linguistics, which is based on searching large electronic databases (see Chapter 3), although the first investigations were based on fairly small amounts of data and were qualitatively oriented. Many individual scholars have compiled their own databases, not always small, but a qualitative orientation still predominates in ELF studies. The completion of two large corpora used by a number of researchers enables quantitative studies, which can supplement qualitative analyses, as is common in corpus linguistics. The first large corpus to be finished was the one used for the analyses in this book, the English as a Lingua Franca in Academic Settings (ELFA) corpus (www.helsinki.fi/elfa), which is described more fully in Chapter 3, and soon after it the VOICE corpus (www.univie.ac.at/voice/index.php) was finished in Vienna. More large corpora are being compiled in different parts of the world, including Asia (the ACE Project).

This book is intended as a contribution to the expanding research field. Its main goals are in the realm of theory and description, but an applicational interest in ELF is also pursued. The line taken here is that applications should build on a sound basis of research, and that the ramifications of an ELF approach and ELF research go far beyond foreign-language teaching, central though it is. The potential of ELF in applications is the focus of Chapter 8. The research potential of ELF is vast and reaches out to different research traditions.

The book is organised in the following way: Chapter 2 lays down the general background of ELF and its theoretical underpinnings. It is a long chapter, where the main focus is on the relationship of ELF research to the study of language change and its societal context; the other relevant perspectives that inform the rest of the book are the cognitive viewpoint and the interactional viewpoint, the groundwork for both of which is also laid in Chapter 2. This is followed by the rationale and the nature of the academic data that the empirical analyses are based on, and a description of the corpus in Chapter 3. Chapters 4 to 7 present the main body of the volume, with empirical analyses and findings on some key domains of language and discourse: Chapter 4 looks into vocabulary, with a focus on word frequencies, including their evolutionary aspects, and lexical processes. It is mainly based on corpus linguistic methods. Chapter 5 expands the horizon to the interfaces of lexis and structure; it starts by looking at structures smaller than the word, that is, morphology, and moves on to larger chunks involving more than one word. These multi-word units, or phraseological sequences, reside in the space between the word and the clause, and they occupy a key position in successful ELF and, as will be argued, in language processing and language change. Chapter 6 shifts the approach to discourse analytical methods and looks at how metadiscourse and other strategies of adding to explicitness are used in ongoing ELF interaction; Chapter 7 continues interactional themes and the multifarious uses of repetition and rephrasing in processing and interaction. Finally, Chapter 8 reviews the main results and takes up the potential for applications that findings of these kinds can have in professions where ELF features prominently; the chapter also goes on to look into the future possibilities of ELF research.

Notes

1. In this respect, our definition of ELF overlaps with Dröschel's (2011: 41) definition of 'Lingua Franca English'.

References

Biber, D. (2009) 'Are there linguistic consequences of literacy? Comparing the potentials of language use in speech and writing', in Olson, D. R. and Torrance, N. (eds.) *Cambridge Handbook of Literacy*, Cambridge: Cambridge University Press, 75–91.

Björkman, B. (2010) 'Spoken lingua franca English in tertiary education at a Swedish technical university: an investigation of form and communicative/pedagogical effectiveness', unpublished PhD thesis, University of Stockholm.

Brutt-Griffler, J. (2002) *World English: A Study of its Development*, Clevedon: Multilingual Matters.

Cogo, A. (2007) 'Intercultural communication in English as a Lingua Franca: a case study', unpublished PhD thesis, King's College London.

Croft, W. (2000) *Explaining Language Change: An Evolutionary Approach*, London: Longman.

Crystal, D. (1997) *English as a Global Language*, Cambridge: Cambridge University Press.

Dewey, M. (2006) 'English as a Lingua Franca: an empirical study of innovation in lexis and grammar', unpublished PhD thesis, King's College London.

Dröschel, Y. (2011) *Lingua Franca English: The Role of Simplification and Transfer*, Bern: Peter Lang.

Ehrenreich, S. (2009) 'English as a lingua franca in multinational corporations: exploring business communities of practice', in Mauranen, A. and Ranta, E. (eds.) *English as a Lingua Franca: Studies and Findings*, Newcastle upon Tyne: Cambridge Scholars Publishing, 126–51.

Firth, A. (1996) 'The discursive accomplishment of normality: on "lingua franca" English and conversation analysis', *Journal of Pragmatics* 26: 237–59.

Firth, A. and Wagner, J. (1997) 'On discourse, communication, and (some) fundamental concepts in SLA research', *The Modern Language Journal* 81: 285–300.

Graddoll, D. (1997) *The Future of English?* London: British Council.

Graddoll, D. (2006) *English Next*, London: British Council.

Guido, M. G. (2008) *English as a Lingua Franca in Cross-Cultural Immigration Domains*, Frankfurt: Peter Lang.

Hülmbauer, C. (2009) '"We don't take the right way. We just take the way we think you will understand": the shifting relationship between correctness and effectiveness in ELF', in Mauranen, A. and Ranta, E. (eds.) *English as a Lingua Franca: Studies and Findings*, Newcastle upon Tyne: Cambridge Scholars Publishing, 323–47.

Hynninen, N. (2011) 'The practice of "mediation" in English as a lingua franca interaction', *Journal of Pragmatics* 43 (4): 965–77.

Hynninen, N. (forthcoming) 'Expressing one's SELF: case studies of using English as a lingua franca in international study programmes', PhD thesis, University of Helsinki.

Jenkins, J. (2000) *The Phonology of English as an International Language*, Oxford: Oxford University Press.

Jenkins, J. (2007) *English as a Lingua Franca: Attitude and Identity*, Oxford: Oxford University Press.

Jenkins, J. (2009) *World Englishes* (2nd edn), London: Routledge.

Kachru, B. (1985) 'Standards, codification, and sociolinguistic realism: the English language in the outer circle', in Quirk, R., Widdowson, H. G. and Cantù, Y. (eds.) *English in the World: Teaching and Learning the Language and Literatures*, Cambridge: Cambridge University Press, 11–30.

Kachru, B. (1990) *The Alchemy of English: The Spread, Functions, and Models of Non-Native Englishes*, Champaign, IL: University of Illinois Press.

Karhukorpi, J. (2006) 'Negotiating opinions in Lingua Franca e-mail discussion groups, discourse structure, hedges and repair in online communication', unpublished licenciate thesis, University of Turku.

Kaur, J. (2009) 'Pre-empting problems of understanding in English as a lingua franca', in Mauranen, A. and Ranta, E. (eds.) *English as a Lingua Franca: Studies and Findings*, Newcastle upon Tyne: Cambridge Scholars Publishing, 107–25.

Kirkpatrick, A. (2007) *World Englishes*, Cambridge: Cambridge University Press.

Kirkpatrick, A. (ed.) (2010) *The Routledge Handbook of World Englishes*, London: Routledge.

Kirkpatrick, A. (2011) *English as a Lingua Franca in ASEAN*, Hong Kong: Hong Kong University Press.

Klimpfinger, T. (2009) '"She's mixing the two languages together": forms and functions of code-switching in English as a lingua franca', in Mauranen, A. and Ranta, E. (eds.) *English as a Lingua Franca: Studies and Findings*, Newcastle upon Tyne: Cambridge Scholars Publishing, 348–71.

Knapp, K. (1987) 'English as an international Lingua Franca and the teaching of intercultural communication', in Lörsche, W. and Schulze, R. (eds.) *Perspectives on Language in Performance*, Tübingen: Narr, 1022–39.

Knapp, K. and Meierkord, C. (eds.) (2002) *Lingua Franca Communication*, Frankfurt: Peter Lang.

Kortmann, B., Burridge, K., Mesthrie, R., Schneider, E. W. and Upton, C. (eds.) (2004) *A Handbook of Varieties of English*, Berlin: Mouton de Gruyter.

Kurhila, S. (2003) *Co-Constructing Understanding in Second Language Conversation*, Helsinki: University of Helsinki.

Kurhila, S. (2006) *Second Language Interaction*, Amsterdam: John Benjamins.

Lesznyák, Á. (2004) *Communication in English as an International Lingua Franca: An Exploratory Case Study*, Norderstedt: Books on Demand GmbH.

Mair, C. (2006) *Twentieth-Century English: History, Variation and Standardization*, Cambridge: Cambridge University Press.

Mauranen, A. (2004a) 'Spoken corpus for an ordinary learner', in Sinclair, J. McH. (ed.) *How to Use Corpora in Language Teaching*, Amsterdam: John Benjamins, 89–105.

Mauranen, A. (2006a) 'Signalling and preventing misunderstanding in English as lingua franca communication', *International Journal of the Sociology of Language* 177: 123–50.

Mauranen, A. and Hynninen, N. (eds.) (2010) *English as a Lingua Franca*. Special issue of *Helsinki English Studies* vol. 6 (http://blogs.helsinki.fi/hes-eng/volumes/volume-6/).

Mauranen, A. and Metsä-Ketelä M. (eds.) (2006) *English as a Lingua Franca*. Special issue of *The Nordic Journal of English Studies* 5 (2).

Mauranen, A. and Ranta, E. (eds.) (2009) *English as a Lingua Franca: Studies and Findings*, Newcastle upon Tyne: Cambridge Scholars Publishing.

Meierkord, C. (1998) 'Lingua franca English: characteristics of successful non-native – non-native speaker discourse', *Erfurt Electronic Studies in English* 1998 (http://webdoc.sub.gwdg.de/edoc/ia/eese/eese.html).

Meierkord, C. (2000) 'Interpreting successful lingua franca interaction: an analysis of non-native-/non-native small talk conversations in English', *Conversation Analysis: New Developments, Linguistik online* 5 (1/00). Special issue (ed. A. Fetzer and K. Pittner) (www.linguistik-online.com).

Mesthrie, R. and Bhatt, R. M. (2008) *World Englishes: The Study of New Linguistic Varieties*, Cambridge: Cambridge University Press.

Mortensen, J. (2010) 'Epistemic stance marking in the use of English as a lingua franca: a comparative study of the pragmatic functions of epistemic stance', PhD thesis, University of Roskilde.

Mukherjee, J. and Hundt, M. (eds.) (2011) *Exploring Second-Language Varieties of English and Learner Englishes*, Amsterdam: John Benjamins.

Myers, G. (2010) *The Discourse of Blogs and Wikis*, London: Continuum.

Pitzl, M.-L. (2011) 'Creativity in English as a lingua franca: idiom and metaphor', unpublished PhD thesis, University of Vienna.

Quirk, R. (1985) 'The English language in a global context', in Quirk, R. and Widdowson, H. G. (eds.) *English in the World: Teaching and Learning the Language and Literatures*, Cambridge: Cambridge University Press, 1–6.

Ranta, E. (2006) 'The "attractive" progressive: why use the *-ing* form in English as a lingua franca?' *English as a Lingua Franca*. Special issue of *The Nordic Journal of English Studies* (ed. A. Mauranen and M. Metsä-Ketelä), 5 (2): 95–116.

Schneider, E. (2006) *Postcolonial Englishes*, Cambridge: Cambridge University Press.

Seidlhofer, B. (2011) *Understanding English as a Lingua Franca*, Oxford: Oxford University Press.

Smit, U. (2010) *English as a Lingua Franca in Higher Education*, Berlin: De Gruyter Mouton.

Smith, N. (2005) 'A corpus-based investigation of recent change in the use of the progressive in British English', unpublished PhD thesis, Department of Linguistics and English Language, University of Lancaster.

Widdowson, H. G. (1994) 'The ownership of English', *TESOL Quarterly* 28: 377–89.

Widdowson, H. G. (2000) 'On the limitations of linguistics applied', *Applied Linguistics* 21 (1): 3–25.

2 *Three perspectives on ELF*

A lingua franca arises out of situations where speakers of different first languages need to talk: they have to choose a medium for communication, and with any luck, they have at least one language in common in their repertoires. They may not know the common language equally well, they may have different versions of it, and at the very least they are likely to have different accents. They will probably also have different expectations of what kinds of things are appropriate to say, how to express or interpret friendliness, social distance, or their interlocutors' wish to continue or close the conversation. However, humans tend to be good at adapting to new situations, and adept at communicating. With a modicum of a shared code, they will find a way of not only carrying out their business with each other, but also dealing with the subtler aspects of social interaction. In brief, they will bring their linguistic, cognitive, and social resources to bear on the communicative task whatever language they are operating in, to achieve the purposes they have. All this will bring not only language but all levels of communication into contact. To get a handle on the complex reality of communicating in a lingua franca, it is a good idea to look at it in different ways. This chapter seeks to lay down a backdrop for analysing such linguistic contact from three perspectives: macrosocial, cognitive, and microsocial.

The three perspectives are different, but interconnected. They converge on focal points: the individual, the speech event, and the wider language community. The speaker engages in social interaction, where participation requires active cognitive processing of language and of the social aspects of the ongoing speech event. The speech event constitutes the immediate social environment for speakers and is embedded in larger social structures, which, in turn, are constructed and reproduced in social interaction between individual actors. The objective in this chapter is therefore not only to look at lingua franca communication from three viewpoints, one after the other, but also to look for their interconnections where possible. This integrative approach is then applied to interpreting the outcomes of the analyses of linguistic features that are taken up in the later chapters (Chapters 4 to 7), which are based on empirical work.

The need to distinguish different levels of language contact was recognised 60 years ago in Weinreich's (1953/1963) classic work on bilingualism. He drew a distinction between transfer at the level of the individual ('speech') and at the level of society ('language'). As Weinreich saw it, transfer in the former was expected to trickle gradually into the latter through repeated use, connecting the speech of individuals to language in society. The movement was thus seen to move 'upwards' from the individual to society. More recent work on language transfer follows in Weinreich's footsteps: Jarvis and Pavlenko (2007) make a distinction between 'cross-linguistic influence' at the level of the individual and 'transfer' at the level of society. As psycholinguists their primary concern at the individual level is with cognition.

A distinction between two levels in language contact is also made in sociolinguistics: for example, Milroy (2002) and Trudgill (1986) talk about the societal level of the language community and the individual level of speakers in interaction. Putting together these viewpoints from transfer studies and sociolinguistics, we get in all three interrelated levels, those that were already introduced as the backbone of this book: the societal or macrosocial, the individual or cognitive, and the inter-individual microsocial level of face-to-face interaction between speakers. The assumption here is that they are all interconnected, and that the connections work in two directions at each interface, constituting a complex whole.

This chapter starts out by looking at lingua francas as a form of language contact from a macrosocial perspective, which shows the big picture and sets the general scene. It forms a kind of backdrop to the whole but does not feature closely in the language analyses in the other chapters. This is why it occupies a larger share of this chapter than the two other perspectives, which are more directly drawn on in the linguistic analyses carried out in the later chapters dealing with empirical research.

The chapter need not be read in the order in which it is written. The sections are relatively self-standing, and for a reader interested in only one perspective on ELF, it should not be too difficult to pick just one section. The subheadings and cross-references should make it easy to check related issues in other sections according to the reader's interest.

2.1 The macrosocial perspective

The huge wave of globalisation that we have felt in the last couple of decades and that is still taking shape has altered many things in life as we experience it, many of them changing the conditions of language use dramatically. With an enormous increase in international mobility and migration, more and more languages are used as lingua francas, English more than any other. We can without hesitation place ELF among one of the most important social phenomena that operate on a global scale; it is on a par with things like global economy, mobility, and the Internet, and closely intertwined with them. The emergence of one language that is the default lingua franca in all corners of the earth is both a consequence and a prerequisite of globalisation. The historical spread of English across continents has been described in detail by many scholars, recently, for instance, by Phillipson (1992), Crystal (1997), Graddoll (1997), Brutt-Griffler (2002), Melchers and Shaw (2003), and Jenkins (2009). The descriptions are not all neutral, but whatever stand one takes on the motives or mechanisms, it is clear that there is nothing in the English language itself that destined it to linguistic world dominance; the reasons lie in social and economic factors.

Lingua francas are ubiquitous, vary from very local to highly international, and have been known throughout historical time; widespread lingua francas such as Sanskrit, Arabic, Aramaic, Latin, and Greek have enjoyed their days of power and influence (see e.g. Weber 1997). What separates English from these is scale: it is the first truly global lingua franca. This scale effect is so massive that it transforms itself into a qualitative difference: socially the range of activities and environments that English is used in covers more ground than has been possible in the past, in part as a consequence of technological advances; English comes into contact with virtually the entire range of human languages.

A social perspective on ELF addresses these wide issues along with smaller-scale social aspects of language contact. It contributes to the theoretical framework two major conceptual domains: language community and language change. I shall discuss each in turn, starting with language communities, which are the social units that regulate linguistic stability and change, and provide a home to all language use.

2.1.1 Communities of speakers

Languages arise for purposes of social communication. Their development and regulation are central concerns among communities of speakers. Negotiations about forms and the meanings associated with them are achieved in speaker communities as a part of speakers' normal dealings with other members of the community. The notion of community is thus central to the description of language. This holds even when there is no firmly established community in sight at the outset, or a readily definable community language, as in the case of a lingua franca. An ELF community looks potentially enormous, even amorphous. From multinational organisations to web-based interest groups and social media, ELF-based groupings can command worldwide reach. Although 'global community' has become a cliché, the meaning of the term is hazy, because it does not in effect denote a single community that would unite the world under some common denominator, but rather a number of specific communities scattered around different parts of the world, such as international organisations, virtual communities, or multinational companies. In the same way, there is no single identifiable ELF community although nearly the whole world uses ELF to a notable degree in their communicative activities.

IMAGINED COMMUNITIES

We can think of global communities perhaps, at best, as kinds of imagined communities along the lines that Benedict Anderson (1991) described the nation. The resemblance lies in patterns of interaction: members of imagined communities do not directly interact with all other members of the community, even in principle. In contrast, traditional notions of 'community' are anchored in a group of individuals who live in close proximity and engage in regular face-to-face contact. Imagined communities are based on people's mental images of their affinity. Such images are fostered through communication, which in turn requires a common language that is able to maintain a sufficient level of mutual comprehensibility. In Anderson's interpretation of modern European nation-building, important factors included 'national print-languages'. In a similar fashion, present-day international communities also crucially depend on communication, and the more global they are, the more likely that they adopt English as their lingua franca.

Traditional definitions of language communities have tended to invoke location and mutual interaction by members. As both Chambers (1992) and Milroy (2002) have pointed out, sociolinguistics and dialectology have been generally oriented to non-mobile speakers in isolated communities. Such conceptualisations, based on location and low mobility, are clearly inadequate to account for communities today, which have become more and more global, fragmented, and ephemeral. Croft (2000) talks about 'intersocietal communities'. Recent developments have nevertheless not wiped out local communities, which stride along with newer societal formations, and the ensuing complexity of social structures calls for analytical frameworks that assimilate the new developments without discarding the continuing structures. A useful general-level concept that captures the bidirectionality of contemporary social influences is Robertson's (1995) 'glocalization', a notion which combines the global and the local, recognising that they are closely intertwined. Global trends draw on the local, and as is familiar from cultural studies, phenomena of the global culture get adapted in the process of local adoption.

What this entails for language communities is the need to adopt non-local models. Relevant to our present concerns are the concepts of *community of practice*, *discourse community*, and *social networks*, which are briefly discussed in turn now.

COMMUNITIES OF PRACTICE

Community of practice (CoP), a concept originally developed by Lave and Wenger (1991), has gained a strong foothold in sociolinguistic studies (e.g. Eckert 2000; Meyerhoff 2002). It has also been adopted by several scholars for conceptualising ELF (e.g. Dewey 2006; Seidlhofer 2007; Ehrenreich 2009, Hülmbauer 2009; Smit 2010; Hynninen 2011). Lave and Wegner's theory is concerned with learning in diverse organisations, from educational institutions to business enterprises. In Wenger's (2006) definition: 'Communities of practice are groups of people who share a concern or a passion for something they do and learn how to do it better as they interact regularly.' Penelope Eckert puts the idea in more succinct and general terms, without evoking learning or passion, placing the emphasis on common activity as a group: 'A community of practice may be defined as an aggregate of people coming together around a particular enterprise' (Eckert 2000: 35). A less precise definition, it is also less limiting, and therefore well suited to language communities. The CoP concept does not invoke locality, therefore groupings in academia or business qualify. A CoP is nevertheless a real community in contrast to imagined communities in that it is based on members' direct interaction with one another; communities of practice consist of members who know each other. Many ELF communities fall into this category, even if they are non-local, because they meet face to face, for instance in meetings or conferences.

Participants in ELF communities may come together as working groups, teams, student groups in international programmes, task forces in international organisations (e.g. Penz 2008), or research teams in the academy. ELF groupings are often temporary, thus easily compatible with the notion of a CoP, which is not limited to long-term stability.

We need to be careful, though, not to overemphasise the ephemerality of ELF communities. Although the fleeting nature of ELF groups is often stressed, impermanence is only part of the story: groups like research teams can last for years. The effect on language is likely to be different in shorter- and longer-living groups. While participants even in short-lived groups work towards practicable levels of mutual comprehensibility and shape linguistic practices, communities of longer duration are more likely to regulate their language towards group norms. Group norms transcend individuals (just as groups often do), so that when individual members change, the ways of speaking within the group tend to remain largely intact, adapting just slightly to each individual. Norms of usage established in one group can also transfer via individuals to similar situations and spread further, competing with other norms. Individuals moving from one group to another thus become agents of diffusing linguistic innovation, as social network theory predicts (see Section 2.1.4 below).

DISCOURSE COMMUNITIES

The idea of a community of practice bears a relation to that of a discourse community (DC), a concept developed by Swales (1990) to characterise social formations in academia. Swales's primary interest was in defining genre in a way that anchors it in social action, as in Miller (1984; see also Martin 1985; Ventola 1987). Discourse community was a notion that helped in linking texts to their social environments: it pinned down the social end of the connection between texts, which can be observed to have fairly predictable shapes, and the social environments that regulate their conventions of expression. DCs are not in principle confined to the academy, but it is in academic genre research where the concept has become influential.

A discourse community shares features with a community of practice. Both terms refer to communities whose membership can be delimited and defined by knowable criteria. Both are also self-regulated communities, unlike imagined communities, which for the vast majority of members are externally imposed and regulated. So, for example, nations, as imagined communities, are normally not chosen by most of their members, and relatively small minorities of speakers regulate standard languages. Importantly, communities of practice and discourse communities are sites where participants co-construct social meanings and linguistic norms as part of their common activity. Language plays a more prominent role in the conceptualisation of a DC, although the notion of a CoP has also been successfully used for describing linguistic practices. The principal difference is the role of face-to-face interaction. Members of discourse communities do not have to meet face to face to exist, as academic discourse communities show (Swales 1990). This is a point of contact between discourse communities and imagined communities. Discourse communities nevertheless take many forms, some of which can be local, such as universities or their departments. On the other hand, universities can alternatively be seen as aggregates of communities of practice. In this way, the two models can converge when we describe complex social formations.

NETWORKS OF SPEAKERS

Communities of practice and discourse communities are frameworks for understanding how groups function in joint activities. If we want to see how influences spread in and between groups, we need a model that shifts the perspective from the group to the individual. A well-established model of this kind is social network analysis (Granovetter 1973; Milroy & Milroy 1985). Network analysis focuses on links that speakers have with others, attending to ties that make up people's personal networks. It provides a participant perspective on social entities, which helps analyse the internal structures and interrelations of groups. In this way, likely routes of linguistic influence can be envisioned more readily than by looking at the groups alone. Networks that are dense and close-knit are essentially much like communities, and such networks can describe similar kinds of social entities that are dealt with by concepts like community of practice or discourse community. Any of these can be used for describing group norms. However, if in addition to the shaping of group norms we need to understand how norms are spread and distributed further by individuals and their networks, social network analysis makes a vital contribution.

An important distinction in network theory is made between weak and strong ties (Granovetter 1973; Milroy & Milroy 1985). Strong ties are both dense and multiplex; they involve emotions, intimacy, long duration, and reciprocity, as between friends. Weak ties on the other hand are more intermittent, involve less commitment, and rest on a narrower basis, like those between acquaintances. Strong ties characterise traditional, local, close-knit communities, typified by little mobility. Weak ties are more typical of looser social formations, and mobile individuals are likely to contract many ties of the weak kind. The mobile individual with wide social networks is also one who is likely to use lingua francas these days, as social networks tend to get more and more international. As will be discussed below

(Section 2.1.4), Milroy and Milroy (1985) suggest that weak ties are conducive to linguistic innovation and change, which are central concerns of processes in ELF. The network model thus captures important social and linguistic facets of ELF, together with connections between them. In principle the model could be applied beyond individuals as well, because it is not only individuals who maintain contact networks, but also collectives like universities, learned societies, or student unions, to take examples from the academic world. Social ties at group level can probably also be conducive to spreading and consolidating linguistic changes.

MULTILINGUAL ENVIRONMENTS

ELF communities and networks are immersed in environments that are multilingual. Awareness of the multilingual reality that surrounds most of us is growing, but models of speech communities have tended to ignore or downplay this, and, as Sankoff (2002) points out, even in sociolinguistics the dominant trend has been the study of monolingual speech communities. This parallels the notion of the ideal monolingual speaker that dominated linguistic research in the latter half of the twentieth century, transposed to the social level. Multi- and plurilingualism nevertheless need to be addressed in adequate social models of language, as has become particularly clear in present-day communities. Individuals possess different linguistic repertoires, whether they are monolingual or multilingual; monolinguals employ different registers, dialects, or sociolects as part of their normal language use, and multilinguals add to this their resources in more than one language. We can think of this as a cline from repertoires in a single language to those in several. Zentella's (1997) work on bilingual Spanish–English speakers' highly complex multidialectal repertoires illuminates the nature of multiple-code repertoires that speakers use in response to different interlocutors and situations. The recently widespread concept of plurilingualism (Denison 1971; Coste et al. 2009) is a useful way of looking at this: as applied in the Council of Europe (2007) it refers to composite bilingualism in individuals, who are recognised as social actors.

Speakers of ELF are mostly bi- or plurilingual and thus usually have at least one other, usually stronger, language in their repertoire. ELF is also commonly used in environments where English is not a dominant language. As Sankoff (2002: 640) points out, the description of a bilingual community involves more social parameters and more inter-individual variation than the description of a monolingual community: members do not share the invariant structural base typical of monolingual communities, and speakers vary across continua of proficiency. This is also true of ELF communities.

As the discussion in this section has sought to point out, certain vital properties need to be taken on board in a successful conceptual model of the social groupings that typically use English as a lingua franca. One is the possibility of non-locality. This requirement is compatible with all the main models presented above. The second is mobility. This is addressed by the network model very well, but not touched upon in the others. Yet none of the models attends to the variable duration of ELF communities themselves, as stability and permanence seem to be underlying assumptions made in the conceptualisation of language communities. The third vital aspect is multilingualism, but none of the models takes this into account; a tacit assumption seems to prevail that members of language communities or networks are monolingual. In brief, we need to conceptualise an ELF community as one that builds on the strengths of the established notion of language community as the site of shaping language and regulating norms, but with strong components that add non-locality, non-permanence, speaker mobility, and multilingualism to it.

2.1.2 Community of ELF?

As was discussed above, traditional notions of language or a speech community are somewhat unhelpful for setting descriptive parameters for ELF as a social phenomenon. Looking at a particular type of community in sharper focus helps us to see the issues more precisely. The specific case we have at hand is academic communities using ELF – albeit in itself an agglomeration of widely diverse component communities.

Academia is in many ways a domain well suited for ELF research: it is international by nature and has used other lingua francas before adopting English as its main language in the years following the Second World War. It is a domain that has arisen 'naturally', without an international master plan underlying institutions like the United Nations (UN), the European Union (EU), or the Association of South East Asian Nations (ASEAN). Unlike such organisations, academia has not adopted a common language by decree or political decision, but the choice of language has developed through a kind of evolutionary process.

The academy is not a clear-cut community, although it is not difficult to pinpoint its main institutional actors, such as universities, research teams, scientific publications, and research institutions. Academia as a whole is an imagined community, and so are many of its constituent social formations – disciplinary communities or 'the research community' often appealed to in scholarly argumentation – but it has also more tangible bases. Innumerable international groups of scientists and scholars work in close collaboration in joint projects and constitute more or less temporal communities of their own. They change and take new shapes, but may live much longer than their three- or five-year funding periods, and some institutions have research centres that recruit internationally but are located in one place (e.g. the Max Planck Institute; CERN). The most stable institutional foundations tend to be universities. It is within such tangible institutions and groupings as these that real individuals come together around common objectives. Universities are themselves multifaceted clusters, which comprise educational institutes and research units in a single whole, spreading over a vast number of disciplinary divisions and combinations.

Cutting across local hierarchies but at the heart of academic collaboration and competition are publishing systems, whose influence is felt at all levels of academic life. The general influence of publishing on language tends to be conservative, as is characteristic of high-prestige formal registers, but as new digital channels of publishing are reaching academia (Russell 2010), these will probably impact on language in the same way as they have made their mark on related channel, such as Wikipedia (Myers 2010). A vast research area has developed around academic publishing in English, including its historical dimensions, but as yet there are no publications on ELF or its impact.

Academic communities can be described from several valid viewpoints and the choice must reflect the research objectives at hand. For this, it is useful to draw on several of the models discussed above. The key aspects to be addressed in connection with ELF are the global–local alternation in practices, mobility connected to variable duration of communities, and the omnipresent other languages in social environments and individuals' repertoires. Apart from the overarching imagined communities, we have discourse communities, which are essentially non-local and mainly discipline-driven communities that are drawn together by the joint pursuit of certain research goals, even if most members may never meet face to face. Communities of practice emerge in the face-to face contacts of research groups, study programmes, or task forces, which may be locally or more widely based. Academic mobility is, again, in terms of its linguistic influence, best captured by network analysis. Multilingualism is an inherent characteristic of all contemporary academic communities, even though virtually ignored so far by established models of community. The same is true of the variable duration of communities, which is an important consideration where ELF is used because it is likely to affect language change.

2.1.3 Lingua franca and language change

As sites of contact but with relatively little long-term stability, ELF communities lie towards the 'diffuse' end of speech communities (LePage & Tabouret-Keller 1985) in that they do not have very stable or clear norms. We could say that they have indeterminate standards – at least in principle. In practice, the tacit standards appear to draw on a common-sense notion of a 'native speaker', and thus to be exonormative in relation to the actual community of speakers, that is, to look to native-speaker communities for standards, usually those Kachru (1985) calls 'inner circle'. This is particularly so when speakers talk about written text or what they regard as 'good' language (Pilkinton-Pihko 2010; Hynninen 2011). Yet at the same time, communities of practice engaged in spoken interaction gravitate much more towards endonormativity (arising from their community-internal needs), prompted by the exigencies of ongoing situations. Such communities, which in the case of academic ELF would fall into Kachru's 'expanding circle' as often or even more frequently than 'outer circle', can, for example, adopt ad hoc terms or usages between themselves (e.g. Lammi 2010). Interview studies show that speakers have some uncertainty about evaluating different kinds of Englishes: while non-native speech is regarded as easily comprehensible, functional, and appropriate in its contexts, native speakers' language is nevertheless set up as an ideal, even if unattainable, model (see e.g. Hynninen 2010; Pilkinton-Pihko 2010). The same people typically hold up both discourses, for example, by saying that their (L2) English is good enough but a little later criticising it for various shortcomings. Such variable attitudes are of course common among people and often come up in interviews, but to some extent they may also reflect speakers' awareness of the transition that English is currently undergoing. The status shift of English into a language of predominantly second-language users has been too fast for language teaching and popular notions to keep pace, and some degree of uncertainty or confusion is only to be expected.

INNOVATION AND CHANGE

Change is a normal and constant part of language, which makes it impossible to keep track of all its different causes and effects: the same effects may result from different causes and they may interact in highly intricate ways. Language change is generally taken to have two necessary components or stages: innovation and diffusion (or 'propagation'). Change is thus an innovation that has spread enough in the language to become established. Yet how widely an innovation is to be diffused and how long it takes before it is accepted as an established part of a language are far from clear; random alterations can occur for a long time before they may start acquiring social value and begin to spread more widely (e.g. Croft 2000).

Innovations are part of normal language use, yet only a fraction of them ever diffuses into general usage. Ordinary speech is peppered with fleeting innovations that pass unnoticed unless they begin to take hold in some community or another. By that time their true origin is lost, and the route from origins to establishment becomes a matter of reconstruction. With present-day web-linked corpus tools (e.g. WebCorp), it is possible to detect first occurrences – at least in the data we have access to. Even so, change is notoriously hard to capture in the process of happening. When an innovation has diffused sufficiently widely to be observable, change has already taken place. The difficulty of pinning it down is aggravated by the fact that new forms can live side by side with older forms for long periods of time (Hopper & Traugott 2003). Despite all this indeterminacy, it is clear that innovations originate with individuals, and their wider acceptance to larger communities spreads through social interaction.

INTERNAL AND EXTERNAL FACTORS

Origins of change have been attributed to both internal and external sources. Language-internal change is foregrounded by, for example, Andersen (1989) and Lass (1997), whereas others such as Thomason (2001) emphasise contact-based explanations. At the level of theory, researchers such as Milroy and Milroy (1985), Trudgill (1986), and Britain (2002a,b) put a lot of weight on the effects of language contact, but most of their work is language-internal in that it is concerned with contacts between dialects or sociolects within the same language. If change is due solely to internal causes, one way of explaining it is by attributing it to children's language acquisition processes, as, for example, Andersen (1989) does. Some types of acquisition are particularly conducive to phonetic changes, and innovations will then spread generation by generation. There is a good amount of evidence to support the central role of the generation in establishing change (e.g. Palander 1987; Vaattovaara 2003). However, there is also ample evidence to support the interpretation that external influences set changes in motion. As Thomason reminds us, language contact is ubiquitous; this is the norm rather than the exception, and the most common result of language contact is change in some or all of the languages (Thomason 2001: 10).

A lingua franca is a site of intense language contact, so any influence that widespread lingua franca use may have on a language falls into the external category of contact-induced change, insofar as the distinction into external and internal is to be maintained. As Filppula (2003) shows, for instance, there is no clear methodological basis for prioritising internal to external explanations. An observed change in usage can sometimes be supported by arguments and evidence from either source. Moreover, as some scholars have also done earlier (e.g. Thomason & Kaufman 1988), he notes that the two can get fused. This renders disputes over single-cause explanations somewhat trivial. What is important for our present purposes is the connection between change and social factors, since the diffusion and acceptance of an innovation lies with language communities. Sociolinguistics and its offshoot historical sociolinguistics (Romaine 1982) have been influential in bringing a social perspective to bear on the close relationship between language variation and change, and social factors are similarly central to the study of language contact (Thomason 2001; Winford 2003).

2.1.4 Contact-induced language change

Why widespread lingua franca use can be expected to exert influence on the language as a whole is in part a matter of scale, but perhaps at least as much one of mobility. Periods of increased mobility tend to result in accelerated language change. In contemporary environments of work or study, heavily permeated by internationalism, talk about networks has become commonplace, and it would seem apt to tackle these environments as networks along the lines of social network theory. Social ties that typify today's international academia are often temporary or intermittent, and would count as 'weak ties' (Granovetter 1973, 1983). Since most novel information travels through weak ties, they position mobile individuals as likely carriers and diffusers of innovations. Milroy and Milroy (1985) have applied social network theory successfully to sociolinguistic analysis and posit that networks consisting of largely weak ties are favourable to linguistic innovation and change, as compared to stable social networks characterised by strong ties: 'Linguistic change is slow to the extent that the relevant populations are well established and bound by strong ties, whereas it is rapid to the extent that weak ties exist in populations' (Milroy & Milroy 1985: 375). Close-knit communities with dense and multiplex ties roughly correspond to stable traditional communities associated with a location. As discussed in Section 2.1.3, this has constituted the dominant conceptualisation of a speech community, but is becoming less and less pertinent for present-day communities.

HOMOGENEITY AND 'SIMILECTS'

Among the linguistic consequences of the social network theory that Milroy and Milroy put forward is that closely knit networks are conducive to maintaining complex, localised linguistic structures. In contrast, when such structures loosen, 'the social prerequisites for supporting highly localised norms disappear, and dialect levelling takes place' (Milroy 2002: 566). The weak links of social network theory thus seem to be involved in language change in two principal ways: promoting innovation and giving rise to levelling.

The increased geographical mobility and urbanisation that have been evident in Europe have been predicted to lead to dialect levelling, homogenisation, or koinéisation (new dialect formation) on a large scale (e.g. Milroy 2002; Trudgill 2002). There may well be such processes in evidence, but there are nevertheless caveats for predicting sweeping homogenisation. To begin with, such a general assumption is probably too simple: while regional dialects seem to be fading out in many places, other communal formations may replace them as close-knit networks that reflect the ongoing social transformations – new social hierarchies, mobile work cultures, social media networks. Re-grouping and its linguistic repercussions can be likened to the process of glocalization (Robertson 1995), where all-pervasive trends of global culture find their way to every part of the world, but simultaneously and in parallel get altered by local particularities and develop into local variants of imported cultural trends (just think of food culture as an example: Indian cuisine has its own flavour in the UK, and an American pizza is a far cry from an Italian one). Communities assimilating global influences adapt them to their local circumstances, thereby generating new heterogeneity. Moreover, processes like mobility do not concern all communities, let alone all members of all communities, in the same way, and if communities have internal social variation, this is reflected in language.

The second caveat against predicting overall homogenisation for ELF arises from the nature of contact in ELF. SLA studies have shown recognisable features attributable to L1 transfer in the English of speakers from different backgrounds (e.g. Ringbom 1992, 2007; papers in Granger 1998). Such 'varieties' are often known in popular terms as Swinglish, Finglish, or Dunglish for Swedish, Finnish, or

Dutch-influenced English. These 'varieties', or lects, resemble mutually comprehensible dialects, and we might predict processes similar to koinéisation between them when they are in prolonged contact with each other. However, there is a crucial difference between these L2 lects and regional dialects: unlike dialects, which arise in communities of speakers talking to each other, L2 lects result from parallel L1 influence on their speakers. Speakers of Finnish, for example, have no reason to talk to each other in English. The shared features of 'Finglish' result from many speakers having the same language combination in their repertoire, and thereby similar transfer from their first language. We cannot simply equate the L1-based lects with dialects, but could speak of them instead as 'similects', because they arise in parallel, not in mutual interaction. In short, there is no community of similect speakers. Similects do not develop new features or new discourse practices in the same way that language communities do – in interaction, from one linguistic generation to another. They remain forever first-generation hybrids: each generation's, each speaker's idiolect is a new hybrid. Similects do not become more complex, simpler, undergo sound changes, accent diversification, develop sociolects, or in general develop like dialects and languages in communities. Because similects originate in cross-linguistic influence, they comprise a renewable resource for the mix that ELF is made of.

SECOND-ORDER LANGUAGE CONTACT

In contrast to similects, ELF takes shape in speaker interaction; interactants come together with their own hybrid variants, variants that resemble those of people who share their background (that is who speak their similect) but are different from those used by the people with whom they speak. ELF groups consist of speakers with hybrid repertoires where each individual may represent a different hybrid. Linguistic complexity in ELF communities and groupings is enhanced by the wider environments where ELF is spoken, which are usually multilingual. The setting typically has some dominant language other than English, and speakers possess other language resources that may become salient in different ways and at different stages over the duration of the interaction. Local languages may gain ground in the longer term in more established groups. All this makes the communities linguistically heterogeneous, and ELF a site of an unusually complex contact. Therefore, ELF might be termed 'second-order language contact': a contact between hybrids. The ordinary language contact situation involves speakers of two languages or varieties, who usually choose one of them as their principal means of communication, but sometimes make do with a mix, or a pidgin. Second-order contact means that instead of a typical contact situation where speakers of two different languages use one of them in communication ('first-order contact'), a large number of languages are each in contact with English, and it is these contact varieties (similects) that are, in turn, in contact with each other. Their special features, resulting from cross-linguistic transfer, come together much like dialects in contact. To add complexity to the mix, ENL speakers of different origins participate in ELF communities. The distinctive feature of ELF is nevertheless its character as a hybrid of similects.

We can reasonably think of the similect contact in ELF as being in many ways analogous to dialect contact, albeit less stable and more complex than between ordinary regional dialects. Both ELF and dialects rest on contact between mutually comprehensible varieties, tapping speakers' adaptive strategies. It makes sense to assume that processes and mechanisms discovered in dialect contact studies should by and large apply to ELF as well, and the same goes for contact research more generally, especially where the languages are typologically relatively close to each other (see Winford 2003). The hybrid similects that come together in ELF are related through being kinds of English, which makes major contact phenomena a good point of departure for making macrosocial predictions for ELF.

SIMPLIFICATION

The most frequently proposed contact-induced change is simplification. Simplification implies regularisation and loss of markedness in the affected language systems, notably in their grammar and phonology. Simplification has also been put forward as a general consequence of contact-induced change. Or, as Thomason puts it: '[a] common proposed constraint is that contact-induced change always makes the receiving system "more natural" – that is, less marked overall' (2001: 64). Although Thomason also notes counterexamples and opposite claims, simplification is the most widely observed and accepted outcome of language or dialect contact. It has been attributed primarily to situations dominated by adult language contact, and it seems to affect grammar and phonology rather than lexis. As far as vocabulary is concerned, lexical borrowing is very common and tends to lead to an increase of lexis, rather than reduction or simplification. However, lexis is a highly varied and heterogeneous category (as will be discussed in more detail in Chapters 4 and 5).

Simplification, or simplicity in language, is an elusive concept. One way in which simplicity and complexity have been approached as attributes of structure is in connection with the ease with which features are learnable for foreign-language learners (see also Thomason & Kaufman 1988). While this is by no means an established matter, one might assume that those aspects of a language that are already simple will remain intact if it is learned as a foreign language on a large scale, while those that are very complex are likely to undergo simplification in the hands of new users. As Winford (2003) points out, notions like structural transparency and naturalness are related to more general cognitive principles. Whether a language can be seen as structurally more transparent or 'natural' irrespective of its learner's earlier languages is questionable, but features generally taken to contribute to transparency, such as regularity and compositionality, may well facilitate a learner's task. English has gone through major simplification processes during its history, largely on account of its contacts with other languages; now that it has a massive number of L2 users, the same trend may continue. Simplification of the target language is also a well-established feature of L2 acquisition. It has also been put forward as a translation universal, even though not accepted as unequivocally as in SLA research (e.g. Baker 1993; Olohan 2004; Mauranen 2007a). All this suggests it is a major phenomenon in situations where two languages come into contact.

LEVELLING

Along with simplification, processes of levelling (Trudgill 1986), or convergence of grammatical systems in contact (Winford 2003), have been suggested as typical consequences of language contact. Levelling is particularly characteristic of contact between dialects (Trudgill 1986; Britain 2002c; Chambers 2002), and between languages with a close typological fit (e.g. Winford 2003). It would thus appear to be a good candidate for similect contact in ELF. Apart from the differences between similects and dialects already discussed, one difference that is particularly relevant to dialect levelling and pertinent to other hypotheses of contact-induced change is the duration of the contact. Most of the research has been concerned with situations of prolonged dialect contact, which is untypical of lingua francas. I shall return to this below.

Dialect levelling usually entails a reduction in variants. Marked forms have been observed to lose out to those that are unmarked, minority forms to majority and shared ones. In other words, choices that are basic, neutral, and dominant are favoured over derived, rarer, and non-dominant ones. While such distinctions are drawn in many linguistic traditions, they have different origins and rationales. They are hard, if possible at all, to determine for an unstable language form such as a lingua franca, but we may yet at a general level assume that when speakers seek optimal common denominators, a globally valid solution is in all probability one that is as widely unmarked as possible. So speakers could be expected to prefer *run* rather than *scurry*, *big* more than *immense*, or *may go* over *might be going*. Here the macrosocial meets the microsocial: changes that are observed at macrosocial levels in the course of time originate in processes of negotiating forms and meanings in interaction. Safe guesses in respect of what an interlocutor might find comprehensible are likely to be features that are widely shared among the world's English speakers. The successful guesses may draw on the kinds of features that are widespread in all languages, because they are probably acquired comparatively easily in English as an additional language (see also Mauranen 2003b). If this is what happens, lingua franca use tends towards what Hunston and Francis (2000: 270) called 'necessary features of language'. In this way, ELF should throw light on vital, possibly universal, features of communication and language. Examples of features that might be affected in English through loss of marked features are things like highly idiomatic phraseology, irregular plural or past tense forms, word order in indirect questions, or the third singular *-s* ending.

It is interesting to note in this connection that 'levelling' is also implicated in translation research, and, like simplification, it has been postulated as a translation universal (Baker 1993). This suggests that this feature may also be relevant to bilingual contact more generally.

In observing dialect contact in the development of new dialects, or koinés, scholars have also observed other processes, such as 'reallocation' (Trudgill 1986; Britain 2002c), where variants of the interdialectal mix are refunctionalised to serve new roles. Here again, available descriptions are based on long-term contact, where processes like 'focusing', reduction of variants from the large number of variants available, have been observed. Whether such processes can be observed at incipient stages is not clear; some initial observations have been made of ELF speech focusing the use of some lexical items in a different way (DISCUSS[1]) or more narrowly (BRING UP) from ENL speakers in comparable situations (Mauranen 2005), but whether these will turn out to have more lasting effects on English is impossible to guess at the moment. Such observations raise the question already touched upon in Chapter 1 concerning time perspectives relevant to language change: how long is a long time?

HOW LONG IS A LONG TIME?

Dialect and language contact research has focused on situations with comparative long-term stability, which cannot be assumed for a lingua franca. So, for example, Trudgill (1986) talks about levelling in terms of new dialect formation over generations. A lingua franca is of course not a first language to anyone, so generations in the normal sense do not come into it. Yet the question of the timescale of change is a vital issue: how long should we allow for new forms to take effect, and most crucially, how long is it reasonable to allow ELF to be globally spoken before we make judgements about its influence on English as a whole? It is reasonable to expect the sheer scale of ELF use to have an effect on the English language, but to gauge its potential effect requires some assessment on the temporal dimension as well.

Most important changes in language, such as language shift or language loss, tend to take place over three generations: the simple scheme depicts the first generation as monolingual in language A, with possible acquisition of language B post childhood, the second generation becomes bilingual in A+B, and the third is monolingual in B. An analogical timescale could be posited for ELF development: if first-generation hybrid forms are entirely based on cross-linguistic influence (similects in contact), the second generation of ELF users have available to them a selection of ELF expressions that results from second-order contact and has diffused into common usage. Second-generation speakers are likely to incorporate such expressions in their repertoires as part of the English they encounter, probably developing them further and adding more, and by the time the third generation learns English, we may expect English already to show clear traces of lingua franca influence. We now talk about generations of learning an additional language, not a first language, and the analogy is of course only partial with the trajectory of children acquiring first languages. In the absence of direct evidence, this is a reasonable guess. If we assume the normal estimate that a generation is 25–30 years, and take into account that the first and the third generations must be slightly shorter in this count, we can estimate the effect of ELF to establish itself well enough for detection in about 60–70 years from its beginning. Although English has been used as a lingua franca for centuries, as already pointed out in the Introduction, the most recent, explosive expansion can be timed to coincide with the Internet in the mid-1990s. At present we are experiencing the first generation of global ELF.

FREQUENCY AND CHANGE

A macro-level phenomenon that has long been known in linguistics, even though it may not be at the heart of social phenomena in the most usual sense, is item frequency. The frequency of words and structures reflects and apparently also influences language change. As far as very large-scale trajectories are concerned, this opens a fascinating perspective on languages and their uses. It has been well established that frequent items behave differently from infrequent ones (see e.g. Bybee & Hopper 2001). Recently, a large quantitative study of several Indo-European languages by a group of evolutionary biologists over a very long time (Pagel et al. 2007; Pagel 2009) presented strong evidence on the relationship between the frequency with which an item is used and its survival in language: the most frequently used items survive the longest. They are also likely to retain irregularity best. This may go some way towards explaining why the general tendency of irregular verb forms to regularise over very long periods of time (Lieberman et al. 2007) has not led to complete regularity. Even though the tacit assumption in much of this research is that speakers are monolingual, it is far more probable that a fair proportion if not most of the people whose language is on the databases have been multilingual. Be that as it may, there is no obvious reason why multilinguals would be differently affected by such tendencies. If frequency is a central factor in predicting the survival of items and forms, it would be odd if it was limited to speakers' first languages only (see Chapter 4, Section 4.1.3).

Frequency of usage relates back to language communities: as network analysis argues, frequently encountered forms tend to survive intact for long periods of time, even if they are complex and irregular. Strong and multiplex social ties in close-knit communities create favourable conditions for frequent exposure to the same items and forms. Conditions of more sporadic encounters are conducive to faster change, but frequency effects apply there as well, since repeated encounters are a prerequisite for effective diffusion (see Milroy & Milroy 1985). If we think of second language use, it is clear that exposure patterns to an additional language differ from those in first languages, especially where speakers' first languages coincide with that of the communal majority language. It would seem clear, though, that frequency affects second language use as well, since frequent items would appear to be easier to memorise and a safer option in communicating with other second-language speakers. The mechanisms involved ought to be similar to the use of unmarked forms discussed above, even though frequent items do not always coincide with unmarked items. But how does it actually work in ELF? Is the preference curve for frequent items steeper or shallower than in ENL? These questions are discussed further in Chapter 4.

WHAT ASPECTS OF LANGUAGE ARE INVOLVED

Contact research has tended to focus its investigation on phonological and lexicogrammatical aspects of language. There is thus much less to go on for making hypotheses on other features of ELF. Nevertheless, it is not difficult to see that crossing boundaries in the lexicogrammatical domain alone can yield insights into change and its counterforces; views on grammar that take lexis on board (for instance Fillmore et al. 1988; Sinclair 1996/2004; Hunston & Francis 2000; Östman & Fried 2005) reveal patterning that pertains to multi-word units. These have been found to occupy a central position in users' processes, and it seems highly plausible that they should also play a significant role in language change. Many scholars have attached considerable importance to calquing in language change, which already operates at the interface of lexis and grammar (e.g. Winford 2003). Phraseological sequences are taken up in Chapter 5.

Discourse phenomena have not attracted much attention from language change research. They would perhaps seem to fall into the domain of interaction, and be more naturally grouped among microsocial than macrosocial phenomena. Yet some macrosocial hypotheses, such as Trudgill's (1986) long-term accommodation, depend for their success on observing speakers in ongoing discourse, face-to-face interaction. Perhaps more importantly, patterns in discourse can throw light on wider social structures and patterns, such as the relative homogeneity of communities and their dominant network types. We can hypothesise, for instance, that discourse features which enhance explicitness characterise communities where weaker ties predominate, and conversely those communities where ties are strong and multiplex do not need much explicitness. Close-knit communities can rely on a large amount of information being shared between their members, and discourse devices such as metadiscourse, referent negotiation, or rephrasing are comparatively redundant (cf. Mauranen 1993b, 2007b). In contrast, more loosely structured communities, or people spending much of their time talking to a large number of acquaintances or strangers, can be expected to require much more explicitation to achieve fluent communication. In this book, such matters are discussed in several chapters, particularly 6 and 7, and while the perspective is mainly that of interaction (see also Section 2.3 in this chapter), it is worth keeping in mind that these practices have repercussions beyond the immediate microsocial environment.

When we look at ELF as a site of contact and change, its special features as second-order contact between similects are probably conducive to rapid diffusion of innovations in many domains. At the same time, a global language has a strong interest in maintaining comprehensibility. Processes that support comprehensibility can in themselves lead to changes or alternatively to attempts at maintaining as much of the shared usages as possible. Simplification and levelling would certainly seem to converge on the smallest common denominator, while innovative hybridity could open up to untraditional expressions that meet the needs of communication in circumstances of unpredictability. Discourse strategies furthering explicitness also serve the interests of comprehensibility. Before we go on to explore the microsocial environment where speakers engage in interaction with each other, let us take another step back and adopt the individual's angle for a moment.

2.2 The cognitive perspective

The relationship of the individual mind to language is puzzling. All language processing takes place in the individual cognition, in individual brains, so that in some sense language resides in individual minds, but the mind has only very limited access to its own workings. We can tap very little of our own language processing by introspection. What we can observe and analyse is only the recorded output of what the mind has processed – as digitised sound, marks on papyrus, paper, or a computer screen. The existence of language outside the individual mind is an abstraction from such outputs. Yet an individual deprived of a social environment would have no language. Thus, when we dip into the cognitive dimension of ELF, it is good to bear in mind that it is deeply intertwined with the social nature of language in every respect. The social orientation starts from the brain itself, which is attuned to its social environment, to other people, as will be discussed at the end of this section.

In this section the individual takes centre stage, along with some basic issues of online processing. Typical spoken language phenomena like hesitating, pausing, turn-taking, certain syntactic features, other-repetition, and searching for items probably result from the same processes whichever of his or her languages the speaker is using. Speech phenomena that can be observed directly as overt behaviour or as distinguishable linguistic features provide clues to ongoing cognitive processing, which we cannot access directly. For a general sketch of the speaker's processing conditions, we can start from the three principles sketched out by Biber et al. (1999: 1067) that help interpret features in speech grammar:

- keep talking
- limited planning ahead
- qualification of what has been said.

These principles shed light on a speaker's simultaneous tasks of keeping the floor and planning the output, together with recognising the temporal nature of speaking, which allows corrections, amendments, and additions to what has already been said but without the real possibility of taking anything back. These conditions affect the grammar of speaking. More recently, usage-based models have made bolder and more specific claims about the fundamental role that cognitive processes have in shaping grammars, in effect saying that a speaker's experience of language is a central building block of grammar; as this experience accumulates, it gets categorised, and gradually the categorisation increases in abstractness. As the levels of abstractness get higher, they eventually result in grammar (Croft 2000; Langacker 2000; Tomasello 2000; Bybee 2006). The accumulated lifetime experience of language is also emphasised in older psycholinguistic models (Levelt 1989) and other cognitively and interactively oriented linguistic models (Du Bois 1987; Ford et al. 2003). On these accounts, then, it is people's cognitive processes in response to repeated exposure that largely determine the ways in which language is represented, and how it probably is acquired.

2.2.1 *Entrenchment and abstraction*

While the most general principles like those outlined above probably govern all speech and its grammatical properties, in some respects we can expect first and later acquired languages to differ. These relate to the individual's accumulated experience, which must be different for languages that are acquired from infancy (whether there is one or more of them) and those learned later. Two central processes are involved in usage-based accounts of the representation of a language in an individual's cognitive makeup: entrenchment (see e.g. Dabrowska 2004; MacWhinney 2008) and abstraction, both of which rest on a speaker's aggregate experience. It is clear that speakers normally have much less exposure to their additional languages than their first, and this lesser experience is likely to be reflected in less deeply entrenched memory representations. Less extensive exposure may also result in more limited repertoires. Production and reception in a limited repertoire may impose a greater strain on working memory, slow down memory retrieval and schema accessibility, and make heavier demands on adaptive strategies. Moreover, recent psycholinguistic research has shown convincingly that frequency effects in language acquisition and use are considerable at all levels (e.g. Bybee & Hopper 2001; Ellis 2002).

The second process, abstraction, is typically assumed for first language acquisition and tallies best with children's learning and models of language change based on generational succession (Andersen 1989).

In Western societies, most second language acquisition takes place in classrooms, where linguistic abstractions in the form of rules are given to learners ready-made. Spontaneous SLA outside formal teaching tends to disregard grammatical phenomena to a degree (Ellis 2006), but learning chunks of language is open to adults as well as children (Bybee 2008), which should enable the acquisition of new patterns along with new lexis. Speakers' language repertoires are dynamic in the sense of being subject to constant change during their whole lifetime. Since most people's language repertoires comprise elements from more than one language, fairly similar processes of abstraction from repeatedly encountered material should be in operation for their entire repertoires even at post-childhood stages. It is also possible, as Dabrowska observes, that speakers' knowledge about their language may be less abstract than is commonly believed (2004: 228). If this is so, it would seem to have important implications for language-learning models, but should not differentiate between an individual's languages.

2.2.2 Fluency or the lack of it

A common experience of second-language speech is that it is less fluent than speaking in the native language. By extension, all dysfluencies in second-language speech are easily attributed to difficulties ensuing from speakers' non-nativeness even for perfectly normal speech phenomena. A useful reminder of the nature of spoken grammar is found in Biber et al.'s work: 'We may refer to the grammar of speech as "dynamic", in the sense that it is constructed and interpreted under real-time pressure, and correction or reformulation is possible only through hesitations, false starts, and other dysfluencies' (Biber et al. 1999: 1066). The descriptive grammar this quotation comes from deals exclusively with English as used by its 'core' native speakers, and was one of the first to dedicate considerable space to grammatical features of speech. While it is quite reasonable to assume that L2 speech has more of these 'dysfluent' features than L1, this is more likely to be a difference of degree than a dichotomy.

Reasons typically given for hesitation phenomena are that they either indicate processing problems or mark boundaries in the speech stream. Reasons of the first type include lexical searches (e.g. Field 2003; Chapter 4 below) and the speaker's need to play for time while planning. On the whole, hesitations are seen as indicators of trouble in speech execution, and responses to pressures of planning under time limitations. It is also likely that speech involves parallel but non-coextensive processing of different facets of language, such as intonation units and syntactic units. This is reflected in 'staggered' segmentation between syntagms and prosodic units (Mukherjee 2001). Similarly, pausing often occurs elsewhere than at clause boundaries in spontaneous speech, and mismatches between syntactic, intonational, and functional boundaries are not infrequently found (Chafe 1994). In all these respects second language use is presumably no different from first-language processing. Most research has been carried out on L1 users, with the unspoken assumption that L1 speakers are monolingual and that this is 'normal' speech processing, which serves as a legitimate basis for generalisation.

Attention to speech taxes the working memory. The contents of the working memory are the information the speaker currently attends to, and its two significant properties are limited capacity and limited duration. Retrieval from long-term memory is presumably a heavier task in SLU, where on account of less extensive exposure many elements of the language are less deeply entrenched than in a first-acquired language. This may be exacerbated by simultaneous competition from two (or more) language systems (cf. Jarvis & Pavlenko 2007; Riionheimo 2009). Second language use thus carries extra processing pressure: in addition to normal conditions of limited planning, speakers operate under conditions of limited resources and multi-source competition.

The second kind of reason attributed to hesitation is less accidental and invokes a purpose: many researchers have noted the tendency of hesitations, pauses, and repeats to take place at junctures. Beginnings and ends of units have been implicated as the most likely locations for them to occur. However, the units that have been investigated have been of different kinds; apparently they can be words, clauses, utterances, or something else. Moreover, different components need not be processed coextensively, as noted above. Hesitation indicators may also take place at the planning stage, thus *before* the output. What Levelt says about interruptions in connection with overt repairs seems to be a fair summary of a general understanding of the placement of indicators of processing trouble: 'In overt repairs, interruption can take place during the utterance of the troublesome item, or right after it, or one or more syllables later ... But interruption can also be delayed by one or more words' (Levelt 1989: 479–80). The processing evidence from interruptions for hesitation or repair thus remains open to several kinds of interpretations. Socially oriented reasons have also been proposed. Among other purposes suggested for pauses and hesitations are indications of the speaker's willingness to hand over the turn to the listener, to help the non-native listener by marking proportionately more word boundaries (Field 2003), anticipating self-repairs (Laakso & Sorjonen 2010), or managing strategic tensions (Laitinen et al. forthcoming). In this way, hesitation phenomena occupy some of the common territory between the cognitive and the interactional, and serve in both kinds of roles, as will be discussed further in Chapter 7.

Speaking is not always peppered with hesitations and signs of trouble. It can proceed without much apparent difficulty even when quite complex utterances are produced. Characteristically, fluent and less fluent stretches alternate, and my ELF data contains plenty of evidence of complex speech with few or no signs of processing difficulties (Example 2.1): a clear shift appears in line 5, following a stretch with many hesitations (*er*), repeats (*or or, from from…*). The speaker then coughs, pauses for seven seconds, and continues with another stretch which, despite equal complexity in content, proceeds with notable fluency (see Appendix 1 for the basic transcription conventions used).

(2.1)

... and in the in the 19th century or or early 20th century er frozen lakes and 2 frozen rivers er er very much helped to er to move er timber from from forest to to saw mills and you also certainly know that the first saw mills were er located by rivers and produced er hydropower of the rivers for sawing <COUGH> <P:07> if we try to er define modernisation i would say first that it is a very complicated thing, and modernisation is not just a change of social structures, towards what we have now but i would emphasise that modernisation includes also change in the ways of thinking, and that is important, and that means that during the past 150 years people have understood that the society is changing, and they have wanted to change things and change as such has been evaluated as a positive matter, because change has been seen as a promise of better future, so that people could have better future on earth not only in heaven, and this way of thinking has changed rapidly let's say since the 18th century

Oscillation of this kind may of course have diverse origins, but one thing it does is indicate rhythmic changes in attention and concentration, which probably works well for speakers and hearers alike. Both need sequences of less concentration and less importance to punctuate focal stretches, which require more processing effort.

2.2.3 Units of processing

The processing load associated with limited planning is reduced by schematic units variously known as formulaic sequences (Wray 2002, 2008; papers in Schmitt 2004), prefabricated elements (Pawley & Syder 1983; Erman & Warren 2000), fixed expressions (Moon 1998), or simply discussed under 'phraseology' (Granger & Meunier 2008). These are conventionalised lexicogrammatical units, which typically consist of lexical words as well as grammatical elements, with fixed and variable parts. Unlike traditional idioms, they can also be compositional and transparent. They have been reported to make processing easier and more fluent, but only for first-language users (Pawley & Syder 1983; Nattinger & DeCarrico 1992; Wray 2002). Like idioms, they are not very frequent (Moon 1998), which has been drawn on as an explanation of why they seem to be so inaccessible to learners (Bybee 2008). If it is indeed the case, as Wray (2002) argues, that non-native users have to build every utterance from its smallest components without access to larger schematic units, this must greatly obstruct their fluency and aggravate the task of achieving communicative competence in a foreign language. However, counterevidence has also been found, in ELF speech (Mauranen 2005) as well as in the performance of learners of English in word association tasks and in text production (Vetchinnikova forthcoming). Evidence from ELF will be brought to bear on the issue in Chapter 5, where it looks quite clear that ELF speech uses multi-word sequences just as ENL speech does, and that ELF speakers also generate their own preferences.

2.2.4 Approximation strategies

In view of all the apparent adversities L2 users face, one option for using limited resources economically is to take processing shortcuts and resort to approximate forms of the language. By approximating target forms well enough, speakers can contribute to communicative success. In untutored SLA, known as 'naturalistic' learning, speakers commonly make do without grammatical elements in English even at otherwise high levels of proficiency, ignoring grammatical markers normally used in the standard language (Ellis 2006). Approximation is beneficial because the nature of processing is fuzzy in most areas of cognition, including speech perception and production. Precision in memory can be achieved to a higher degree when items are firmly entrenched in long-term declarative memory, but with less deep entrenchment, the connections may remain less stable. We can posit that at cognitive level, approximation is involuntary and results from realities of perception, memory, and access. At the same time, it tends to work as a communicative strategy, and to the extent that it does, the positive feedback strengthens the items that have been generated. A complex environment like ELF seems to require stretching the tolerance of fuzziness wider than usual, but speakers seem to adapt to this, as is shown in research that has observed less miscommunication in ELF than expected (House 2003; Mauranen 2006a; Kaur 2009).

An item that deviates from or falls short of the target (say, *assimilisation* for *assimilation*) in a speaker's output may result from either insufficient or partial representation or from insufficient access routes to the target item. Memory representations are less than perfect, as can be seen from people's partial or approximate representations of precise shapes or proportions of familiar objects (try drawing a picture of the chair you mostly sit on from memory), melodies, etc., not to speak of memory for events. Access routes may be more precarious in a less entrenched language and on the whole for less frequent items. Yet it is possible that approximation works because a speaker's output has enough for the interlocutor to go on, and they can manage with less accurate detail than would seem to be the case if standard written language were taken as the benchmark. Ordinary language comprehension relies heavily on preceding context and prospection, which means that as speech unfolds, hearers have usually already made guesses about what is coming next, and need only confirm that their guesses were right (Sinclair & Mauranen 2006). They do not start working out bottom-up the meaning of each individual item as it comes up. Along similar lines, recent psychological research into processing suggests that ordinary comprehension may rest on relatively shallow processing, which would seem to go a long way towards explaining why it is possible to arrive at mutual understanding in lingua franca communication despite its many non-standard features:

> There is growing evidence that the processing involved in ordinary language comprehension is, in fact, fairly shallow: that is to say, people may integrate the meanings of the most salient lexical items, some easily accessible grammatical cues, and contextual information to arrive at a semantic interpretation without fully parsing the sentence. (Dabrowska 2004: 23)

Memory for sense overrides memory for form in language, and a relatively small proportion of utterances are remembered verbatim. Approximations may retain the meaning but only part of the conventional expression, as in *building stones* (cf. *building blocks*) or *the hen or the egg* (cf. *the chicken or the egg*). The longer the unit considered, the easier it seems to accept that mental representations are partial and skewed towards meaning rather than form (we do not expect to remember sentences verbatim, let alone books or even their chapters), but for smaller units it is not so clear. Do morphemes necessarily get stored whole? Words? The controversy around conventionalised sequences has already been touched upon. If chunks are learned and remembered (Ellis 2006; Bybee 2008), do they have limitations of size? A reasonable guess would be that chunks of processing cannot exceed the capacity of working memory, and there is some evidence to support this (Sinclair & Mauranen 2006), but more is needed. Chapters 4 and 5 below will discuss these issues further in the light of evidence from transcriptions and corpus data. The issue of regularities in approximation is also taken up there: if approximations, or other non-standard forms in ELF are random and show no regularities or directionality, it means that ELF amounts to an arbitrary collection of L2 errors, as has been suggested by Mollin (2006) and Shaw et al. (2009). Yet, as will be seen, there is regularity in ELF, despite large numbers of non-standard features.

Some items are more salient than others, and presumably better remembered. To what degree salience is a product of the current context, previous experience, or other cognitive factors is controversial (see e.g. Giora 2004), but some aspects of language, such as content words, would seem to be stored and context-independent, while contextual salience is likely to result from an interplay of the stored and the instantial. An effective approximation is a matter of shared ground between interlocutors, be it based on stored or contextual elements. A noun such as *comment* is a good candidate for being salient, because it is frequent and presumably because it has existing cognates in many languages. It is also easily accessible because it is both well entrenched and specific (Dabrowska 2004). ELF speakers use it in the same functions as ENL speakers, but often with verbs that would be untypical in ENL such as ***say** some brief **comments*** (Mauranen 2007c). Such verbs nevertheless fall within the semantic field of speaking; the combination approximates a more conventional collocation (*make/add comments*) and may be readily comprehensible to interlocutors. Another typical approximation is using non-standard prepositions (*a brief comment of this*), where the approximation concerns form but is not focal or particularly central to the meaning of the whole unit. Precise forms would seem harder to approximate than meanings – which presumably lend themselves to inference more readily. Morphological complexity also makes lexis more resistant to borrowing, which is why verbs get borrowed less than other kinds of open-class words (Winford 2003).

2.2.5 *Cognition and intersubjectivity*

The cognitive and the interactional are closely intertwined. Multilingual proficiency is dynamic (Herdina & Jessner 2002), and if we view language as a system, it is perhaps best seen as a complex system showing many features typical of complex (or 'chaotic') systems in general. Language systems influence each other in multilingual cognition, and in addition to this mutual influence, they act like other complex systems in interaction with their environment (Larsen-Freeman & Cameron 2008). For language systems, the crucial environment is social.

Human cognition is strikingly attuned to intersubjectivity from the start; consciousness develops together with dialogical competence, as much research on early language development (e.g. Tomasello 2003) and research on mirror neuron systems (e.g. Bråten & Trevarthen 2007) have been showing over the last few years. For understanding the mind, contemporary brain research seeks ways to observe people in interaction with their social environment, because other people are the most important constituent of the environment for humans (Hari 2007). For the present purpose of describing ELF speech, it is important to keep in mind that the same phenomena can be viewed from either side. So, for example, collaborative completions (cf. Section 2.3 below; Chapter 4, Section 4.3.2), which are quite common in dialogic speech, can be seen as reflecting other-centred (altricentric) systems of the mind (Bråten 2007). At the same time, they can equally well be couched in interactional linguistic terms as affiliative cooperative acts (e.g. Couper-Kuhlen & Selting 2001). In the next section, the viewpoint shifts to the interactive perspective, with other-oriented individuals engaged in interaction through language.

2.3 The microsocial perspective

Language is used primarily in face-to-face interaction between individuals. This is where meaning gets constructed and negotiated, and where linguistic influences and innovations are passed on. Individuals engaged in talk contribute to a common pool of shared knowledge, simultaneously attending to the needs of the situation as it unfolds, where interactional aspects like speakers' interests in maintaining face, taking turns, and responding to each other's contributions enmesh with extralinguistic events like people coming and going, meals being served, technological equipment playing up, etc. It is a complex task to handle, involving both content-related and interactional matters to be managed through language. Yet it is to serve such complex interactional needs that language has evolved, and interaction is unquestionably its most fundamental mode of existence.

The primacy of speech has been emphasised above all by conversation analysts from the 1970s onwards, and as Goodwin (1981) put it, speech production is an interactional achievement. Similar ideas have found a foothold in other research traditions as well, such as early forms of Discourse Analysis (Sinclair & Coulthard 1975), and generally among researchers who have made spoken language their focus (e.g. Tannen 1989; Chafe 1994; Aijmer 2002a; Linell 2005). As Du Bois (2003: 52) puts it: 'face-to-face-conversation ... is pervasive, constituting the commonest use of language for virtually all language users, the first learned by children, and one of the few forms of language use found in all languages, at all stages of human history'. Talk in interaction is the microsocial perspective that most immediately captures language in the making. At the same time, it is the meeting point of the macrosocial and the individual. The final section in this chapter discusses the interface of the two perspectives already discussed, and identifies their connections.

2.3.1 Inherent intersubjectivity of language

Awareness of language use and form as permeated by social interaction and intersubjectivity has moved to the centre of linguistic research in the last few decades. Many linguistic traditions, especially those focusing on spoken language, have stressed the nature of speech as a joint activity since the mid-1970s, although interestingly, the interactional orientation has not been confined to speech. Traditions emanating from Bakhtin's thinking (Voloshinov 1973; Bakhtin 1986) have made a significant contribution to conceptualising language as a dialogic phenomenon, whose dialogism is inherent, independently of whether it manifests itself in written or spoken form. In practice, Bakhtinian dialogism is primarily concerned with written text, and one of the central manifestations of dialogism in this tradition is intertextuality, much investigated in Critical Discourse Analysis.

An offshoot of the awakened interest in spoken interaction was an 'interpersonal turn' in the analysis of academic writing in the early 1990s. Written academic discourse began to be analysed in terms of interaction between writers and readers, with concepts such as hedging

(Salager-Meyer 1994) and metadiscourse (Mauranen 1993b). This focus on writer–reader relationship continues as a strong research tradition, which has lead to important insights about interpersonal aspects in academic text (e.g. Hyland 2000, 2005). The interpersonal turn was no doubt also greatly influenced by developments in the sociology of science (Knorr-Cetina et al. 1981; Gilbert & Mulkay 1984; Schaeffer & Shapin 1985; Latour & Woolgar 1986), where scientific research was seen as a social and rhetorical, not solely intellectual activity, as the traditional fields of history and philosophy of science had taken it to be. It nevertheless took several years before the interest in interactional linguistic features found its way to spoken discourse in the academy, reflected in the compilation of corpora of academic speaking in the late 1990s (cf. Chapter 3).

As already observed in the previous section (Section 2.2) on cognition, intersubjectivity has also been enthusiastically embraced in brain research and neuroscience. From this angle, it is seen as an element of altricentric behaviour, manifesting the inherently social orientation of the brain (Bråten & Trevarthen 2007). This research has given intersubjectivity a new kind of empirical basis. Interactional linguistics has also made steady progress since the early 1990s (e.g. Couper-Kuhlen & Selting 2001) and maintains a steady position as one of the core approaches to investigating talk in interaction.

As a new field, relatively unburdened by the traditional 'written language bias' in linguistics (Linell 2005), ELF research has almost exclusively focused on exploring spoken language. This is a natural route to take even if it is not the traditional one, because it is in interactional discourse that we can best see language and linguistic norms in the making, and because it has been technically possible to record authentic speech throughout the short history of ELF research. A speech-in-interaction approach is particularly valuable to ELF, because ELF communities are unusually heterogeneous in terms of linguistic and cultural backgrounds, and it is when the speakers come together and negotiate their differences and commonalities that we can capture their mutual influence and adaptation as these processes take place. Crucially, interaction is the only situation where we can observe miscommunication taking place: monologues (such as lectures or sermons) may or may not be understood by their hearers, but there is no way in which this can be ascertained from speech data, unless we also have access to interlocutors' responses.

Perfect understanding is hardly ever possible to achieve in the sense that participants' representations of what was said or meant would be identical. As long as the match is good enough for participants to proceed, discrepancies between representations are not likely to surface. Instances of non-understanding or partial understanding are nevertheless mostly easy to detect in speech recordings, because interlocutors who need to respond appropriately are usually quick to take up the problematic expressions; if they are to be corrected, they must be retrievable, which implies they must remain in participants' short-term memories.

2.3.2 Language change in action

Macrosocial theories make assumptions about the microsocial level to the effect that they set up face-to-face interaction as the principal site where language change will begin and be consolidated. Innovations are first accepted (or rejected) in interaction, and as they are carried over to other interactions, with time the new uses that have spread can be seen at the level of mainstream usage (e.g. Milroy & Milroy 1985; Trudgill 1986). Something like this probably happens in spoken discourse, although written media obviously must play an important and increasingly influential role in diffusing innovations, with its current interactive digital modes.

Many researchers have noted that it is impossible to notice language change before it has already taken place (e.g. Thomason 2001; Milroy 2003), because there is no way of predicting which of all innovations that speakers come up with will actually find a foothold in a speech community and eventually diffuse widely enough to establish themselves as part of the language. Croft (2000) criticises theoretical accounts of language change for presuming that there is always variability around without presenting an account of mechanisms of innovation itself. As an alternative, he adopts Keller's (1994) model based on the 'invisible hand' idea, where innovations arise as unintended consequences of intentional linguistic acts. Such a view would seem to fit in well with ELF observations; it seems that speakers use creative solutions to challenges arising in the heterogeneous and complex language environments that a lingua franca entails (see e.g. Dewey 2006; Cogo 2009; Hülmbauer 2009; Hüttner 2009). The difficulty still holds for analysts detecting innovations that will spread in the community and get accepted into the language. Only time will tell which of the innumerable solutions will be of an enduring kind, and by then change has already taken place. What we nevertheless can observe is how new forms, such as approximations, blends, or neologisms appear, what they are like, and how they develop in the course of the interaction. They can be expected to be particularly common in ELF interactions, given the challenges of the communicative situations. Non-standard or unusual forms can of course arise from many sources, from just one-off slips of the tongue to solutions on which speakers gradually converge. They can even fluctuate in one person's speech.

If we look at the principal mechanisms of contact-induced language change listed by Thomason (2001: 139), we can see that three of the seven mechanisms involve face-to-face interaction (code-switching, code alternation and negotiation), and two have to do with multilingualism (second-language-acquisition strategies and bilingual first-language acquisition). The entire list (Thomason 2001: 139) is as follows:

1. code-switching
2. code alternation
3. passive familiarity
4. negotiation
5. second language acquisition strategies
6. bilingual first language acquisition
7. deliberate decision.

Of these, code-switching and code alteration play important roles in facilitating intelligibility and fluency. They will not be explored in detail in this book, but they have been studied in ELF conversations, where they have been shown to occur frequently and be drawn on as useful and effective communicative resources (Cogo 2009; Hülmbauer 2009). What Thomason calls 'negotiation' is a central concern in the present context. In her definition, this is a mechanism 'when speakers change their language (A) to approximate what they believe to be the patterns of another language or dialect (B)' (Thomason 2001: 142). In effect, this is one of the cornerstones of speaker interaction: a number of processes have been distinguished which involve speakers doing what their interlocutors do, and conversationalists converging on usage in the course of interaction. Such cooperative behaviour has been identified as fulfilling a number of functions, mostly interactional: speakers want to show affiliation, comprehension, encouragement, willingness to cooperate, sharing the same ground, and generally construct and maintain positive interactional space. As a consequence their language use is affected.

2.3.3 Accommodation

People working together for common goals is thus the driving force behind their linguistic adaptation to each other's ways of speaking. One way of looking at this is in terms of the invisible hand model suggested in Keller (1994). Cooperative adaptation may be even more fundamental than its linguistic manifestations. As Meltzhoff and Brooks (2007: 152) note: 'The duplication of the action patterns, mannerisms, and gestures others use is part of the fabric of human communication. It runs in the background and fosters emotional cohesion in everyday interactions, oftentimes outside explicit awareness.' Accommodation theory is the major theoretical framework for dealing with adaptive behaviour in interaction. It started in social psychology in the 1970s (Giles 1973; Giles & Smith 1979) and has since undergone some updates and developments (Gallois et al. 2005). Its main interest has been in situational convergence and divergence of accents, especially in terms of varying social prestige, but in principle its tenets could apply at any level of language.

The possibility of more lasting adaptations in accent through prolonged accommodation was suggested by Trudgill (1986), who saw this 'long-term accommodation' as more interesting to the linguist. His own interest was primarily in regional dialect contact, which should be close to similect contact in ELF, as discussed already in Section 2.1.4. Trudgill's hypothesis is that if similar accommodation is done repeatedly over longer periods of time, it may result in permanent change. This is a plausible hypothesis for explaining dialect levelling, observed commonly as a result of dialect contact situations. But how often will one have to accommodate for the outcome to become permanent, and how long does the process take? Trudgill offers no answers to these questions, but he suggests that the process must be slow, and 'not completed for a number of years' (Trudgill 1986: 22). The problem of timescale, already discussed above, was noted as being hard to pin down for several reasons.

In ongoing interaction, accommodation is readily observable in ELF (Jenkins 2000; Cogo & Dewey 2006; Cogo 2009; Hülmbauer 2009; Hynninen forthcoming). Different studies subsume somewhat different phenomena under its wing. If seen in a wide sense, cooperative acts such as other-repetition (or 'echoing', cf. Chapter 7) and explicitness are integral parts of accommodation. If, on the other hand, we assume a narrower view and only include features where speakers reduce the dissimilarities between their speech patterns and adopt features from each other's speech, then the process is best seen when we can also demonstrate that there was an initial discrepancy between the speakers. This is the interpretation adopted in this book, and I shall illustrate it with an example. The following example (2.2a–b) from the ELFA corpus shows how alternative forms of a word are negotiated, and how speakers accommodate and finally converge on one of them. The example comes from a seminar discussion with several participants. It is a sequence where speakers discuss same-sex marriage in different countries. Example (2.2a) shows where the topic starts, and (2.2b) shows snippets of all turns in the discussion where the term surfaces.

(2.2a)

<S1> [yeah] from time to time I think er it kind of er, first this law for that you can *registrate* your er how you say your (S5: sort of partnership) partnership er I think er you cannot argue for too much in in in Finland you have to, go li- by [steps] (S5:[(it was)]) yeah (S5: yes) with small steps so [that you can]

<S5> [was it] in this, er

<S1> it was [together]

<S5> [this spring], spring 2002 was it 2001 (S1:mhm) that it became possible in Finland that you can *register* you can't [get] (NS2: [ah]) married and you can't you can *register* yourself, to be partners [with]

(2.2b)

<S1> ...you can *registrate* your er how you say your...

<S5> ... you can *register* you can't get married and you can't you can *register* yourself ...

<S5> ... very much against this, er *registration* thing because ...

<S3> ... between *registration* and marriage so

<S5> ... got the right to *registrate* so I suppose in another ten years ...

<S1> ... er getting re- *registrated* was were kept together but then ...

As the example shows, the first time around S1 introduces the topic, using the non-standard *registrate*, which looks like a back-formation derived from the noun *registration*. S5 continues the topic, using the standard form *register*. A little later she shows some uncertainty about the form, with a hesitation marker (*er*) following a short pause, and then opts for a safe solution, a nominalised form that neutralises the difference (*registration thing*). The next time the problematic word surfaces in S3's turn, who also plays safe and opts for the noun. After that, S5 shows accommodation and produces the verb *registrate*. Finally, S1 confirms a past tense version of her own initial form, now adopted by S5 as well. This example is from one speech event, and of course gives no indication whether any of the speakers used this form on a later occasion. Hynninen (forthcoming) nevertheless shows with similar data from students' group work that on repeated meetings of the same group, results of earlier accommodation are confirmed. Even this does not show whether such forms have begun to diffuse more widely, which would mean that accommodation has resulted in something that is on its way to being used in the wider language community.

Accommodation of the kind shown in Example (2.2a–b) is found every now and then in our corpus. The instances are fairly easy to detect when speakers converge on a non-standard form. If the outcome is a standard form, it is more likely to be interpreted as a correction of some kind: other-repair, or if not an immediate response, then what is known as an embedded correction, where the second speaker produces the correct form in his or her turn. Since L2 research has been almost exclusively concerned with learner language or, rarely, L1–L2 conversations, the usual models for interpreting such discrepancies and shifts have tended to see them in terms of correction, not negotiation or accommodation. However, taking a 'correction' interpretation implies that the act is seen relative to a standard, and that either both parties agree on the standard or at least one speaker, the one doing the correcting, has the authority to judge what is within the standard and what is not.

Enhanced explicitness is generally taken to be a collaborative strategy, and it has been frequently observed in ELF research (Seidlhofer 2005; Dewey 2006; Mauranen 2007b). Explicitness can be seen as a form of accommodation (e.g. Hynninen forthcoming), as it is a way of accommodating to the hearer's perceived interpretive competence. This would be a wider notion of accommodation than we have been concerned with here, though. Explicitness finds many forms, such as metadiscourse, repetition, and rephrasing, and syntactic strategies such as 'negotiating topics' (Mauranen 2007b; Chapters 6 and 7 below). The tendency to expand explicitness in discourse relates to what Blum-Kulka (1986) termed 'explicitation' in translator's work. Explicitation may relate to a natural response in individuals operating in a language contact situation, anticipating gaps in shared ground. This is a reasonable hypothesis to make in connection with the great cultural heterogeneity of ELF environments, as it is the exact opposite of the implicitness observed in small, relatively homogeneous cultures, where much can be assumed to be shared and less needs to be spelt out to hearers or readers (Mauranen 1993a, 1993b).

A much-debated issue in ELF research has been the willingness of native speakers of English to accommodate in ELF interaction in the interests of comprehensibility. Jenkins (2000, 2007) has generally found them unwilling or incapable of accommodating to non-native speakers' needs. On the other hand, Hynninen (forthcoming) and Carey (2010) found several instances of ENL speakers accommodating to L2 speakers in ELF environments. Carey also detected some negative cases of accommodation, or what Gallois et al. (2005) call 'over-accommodation', i.e. unsolicited and unhelpful accommodation, which can be seen as emanating from group stereotypes and to be patronising, like 'foreigner talk'.

2.3.4 *Enhanced cooperativeness*

Researchers have noticed that ELF interaction shows pronounced cooperativeness. House (2003: 569) is one of those who have emphasised the significance of collaboration, observing that co-construction in particular is one of the most prominent features of ELF discourse. Typical collaborative features are illustrated below (Example 2.3) in the light of another excerpt from the ELFA corpus. The example shows one speaker's (S6) turn in a seminar discussion. Of the other six participants, three (S1, S3, and SU) make inserts into S6's turn:

(2.3)

<S6> about stalin i heard i heard that er during the 70's they had a vote in the city council that should they tear this old toompea castle, @away@ and build
<S1> [pull it down] </S1>
[a new] new techno city and it was like one or two votes that @@
<S3> saved it </S3>
that saved it so it was
<SU> mhm-hm </SU>
pretty close that that @@ those castles wouldn't be there anymore </S6>

Here S1 contributes by an alternative expression (*pull it down*) to S6's's *tear away*, S3's *saved it* is a collaborative completion (see also Chapter 4, Section 4.3.2), anticipating what S6 might be saying next. An unidentified student (SU) engages in back-channelling, one of the basic ways of showing listenership (e.g. McCarthy 1998; Warren 2006), and something that has been often reported to be particularly frequent in ELF interactions. It is important to note, however, that cooperativeness does not necessarily entail consensus or agreement between participants. Cooperation is required even if speakers engage in argument or express divergent views.

2.3.5 *Interaction and content orientation*

Apart from cooperativeness, a strong focus on content has been observed by many early researchers of ELF. Content orientation is sometimes interpreted to mean that interactional features such as hedges tend to go missing in ELF discourse (e.g. Cogo & Dewey 2006: 65–6; Karhukorpi 2006). On the other hand, other researchers have found that interactional language is well represented in ELF interactions (Riekkinen 2010; Suviniitty 2010). The question clearly needs to be settled on the basis of empirical evidence, but it is an important one. If we assume that lingua franca discourse tends to hold on to those features of language that are most crucial to communication, or necessary features of language, the question arises as to whether it is reasonable to assume that the essence of communication is content.

Clearly it makes sense to distinguish aspects of discourse, and one basic line of division would seem to run between content orientation (the 'message' that speakers are co-constructing in conversation) and the 'organising' orientation (speakers organising the discourse and managing the interaction), as suggested by Sinclair and Mauranen (2006). We can then ask whether features that have been put forward as having universal importance, such as discourse markers (McCarthy 2001) or metadiscourse (Mauranen 2010), which clearly fall into the organising type, make their way into ELF discourse (cf. Chapter 4, Section 4.1.3, and Chapter 6). Some of the expressions that fulfil the functions shared by all users may differ from Standard English or ENL preferences, but the function may still find expression. Metadiscourse was, for example, expressed in ELFA data with *sorry last thing what you said; I'm sort of er just making this argument; now we've started to getting into, more closer to what I what I er wa- was a title of the talk today*, none of which are quite standard or routine expressions of discourse reflexivity, but serve the same purpose. Hedges show similar properties (*the thinking of the youths must be different i'm* ***i'm not sure but this is a personal meaning of course****; more benefits than the german one er* ***it's just my idea; but this is my opinion of course***). Importantly, Riekkinen (2009, 2010) analysed lexical hedges in doctoral defences, and noticed that ELF speakers used more of them than ENL speakers in comparable speech events in the MICASE corpus. She also found that the speakers in ELFA often added a hedge as an afterthought when they had started without any hedging, which is what Couper-Kuhlen and Thompson (2005) call 'concessive repairs', also observed in Karhukorpi (2006). Riekkinen felt that the ELF speakers were trying to be very clear about their politeness strategies, as they used more lexical and personal hedges rather than particles. Most interestingly, she noticed a connection to the style of speaking of the opponent in the defences: the more casual and discussion-like the style, the fewer the hedges. The easy-going style thus seemed to reduce some of the face-threat inherent in examining. This worked in the same way in ENL and

ELF, suggesting that register choices are made within the degrees of freedom allowed by genre conventions, and that interaction shapes language in quite subtle ways even if speakers are not using their first language.

It would seem highly unlikely that beyond very basic transactional exchanges language could work well without interactive elements. Therefore situations demanding sophisticated language, such as academic environments, can yield data that is relevant to seeing a bigger picture of ELF than minimal encounters between strangers. Prioritising content does not entail rejection of interactional concerns, although the idea is familiar from the time preceding 'the interpersonal turn' in analysing academic writing, touched on above. In dealing with others in social situations, humans are attuned to the social interaction, and language is shaped accordingly.

As already pointed out, interaction is the meeting place of the social and the cognitive. It is a microsocial phenomenon in the sense of taking place in face-to-face encounters. However, it connects with the macrosocial dimension as the site of linguistic change: it triggers innovative solutions from participants, and it diffuses innovations from one context to another. It is based on cooperation, which provides a key to understanding how speakers achieve communication in situations that would seem to be rife with obstacles to communication: interactants cooperate to co-construct meaning and negotiate the linguistic means of establishing it to mutual satisfaction. Looking into the cognitive from the angle of social interaction is a central interest in contemporary brain research; it is in tune with a general emphasis on top-down processes, where prediction plays a central role in processing information. For ELF research, social interaction occupies a key position, not just because it is observable, but because it is where the complexities of language contact come together. Participants in situations where English is the lingua franca often have little to go on when making predictions about shared knowledge with their interlocutors. This puts more pressure on language than is usual in monolingual interaction: English is the principal shared resource, and communicative success depends on how well interactants can make use of this to achieve mutual comprehensibility.

2.4 Summary

In this chapter, we have discussed linguistic issues relevant to English as a lingua franca from three perspectives: macrosocial, cognitive, and microsocial. The main issues relate to the ways in which speakers manage communicative interaction in communities that use a global lingua franca, how they deal with the contingencies of complex situations with a language that is not the first language for most, and the consequences of all this to language as a whole.

Among the many, often diffuse communities that use English as their contact language, academic discourse communities are among the most prominent. They consist of networks of a growing number of mobile speakers representing different similect groups and simultaneously identifying with different imagined communities: disciplinary communities, national, institutional, and many others. It is reasonable to expect this second-order language contact to result in rapid diffusion of innovations, in other words alterations in English as (we think) we know it.

Change becomes visible when it has surfaced at the macrosocial level; it is only when language communities adopt a usage on a large scale that we speak about change, although it results from smaller-scale activities of individuals and their interaction. Language in interaction is the hub of language in the making – and we must subsume communication through written text under language in interaction. In the end it is individuals who do all the talking, and language is produced and understood by virtue of being somehow stored in their neural systems. In turn, the brain is specially attuned to interaction with its environment, where other individuals constitute the most important environment for us. The different 'levels' at which language takes place, our different perspectives, are thus angles on one phenomenon, language in use. It is easy to accept that such a complex whole can never be static, but its dynamism manifests itself very differently depending on where we are looking from: our three perspectives span an enormous timescale, from the millisecond-rate of real-time processing in the brain to the slow changes of whole languages over centuries or millennia. The perspectives also span a huge range of scale from tiny elements, brain neurons, to large-scale abstractions, and entire language systems. Among these, it is the middle ranges that are best observable to the human analyst, while the extremes are accessible to us only indirectly.

Frequency is one of those large-scale phenomena that are not readily accessible to the speaker, even though interaction is where frequencies get reproduced and thereby established. In fact frequency cuts across all our perspectives. It is implicated in speakers' processing speed and accuracy, accounts for intriguing differences in language-internal patterning, and plays a crucial role in the evolution of vocabulary. Frequent encounters with the same items have been evoked in explaining the maintenance of complex forms in close-knit communities and in long-term accommodation leading to new dialect acquisition. Observing frequent items requires large quantities of data. Now that we have extensive corpus data, it is interesting to see what happens to frequencies in ELF: do they show a different distribution from ENL items, are the items themselves different, and is there more variation or less?

Even a casual look at a speech event using English as a lingua franca shows that it teems with linguistic variation; numerous non-standard forms will be in evidence, which vary, moreover, with speakers and sometimes fluctuate from moment to moment in the same speaker's use.

On the basis of the above, we can posit some more specific hypotheses concerning the linguistic characteristics of ELF. All linguistic features reflect the social environment that they are used in, and to understand ELF, all our perspectives come into play.

First of all, with all this linguistic and cultural diversity and the ensuing reduced predictability in communicative situations, we can hypothesise that a major communicative consequence includes explicitness. Constant similect encounters can be assumed to impinge on use by enhancing transparency: simplicity in grammar, complexity in lexis, and explicitness in discourse. Another general-level hypothesis is that speakers adapt to ELF circumstances by accommodating and converging, but also by adapting to variability. It is a reasonable assumption that speakers with substantial ELF experience learn to live with a more varied selection of English lects than is customary for first- or second-language users in an ENL-speaking environment or a learner exposed to standard varieties.

Much along the lines of increasing explicitness, it is a good strategy to pick up the interlocutor's words or phrases, as they can be assumed to be comprehensible to the speaker who first used them, and repeating them (other-repetition or 'echoing') is one way of indicating comprehension. Like explicitness, echoing promotes efficiency.

Moreover, echoing has an interactional dimension. It shows affiliation, and together with other signals of listenership, such as backchannelling, it contributes to the common ground that speakers need to build in order to achieve communication. This also serves effectiveness. ELF communication, like any other communication, seeks to be effective as well as efficient. We may therefore assume that to be successful, ELF encounters need to attend to interactional requirements in the same way as any communication. Similar tendencies can be expected to work for interactional functions as well as for those conveying a 'message', such as approximation and enhanced explicitness (for instance lexical means instead of pragmatic particles).

From a cognitive point of view, we would expect ELF speakers to approximate English forms because this would allow them to attain reasonable economy in processing while securing a good chance of achieving comprehension. Similarly, they can be expected to resort to processing shortcuts that benefit economy and fluency, such as multi-word sequences.

Communicative practices of these kinds benefit interlocutors in both of their roles: that of a speaker and that of a hearer. They allow processing time for both (for example hesitating, repeating, and pausing), assist in mutual comprehension (for example explicitness, approximation), and help achieve positive social goals (for example repetition, co-construction).

Because language is such a use-based dynamic whole, all its users impact on the way it takes shape. Some researchers allow a role for non-native speakers in language change, others do not. As a rule, research on contact-based change has presumed a comparatively stable language contact environment, with a dominant language of native speakers and a minority of others. Things are radically different with contemporary English. It is now spoken so widely by those for whom it is an additional language that this must have an effect on the language as a whole. Relative numbers of speakers have been implicated as a source of influence, with a sufficiently large majority of non-natives seen as potentially exerting a significant influence on the language they adopt. Whether ELF will have a significant impact on ENL communities is less clear. But it would be surprising if this did not happen.

Note

1. I use small capitals for lemmas, i.e. all the different forms of a given word.

References

Aijmer, K. (2002a) *English Discourse Particles*, Amsterdam: John Benjamins.

Andersen, H. (1989) 'Understanding linguistic innovations', in Breivik, L. E. and Jahr, E. H. (eds.) *Language Change: Contributions to the Study of Its Causes,* Berlin: Walter de Gruyter, 5–28.

Anderson, B. (1991) *Imagined Communities: Reflections on the Origin and Spread of Nationalism*, London: Verso.

Baker, M. (1993) 'Corpus linguistics and translation studies: implications and applications', in Baker, M., Francis, G. and Tognini-Bonelli, E. (eds.) *Text and Technology: In Honour of John Sinclair*, Amsterdam: John Benjamins, 233–50.

Bakhtin, M. M. (1986) *Speech Genres and Other Late Essays by Mikhail Bakhtin*, ed. C. Emerson and M. Holquist, Austin: University of Texas Press.

Biber, D., Johansson, S., Leech, G., Conrad, S. and Finegan E. (1999) *The Longman Grammar of Spoken and Written English*, London: Pearson Education.

Blum-Kulka, S. (1986) 'Shifts of cohesion and coherence in translation', in House, J. and Blum-Kulka, S. (eds.) *Interlingual and Intercultural Communication: Discourse and Cognition in Translation and Second Language Acquisition Studies*, Tübingen: Gunter Narr, 17–35.

Bråten, S. (2007) 'Altricentric infants and adults: on the origin and manifestations of participant perceptions of others' acts and utterances', in Bråten, S. (ed.) *On Being Moved: From Mirror Neurons to Empathy*, Amsterdam: John Benjamins, 111–36.

Bråten, S. and Trevarthen, C. (2007) 'Prologue: from infant intersubjectivity and participant movements to simulation and conversation in cultural common sense', in Bråten, S. (ed.) *On Being Moved: From Mirror Neurons to Empathy*, Amsterdam: John Benjamins, 21–34.

Britain, D. (2002a) 'Space and spatial diffusion', in Chambers, J., Trudgill, P. and Schilling-Estes, N. (eds.) *The Handbook of Variation and Change*, Oxford: Blackwell, 603–37.

Britain, D. (2002b) 'Surviving "Estuary English": innovation diffusion, koinéisation and local dialect differentiation in the English Fenland', *Essex Research Reports in Linguistics* 41: 74–103.

Britain, D. (2002c) 'Diffusion, levelling, simplification and reallocation in past tense BE in the English Fens', *Journal of Sociolinguistics* 6 (1): 16–43.

Brutt-Griffler, J. (2002) *World English: A Study of Its Development*, Clevedon: Multilingual Matters.

Bybee, J. L. (2006) 'From usage to grammar: the mind's response to repetition', *Language* 82: 711–33.

Bybee, J. L. (2008) 'Usage-based grammar and second-language acquisition', in Robinson, P. and Ellis, N. C. (eds.) *Handbook of Cognitive Linguistics and Second Language Acquisition*, New York: Routledge, 216–36.

Bybee, J. L. and Hopper, P. (2001) 'Introduction to frequency and the emergence of linguistic structure', in Bybee, J. L. and Hopper, P. (eds.) *Frequency and the Emergence of Linguistic Structure*, Amsterdam: John Benjamins, 1–24.

Carey, R. (2010) 'Hard to ignore: English native speakers in ELF research', *English as a Lingua* Franca. Special issue of *Helsinki English Studies* (ed. A. Mauranen and N. Hynninen) 6: 88–101.

Chafe, W. (1994) *Discourse, Consciousness, and Time*, Chicago: University of Chicago Press.

Chambers, J. K. (1992) 'Dialect acquisition', *Language* 68: 673–705.

Chambers, J. K. (2002) 'Dynamics of dialect convergence', *Journal of Sociolinguistics* 6 (1): 117–30.

Cogo, A. (2009) 'Accommodating difference in ELF Conversations: a study of pragmatic strategies', in Mauranen, A. and Ranta, E. (eds.) *English as a Lingua Franca: Studies and Findings*, Newcastle upon Tyne: Cambridge Scholars Publishing, 254–73.

Cogo, A. and Dewey, M. (2006) 'Efficiency in ELF communication: from pragmatic motives to lexico-grammatical innovation', *Nordic Journal of English Studies* 5 (2): 59–93 (https://guoa.ub.gu.se/dspace/bitstream/2077/3148/1/5-2-Cogo-Dewey.pdf).

Coste, D., Moore, D. and Zarate, G. (2009) 'Plurilingual and pluricultural competence', Strasbourg: Council of Europe (www.coe.int/lang).

Council of Europe (2007) 'From linguistic diversity to plurilingual education', Strasbourg: Council of Europe, Language Policy Division (www.coe.int/lang).

Couper-Kuhlen, E. and Selting, M. (2001) 'Introducing interactional linguistics', in Selting, M. and Couper-Kuhlen, E. (eds.) *Studies in Interactional Linguistics,* Amsterdam: John Benjamins, 1–22.

Couper-Kuhlen, E. and Thompson, S. A. (2005) 'A linguistic practice for retracting overstatements: "concessive repairs"', in Hakulinen, A. and Selting, M. (eds.) *Syntax and Lexis in Conversation*, Amsterdam: John Benjamins, 257–88.

Croft, W. (2000) *Explaining Language Change: An Evolutionary Approach*, London: Longman.

Crystal, D. (1997) *English as a Global Language*, Cambridge: Cambridge University Press.

Dabrowska, E. (2004) *Language, Mind and Brain: Some Psychological and Neurological Constraints on Theories of Grammar*, Edinburgh: Edinburgh University Press.

Denison, N. (1971) 'Some observations on language variety and plurilingualism', in Ardener, E. (ed.) *Social Anthropology and Language*, London: Routledge, 157–83.

Dewey, M. (2006) 'English as a lingua franca: an empirical study of innovation in lexis and grammar', unpublished PhD thesis, King's College London.

Du Bois, J. W. (1987) 'The discourse basis of ergativity', *Language* 63: 805–55.

Du Bois, J. W. (2003) 'Discourse and grammar', in Tomasello, M. (ed.) *The New Psychology of Language*, vol. II, Mahwah, NJ: Lawrence Erlbaum, 47–87.

Eckert, P. (2000) *Linguistic Variation as Social Practice*, Oxford: Blackwell.

Ehrenreich, S. (2009) 'English as a lingua franca in multinational corporations: exploring business communities of practice', in Mauranen, A. and Ranta, E. (eds.) *English as a Lingua Franca: Studies and Findings*, Newcastle upon Tyne: Cambridge Scholars Publishing, 126–51.

Ellis, N. C. (2002) 'Frequency effects in language processing: a review with implications for theories of implicit and explicit language acquisition', *Studies in Second Language Acquisition* 24 (2): 143–88.

Ellis, N. C. (2006) 'Selective attention and transfer phenomena in SLA: contingency, cue competition, salience, overshadowing, blocking and perceptual learning', *Applied Linguistics* 27: 164–94.

Erman, B. and Warren, B. (2000) 'The Idiom Principle and the Open Choice Principle', *Text* 20 (1): 87–120.

Field, J. (2003) *Psycholinguistics*, London: Routledge.

Fillmore, C. J., Kay P. and O'Connor, M. (1988) 'Regularity and idiomaticity in grammatical constructions: the case of "let alone"', *Language* 64: 501–38.

Filppula, M. (2003) 'The quest for the most "parsimonious" explanations: endogeny vs. contact revisited', in Hickey, R. (ed.) *Motives for Language Change*, Cambridge: Cambridge University Press, 161–73.

Ford, C. E., Fox, B. A. and Thompson, S. A. (2003) 'Social interaction and grammar', in Tomasello, M. (ed.) *The New Psychology of Language*, vol. II, Mahwah, NJ: Lawrence Erlbaum, 119–43.

Gallois, C., Ogay, T. and Giles, H. (2005) 'Communication accommodation theory: a look back and a look ahead', in Gudykunst, W. B. (ed.) *Theorizing About Intercultural Communication*, London: Sage, 121–48.

Gilbert, G. N. and Mulkay, M. (1984) *Opening Pandora's Box: A Sociological Analysis of Scientific Discourse*, Cambridge: Cambridge University Press.

Giles, H. (1973) 'Accent mobility: a model and some data', *Anthropological Linguistics* 33: 27–42.

Giles, H. and Smith, P. (1979) 'Accommodation theory: optimal levels of convergence', in Giles, H. and St Clair, R. (eds.) *Language and Social Psychology*, Oxford: Blackwell, 45–65.

Giora, R. (2004) 'On the graded salience hypothesis', *Intercultural Pragmatics* 1 (1): 93–103.

Goodwin, C. (1981) *Conversational Organization: Interaction Between Speakers and Hearers*, New York: Academic Press.

Graddoll, D. (1997) *The Future of English?* London: British Council.

Granger S. (ed.) (1998) *Learner English on Computer*, London: Longman.

Granger S. and Meunier, F. (eds.) (2008) *Phraseology: An Interdisciplinary Perspective*, Amsterdam: John Benjamins.

Granovetter, M. (1973) 'The strength of weak ties', *American Journal of Sociology* 78 (6): 1360–80.

Granovetter, M. (1983) 'The strength of weak ties: a network theory revisited', *Sociological Theory* 1: 201–33.

Hari, R. (2007) 'Human mirroring systems: on assessing mind by reading brain and body during social interaction', in Bråten, S. (ed.) *On Being Moved: From Mirror Neurons to Empathy*, Amsterdam: John Benjamins, 89–100.

Herdina, P. and Jessner, U. (2002) *A Dynamic Model of Multilingualism: Perspectives of Change in Psycholinguistics*, Clevedon: Multilingual Matters.

Hopper, P. and Traugott, E. (2003) *Grammaticalization* (2nd edn), Cambridge: Cambridge University Press.

House, J. (2003) 'English as a lingua franca: a threat to multilingualism?' *Journal of Sociolinguistics* 7 (4): 556–78.

Hülmbauer, C. (2009) '"We don't take the right way: we just take the way we think you will understand" – the shifting relationship between correctness and effectiveness in ELF', in Mauranen, A. and Ranta, E. (eds.) *English as a Lingua Franca: Studies and Findings*, Newcastle upon Tyne: Cambridge Scholars Publishing, 323–47.

Hunston, S. and Francis, G. (2000) *Pattern Grammar: A Corpus-Driven Approach to the Lexical Grammar of English*, Amsterdam: John Benjamins.

Hüttner, J. (2009) 'Fluent speakers – fluent interactions: on the creation of (co)-fluency in English as a lingua franca', in Mauranen, A. and

Ranta, E. (eds.) *English as a Lingua Franca: Studies and Findings*, Newcastle upon Tyne: Cambridge Scholars Publishing, 274–97.

Hyland, K. (2000) *Disciplinary Discourses: Social Interactions in Academic Writing*, London: Longman.

Hyland, K. (2005) *Metadiscourse*, London: Continuum.

Hynninen, N. (2010) '"We try to to to speak all the time in easy sentences" – student conceptions of ELF interaction', *English as a Lingua Franca*. Special issue of *Helsinki English Studies* (ed. A. Mauranen and N. Hynninen) 6: 29–43.

Hynninen, N. (2011) 'The practice of "mediation" in English as a lingua franca interaction', *Journal of Pragmatics* 43 (4): 965–77.

Hynninen, N. (forthcoming) 'Expressing one's SELF: case studies of using English as a lingua franca in international study programmes', PhD thesis, University of Helsinki.

Jarvis, S. and Pavlenko, A. (2007) *Crosslinguistic Influence in Language and Cognition*, London: Routledge.

Jenkins, J. (2000) *The Phonology of English as an International Language*, Oxford: Oxford University Press.

Jenkins, J. (2007) *English as a Lingua Franca: Attitude and Identity*, Oxford: Oxford University Press.

Jenkins, J. (2009) *World Englishes* (2nd edn), London: Routledge.

Kachru, B. (1985) 'Standards, codification, and sociolinguistic realism: the English language in the outer circle', in Quirk, R., Widdowson, H. G. and Cantù, Y. (eds.) *English in the World: Teaching and Learning the Language and Literatures*, Cambridge: Cambridge University Press, 11–30.

Karhukorpi, J. (2006) 'Negotiating opinions in Lingua Franca e-mail discussion groups, discourse structure, hedges and repair in online communication', unpublished licenciate thesis, University of Turku.

Kaur, J. (2009) 'Pre-empting problems of understanding in English as a lingua franca', in Mauranen, A. and Ranta, E. (eds.) *English as a Lingua Franca: Studies and Findings*, Newcastle on Tyne: Cambridge Scholars Publishing, 107–25.

Keller, R. (1994) *On Language Change: The Invisible Hand in Language*, London: Routledge.

Knorr-Cetina, K., Krohn, R. and Whitley, R. (eds.) (1981) *The Social Process of Scientific Investigation*, Dodrecht: Reidel.

Laakso, M. and Sorjonen, M.-L. (2010) 'Cut-off particle: devices for initiating self-repair in conversation', *Journal of Pragmatics* 42: 1151–72.

Laitinen, H., Mustajoki, A. and Mauranen, A. (forthcoming) 'Hesitation caused by competing intentions in Russian'.

Lammi, R.-L. (2010) 'Backchannels and repetition in ELF in a hairdressing setting', *English as a Lingua Franca*. Special issue of *Helsinki English Studies* (ed. A. Mauranen and N. Hynninen) 6: 118–31.

Langacker, R. (2000) 'A dynamic usage-based model', in Barlow, M. and Kemmer, S. (eds.) *Usage-Based Models of Language*, Stanford: CSLI, 1–63.

Larsen-Freeman, D. and Cameron, L. (2008) *Complex Systems and Applied Linguistics*, Oxford: Oxford University Press.

Lass, R. (1997) *Historical Linguistics and Language Change*, Cambridge: Cambridge University Press.

Latour, B. and Woolgar, S. (1986) *Laboratory Life: The Construction of Scientific Facts*, Princeton: Princeton University Press.

Lave, J. and Wenger, E. (1991) *Situated Learning: Legitimate Peripheral Participation*, Cambridge: Cambridge University Press.

LePage, R. and Tabouret-Keller, A. (1985) *Acts of Identity*, Cambridge: Cambridge University Press.

Levelt, W. (1989) *Speaking*, Cambridge, MA: MIT.

Lieberman, E., Michel, J.-B., Jackson, J., Tang, T. and Nowak, M. A. (2007) 'Quantifying the evolutionary dynamics of language', *Nature* 449 (11): 713–16.

Linell, P. (2005) *The Written Language Bias in Linguistics: Its Nature, Origins, and Transformations*, London: Routledge.

MacWhinney, B. (2008) 'A unified model', in Robinson, P. and Ellis, N. (eds.) *Handbook of Cognitive Linguistics and Second-Language Acquisition*, London: Routledge, 341–71.

McCarthy, M. (1998) *Spoken Language and Applied Linguistics*, Cambridge: Cambridge University Press.

McCarthy, M. (2001) *Issues in Applied Linguistics*, Cambridge: Cambridge University Press.

Martin, J. R. (1985) 'Process and text: two aspects of human semiosis', in Benson, J. and Greaves, W. (eds.) *Systemic Perspectives on Discourse*, New York: Ablex, 248–74.

Mauranen, A. (1993a) *Cultural Differences in Academic Rhetoric: A Textlinguistic Study*, Frankfurt: Peter Lang.

Mauranen, A. (1993b) 'Contrastive ESP rhetoric: metatext in Finnish English economics texts', *English for Specific Purposes* 12 (1): 3–22.

Mauranen, A. (2003b) 'The corpus of English as a lingua franca in academic settings', *TESOL Quarterly* 37 (3): 513–27.

Mauranen, A. (2005) 'English as a lingua franca: an unknown Language?', in Cortese, G. and Duszak A. (eds.) *Identity, Community, Discourse: English in Intercultural Settings*, Frankfurt: Peter Lang, 269–93.

Mauranen, A. (2006a) 'Signalling and preventing misunderstanding in English as a lingua franca communication', *International Journal of the Sociology of Language* 177: 123–50.

Mauranen, A. (2007a) 'Universal tendencies in translation', in Anderman, G. and Rogers, M. (eds.) *Incorporating Corpora: The Linguist and the Translator*, Clevedon: Multilingual Matters, 32–48.

Mauranen, A. (2007b) 'Hybrid voices: English as the lingua franca of academics', in Fløttum, K., Dahl, T. and Kinn, T. (eds.) *Language and Discipline: Perspectives on Academic Discourse*, Newcastle upon Tyne: Cambridge Scholars Publishing, 244–59.

Mauranen, A. (2007c) 'Refleksivnost diskurza pri mednarodnih govorcih – raba v anglescini kot lingui franci' (Discourse reflexivity and international speakers – How is it used in English as a Lingua Franca?), *Jezik in slovstvo* 52: 3–4 (www.jezikinslovstvo.com/pdf/2007-03-04-Razprave-AnnaMauranen-ENG.pdf).

Mauranen, A. (2010) 'Discourse reflexivity: a discourse universal? The case of ELF', *Nordic Journal of English Studies* 9 (2): 13–40.

Melchers, G. and Shaw, P. (2003) *World Englishes*, London: Arnold.

Meltzhoff, A. N. and Brooks, R. (2007) 'Intersubjectivity before language: three windows on preverbal sharing', in Bråten, S. (ed.) *On Being Moved: From Mirror Neurons to Empathy*, Amsterdam: John Benjamins, 149–74.

Meyerhoff, M. (2002) 'Communities of practice', in Chambers, J. K., Trudgill, P. and Schilling-Estes, N. (eds.) *The Handbook of Language Variation and Change*, Oxford: Blackwell, 526–48.

Miller, C. (1984) 'Genre as social action', *Quarterly Journal of Speech* 70: 151–67.

Milroy, L. (2002) 'Social networks', in Chambers, J. K., Trudgill, P. and Schilling-Estes, N. (eds.) *The Handbook of Language Variation and Change*, Oxford: Blackwell, 549–72.

Milroy, J. (2003) 'On the role of the speaker in language change', in Hickey, R. (ed.) *Motives for Language Change*, Cambridge: Cambridge University Press, 143–57.

Milroy, J. and Milroy, L. (1985) 'Linguistic change, social network and speaker innovation', *Journal of Linguistics* 21: 339–84.

Mollin, S. (2006) 'English as a lingua franca: a new variety in the new Expanding Circle?', *English as a Lingua Franca.* Special Issue of *The Nordic Journal of English Studies* (ed. A. Mauranen and M. Metsä-Ketelä M): 5 (2) 41–58.

Moon, R. (1998) *Fixed Expressions and Idioms in English*, Oxford: Clarendon Press.

Mukherjee, J. (2001) *Form and Function of Parasyntactic Presentation Structures: A Corpus-Based Study of Talk Units in Spoken English*, Amsterdam: Rodopi.

Myers, G. (2010) *The Discourse of Blogs and Wikis*, London: Continuum.

Nattinger, J. R. and DeCarrico, J. (1992) *Lexical Phrases and Language Teaching*, Oxford: Oxford University Press.

Olohan, M. (2004) *Introducing Corpora in Translation Studies*, London: Routledge.

Östman, J.-O. and Fried, M. (eds.) (2005) *Construction Grammars: Cognitive Grounding and Theoretical Extensions*, Amsterdam and Philadelphia: John Benjamins.

Pagel, M. (2009) 'Human language as a culturally transmitted replicator', *Nature Reviews Genetics* 10: 405–15 (June 2009) (doi:10.1038/nrg2560).

Pagel, M., Atkinson, D. Q. and Meade, A. (2007) 'Frequency of word-use predicts rates of lexical evolution throughout Indo-European history', *Nature* 449 (11): 717–20.

Palander, M. (1987) *Suomen itämurteiden erikoisgeminaatio*, Helsinki: Suomalaisen kirjallisuuden seura.

Pawley, A. and Syder, F. H. (1983) 'Two puzzles for linguistic theory: nativelike selection and nativelike fluency', in Richards, J. C. and Schmidt, R. W. (eds.) *Language and Communication*, London: Longman, 191–225.

Penz, H. (2008) 'What do we mean by that? ELF in intercultural project work', paper presented in ESSE 9, the Ninth International Conference of the European Society for the Study of English, Aarhus, Denmark, 22–26 August, 2008.

Phillipson, R. (1992) *Linguistic Imperialism*, Oxford: Oxford University Press.

Pilkinton-Pihko, D. (2010) 'English as a lingua franca lecturers' self-perceptions of their language use', *English as a Lingua Franca*. Special issue of *Helsinki English Studies* (ed. A. Mauranen and N. Hynninen) 6: 58–74.

Riekkinen, N. (2009) '"This is not criticism, but..." – softening criticism: the use of lexical hedges in academic spoken interaction', unpublished MA thesis, University of Helsinki (www.helsinki.fi/elfa).

Riekkinen, N. (2010). '"This is not criticism, but..." – softening criticism: the use of lexical hedges in academic spoken interaction', *English as a Lingua Franca*. Special issue of *Helsinki English Studies* (ed. A. Mauranen and N. Hynninen) 6: 75–87.

Riionheimo, H. (2009) 'Interference and attrition in inflectional morphology: a theoretical perspective', in Penttilä, E. and Paulasto, H. (eds.) *Language Contact Meets English Dialects: Studies in Honour of Markku Filppula*, Newcastle upon Tyne: Cambridge Scholars Publishing, 83–106.

Ringbom, H. (1992) 'On L1 transfer, L2 comprehension and L2 production', *Language Learning* 42 (1): 85–112.

Ringbom, H. (2007) *Cross-Linguistic Similarity in Foreign Language Learning,* Clevedon: Multilingual Matters.

Robertson, R. (1995) 'Glocalization: time–space and heterogeneity–homogeneity', in Feathersone, M., Lash, S. and Robertson, R. (eds.) *Global Modernities*, London: Sage, 25–44.

Romaine, S. (1982) *Socio-Historical Linguistics: Its Status and Methodology*, Cambridge: Cambridge University Press.

Russell, N. (2010) *Communicating Science*, Cambridge: Cambridge University Press.

Salager-Meyer, F. (1994) 'Hedges and textual communicative function in medical English written discourse', *English for Specific Purposes* 13 (2): 149–71.

Sankoff, G. (2002) 'Linguistic outcomes of language contact', in Chambers, J. K., Trudgill, P. and Schilling-Estes, N. (eds.) *The Handbook of Language Variation and Change*, Oxford: Blackwell, 638–68.

Schaeffer, S. and Shapin, S. (1985) *Leviathan and the Air Pump: Hobbes, Boyle and the Experimental Life*, Princeton, NJ: Princeton University Press.

Schmitt, N. (ed.) (2004) *Formulaic Sequences: Acquisition, Processing and Use*, Amsterdam: John Benjamins.

Seidlhofer, B. (2005) 'English as a Lingua Franca', in Hornby, A. S. (ed.) *Oxford Advanced Learner's Dictionary of Current English* (7th edn), Oxford: Oxford University Press.

Seidlhofer, B. (2007) 'English as a lingua franca and communities of practice', in Volk-Birke, S. and Lippert, J. (eds.) *Anglistentag 2006 Halle Proceedings*, Trier: Wissenschaftlige Verlag Trier, 307–18.

Shaw, P., Caudery, T. and Petersen, M. (2009) 'Students on exchange in Scandinavia: motivation, interaction, ELF development', in Mauranen, A. and Ranta, E. (eds.) *English as a Lingua Franca: Studies and Findings*, Newcastle upon Tyne: Cambridge Scholars Publishing, 178–99.

Sinclair, J. McH. (1996/2004) 'The search for units of meaning', *Textus* 9 (1): 75–106. Reprinted in Sinclair, *Trust the Text*, London: Routledge, 24–48.

Sinclair, J. and Coulthard M. (1975) *Towards an Analysis of Discourse*, Oxford: Oxford University Press.

Sinclair, J. and Mauranen, A. (2006) *Linear Unit Grammar*, Amsterdam: John Benjamins.

Smit, U. (2010) *English as a Lingua Franca in Higher Education*, Berlin: De Gruyter Mouton.

Suviniitty J. (2010) 'Lecturers' questions and student perception of lecture comprehension', *English as a Lingua* Franca. Special issue of *Helsinki English Studies* (ed. A. Mauranen and N. Hynninen) 6: 44–57.

Swales, J. M. (1990) *Genre Analysis: English in Academic and Research Settings*, Cambridge: Cambridge University Press.

Tannen, D. (1989) *Talking Voices: Repetition, Dialogue, and Imagery in Conversational Discourse*, Cambridge: Cambridge University Press.

Thomason, S. G. (2001) *Language Contact*, Edinburgh: Edinburgh University Press.

Thomason, S. G. and Kaufman, T. (1988), *Language Contact, Creolization, and Genetic Linguistics*, Berkeley: University of California Press.

Tomasello, M. (2000) 'First steps toward a usage-based theory of language acquisition', *Cognitive Linguistics* 11 (1–2): 61–82.

Tomasello, M. (ed.) (2003) *The New Psychology of Language*, vol. II, Mahwah, NJ: Lawrence Erlbaum.

Trudgill, P. (1986) *Dialects in Contact*, Oxford: Blackwell.

Trudgill, P. (2002) *Sociolinguistic Variation and Change*, Edinburgh: Edinburgh University Press.

Vaattovaara, J. (2003) 'Innovaattorin muotokuva', in Laitinen, L., Lappalainen, H., Nieminen, P. and Vaattovaara, J. (eds.) *Muotojen mieli: kirjoituksia morfologiasta ja variaatiosta*, Kieli 15, Helsinki: Helsingin yliopiston suomen kielen ja yleisen kielitieteen laitos, 121–60.

Ventola, E. (1987) *The Structure of Social Interaction: A Systemic Approach to the Semiotics of Service Encounters*, London: Frances Pinter.

Vetchinnikova, S. (forthcoming) 'Productive vocabulary acquisition: EFL users' lexical choices in context and the idiom principle', PhD thesis, University of Helsinki.

Voloshinov, V. N. (1973) *Marxism and the Philosophy of Language*, New York: Seminar Press.

Warren, M. (2006) *Features of Naturalness in Conversation*, Amsterdam: John Benjamins.

Weber, G. (1997) *The Top Ten Languages of the World* (www.andaman.org/BOOK/reprints/textrep.htm).

Weinreich, U. (1953/1963) *Languages in Contact: Findings and Problems*, New York: Linguistic Circle 1953. Reprinted, The Hague: Mouton, 1963.

Wenger, E. (2006) 'Communities of practice and social learning systems' (www.ewenger.com/pub/index.htm).

Winford, D. (2003) *An Introduction to Contact Linguistics*, Oxford: Blackwell.

Wray, A. (2002) *Formulaic Language and the Lexicon*, Cambridge: Cambridge University Press.

Wray, A. (2008) *Formulaic Language: Pushing the Boundaries*, Oxford: Oxford University Press.

Zentella, A. C. (1997) *Growing up Bilingual: Puerto Rican Children in New York*, Oxford: Blackwell.

3 *Academic speech as data*

All examples in this book come from speech in university environments. Why this is a good idea for investigating ELF was already touched upon in the Introduction, but this chapter expands the discussion and explains what such a focus entails and what the data is like. At the outset, it might seem as if there were more exciting alternatives than academia for investigating communities using English as their predominant lingua franca. Tourism, hip-hop culture, Internet chat groups, or on the other hand, high-level business, political and diplomatic negotiations, might all sound like more obvious choices. I agree. Any, or all of these domains of language use are well worth investigating, and I hope that their uses of English will be tackled by large numbers of enthusiastic researchers. Nevertheless, academia has distinct advantages for tracking developments in English as a lingua franca.

A number of things speak for selecting academia, as already pointed out in Chapter 2. To begin with, the academic realm is one of the major domains in today's world that has adopted English as their lingua franca on a large scale. Academia and business are influential, high-stakes environments where language is deeply involved in all their principal activities. Business English was one of the fields where issues related to using a lingua franca were taken up relatively early (for a recent overview, see Louhiala-Salminen & Kankaanranta 2010), but before 2001,when the ELFA project started, ELF in academia did not seem to attract scholarly interest. Things have changed drastically since then. Academic ELF has turned into a lively research field, and in addition to Finnish work on ELFA, other Nordic universities have delved into it (see e.g. Bjørge 2007; Björkman 2008b, 2009, 2010; Haberland et al. 2008; Shaw 2008; Harder 2009; Mortensen 2010; Arnbjörnsdóttir & Ingvarsdóttir (forthcoming)). This keen interest is not surprising in view of recent developments in the university world, where a wave of internationalisation has swept over many countries with a small local language established as the language of higher education. Internationalisation has brought English as a medium of instruction in its wake, alerting researchers to its effect on redefining language policies and practices in universities. An interest in the linguistic consequences is also growing.

Below, I shall expand on the relationship between ELF and academia a little, and then go on to give a brief outline of the ELFA corpus. A more complete description of the corpus, with transcription conventions, header information, and more technical aspects are best found through the corpus website (www.helsinki.fi/elfa). In the final section of this chapter, I give a foretaste of the corpus by listing its commonest words alongside those of a comparable native-English corpus.

3.1 The case of academic ELF

Academic mobility is not a new phenomenon. Universities have been thoroughly international from their inception. In the Middle Ages, scholars and students travelled widely all over Europe, gathering around common interests in universities that had been founded in many cities from the late eleventh century onwards (see e.g. Koski 1993; Mäkinen 2003). For centuries scholars and scientists were recruited to the ranks of a university for their skills and knowledge (with schools of thought and disputes also playing their role) independently of the country they originally came from. For centuries communication in these mobile interregional groupings was facilitated by the existence of a lingua franca of the scientific and scholarly communities: Latin. Gradually vernaculars took over higher education with the rise and growing power of nation-states, and in the late nineteenth century education began to spread to wider societal groups, with an explosive increase in the number of universities in the post-Second World War period. Along with the growing use of national languages in higher education, the learning of modern languages increased among academics who wanted to keep up with developments in international research. An interesting case study shows the rise and fall of multilingualism in Danish higher education and research in the twentieth century (Mortensen & Haberland 2009).

Today we have returned to a largely international context of research and study, with the most notable differences compared to mediaeval times being those of scale. A considerable proportion of the age cohort in very many countries is now involved in higher education as students, teachers and researchers. The mobility of undergraduate and graduate students has become a normal part of university life: they look for opportunities to study outside their own countries while universities compete for good students and cast their nets wide. Even those who take their degrees in their own countries participate in exchange programmes such as the European ERASMUS (http://ec.europa.eu/education/lifelong-learning-programme/doc80_en.htm).

Teaching staff receive more and more international students in their institutions. The need to deploy a lingua franca to make these developments possible has not changed, but now the common language is of course English. Even entire departments or faculties in non-English-speaking countries adopt English as their medium of instruction for Master's programmes (recently, for instance, at the University of Copenhagen, www.ku.dk/english/, or the Aalto University in Helsinki, www.aalto.fi/en/). Whether we talk about exchange programmes or international degree programmes, the trend seems to be towards more English in non-English environments, not less (see e.g. Wächter 2008).

In research it has become normal that international, often intercontinental, projects adopt English as their lingua franca even if there are no participants who speak English as their native language (ENL speakers). The current trend is for research projects in many competitive fields to expand, include more and more partners, and span continents. Large-scale projects are also set up to solve global problems. Under these circumstances, the use of English is likely to escalate, because it has become the language known to most people. Conversely, the dominance of the ENL model is likely to diminish, because the determinants of language use lose their connections to a national basis. Instead, the influence of professional and disciplinary communities is likely to be on the increase.

English is spoken far more by non-native than native speakers. Yet the consequences of this reality are only slowly trickling down to the language practices of academic communities and language professionals who offer them support. Up to now, the unquestioned assumption has been that 'good English' equals that of the educated native speaker, in other words Standard English. Innumerable native speakers have been recruited to help non-native scientists and scholars in their struggle with the language, and it is standard practice in publishers' style sheets to require non-native writers to have their text checked by a native speaker of English prior to publication. The advisability of the exclusive reliance of ENL language revision is beginning to be questioned here and there, but there are still places where doubts have not begun to shake the practices (Owen 2011). Yet international research is a site of activity and communication where accuracy and effectiveness in reporting findings and constructing arguments is crucial – whereas the 'native-likeness' of a text, accent, or turn of phrase has scarcely any relevance. It is not a realm where nationality or national standards and practices take first priority.

Academic discourses and genres are highly specialised, and need to be learned as part of becoming a member of an academic community (e.g. Bourdieu & Passeron 1977). All novices in academic institutions undergo secondary socialisation into academic discourses, regardless of their linguistic background. There are no native speakers of *academic* language. Along with new conceptual systems, novices need not only learn technical and subtechnical terminologies that go with them, but acceptable ways of presenting their knowledge – how to put forth 'strong arguments', ask 'appropriate questions', make 'interesting points', and perform other such speech acts (Väliverronen 1992). This is part of the secondary socialisation that takes place in educational institutions. Much of it is implicit, and not getting it right may result in what Bourdieu and Passeron (1977) called a 'rhetoric of despair', where students imitate their professors' ways of speaking and writing to the point of travesty. The acquisition of academic literacies and ways of talking involves much more than a few surface expressions and poses challenges in students' first languages as well (e.g. Zamel & Spack 1998; Braine 2002). This levels the playing field for those who study in a foreign language, at least to an extent. In international study programmes, much in the way of international research groups, the contact language gets shaped by the needs and contingencies of the situation, loosening and dissolving its ties to a particular culture or origin.

One of the major goals of research into specialised languages, or language for specific purposes (LSP), is to understand language use in specific contexts. It is a large field of study, where English for obvious reasons has the lion's share. Much of the research is aimed at developing workable applications in language teaching, and this practical interest is what gives the field its momentum. Obviously, practical, theoretical, and descriptive interests are closely intertwined in this work where new departures require theoretical insights about language as well as practical experience of what produces desired results. In the current academic world where English is the unquestionable lingua franca, it is clear that to understand how English works, how it is changing, and how it fits into its multilingual settings, we need to find out what English is like in precisely this use – as a lingua franca.

Research into English for specific purposes (ESP) and English for academic purposes (EAP) has traditionally oriented to the native speaker. This was a natural and understandable orientation for a long time, and gave rise to much good work (see e.g. Swales 1985, 1990; Hutchinson & Waters 1987; Johns & Dudley-Evans 1991; Dudley-Evans 1998; Hewings 2002). The all-embracing globalisation of academic activity is comparatively recent, and prior to the explosion of English-language programmes in a variety of environments since the late 1990s, English was learned for international study in

English-speaking countries. The premises that ESP and EAP research previously built on have nevertheless changed as the world has moved on, and new questions must be faced. The vast majority of research and publications in the field have been concerned with non-native uses of English all along, but the approach has essentially been one of contrastive rhetoric (Connor 1996), where the point of comparison, and at least the tacit gold standard, is the ENL speaker. The implications for teaching have accordingly been constructed along the lines of bringing the non-natives closer to perceived ENL conventions, that is, making their texts more 'native-like'. Non-native practices have been set up as problems to be solved, and the solutions have been sought in discovering the differentiating factors and eliminating them.

In the present situation this exclusive orientation to the ENL standard has clearly become inadequate. Since understanding English in its professional and academic use is one of the major goals of EAP research, it is crucial that its current manifestations in complex international circumstances are investigated. How do academics and students manage demanding intellectual tasks using a second language? What discourse features are so vital to academic communication that they accompany successful academic exchanges even when speakers use a lingua franca? What linguistic variation is acceptable in ELF environments even though it might raise eyebrows in ENL contexts?

In brief, in order to understand contemporary academic discourse, it is necessary to study second-language academic writing and speaking in their own right, and for applied purposes extract effective practices from this study. Academic English is of enormous interest in the world for its practical value. We must take seriously the possibility that there are practices that differ from ENL conventions but that could be at least equally effective, or in fact work better for an international readership or in an international conference.

3.2 Why speaking rather than writing?

Spoken language is far more laborious to collect and prepare until it is suitable for research than written text. Speech is ephemeral, and needs to be recorded for scrutiny, and usually even that is not enough, but transcription is needed before analysts are happy to proceed with their work. It seems that we need to see what we analyse, even though the mode of existence of speech is based on sound. Written transcript arrests the flow of speech and gives the analyst time to focus. These days written text can be downloaded directly into electronic databases, which therefore grow into enormous dimensions, whereas with speech, data-gathering still requires manual transcription and normally re-checking a few times over. For this reason speech corpora or spoken components of general reference corpora, such as the BNC, are usually much smaller than written databases. Is it worth all this trouble to collect speech data? There are many good reasons why it is worth all the work invested, beginning from the fundamental fact that speaking is the primary mode of human language, and a large proportion of the world's 6,000 languages still do not exist in a written mode at all. But why would it be relevant to gather speech from a domain like academia, which has developed stunningly complex and sophisticated means of communication in written form?

While going about our ordinary activities as professors, lecturers, or students at university, we are using spoken language most of the time. In their academic core functions, research and education, universities rely on talk. Research groups are typical communities of practice (Wenger 1998; Chapter 2), which cooperate to develop their work together towards common goals. Educational practices by which new generations enter academic and professional communities hinge upon events like lectures, seminars, and supervision. Organisational and administrative structures are routinely run and reproduced and under frequent renegotiation in departmental and faculty meetings, financial negotiations, and consultations. Salary increases and promotions are settled in face-to-face consultation. In all these ordinary everyday practices, we engage in spoken discourse, simultaneously reproducing and enhancing (cf. Giddens 1984) the structures of academic practices, and in these activities we constitute the institutions themselves. Conferences as fora of presenting and discussing research have proliferated in the last few decades, and occupy an increasingly central position at early stages of research careers. They are important sites of networking – also carried out in talk. Even in the more formal kinds of university discourses, such as large lectures, it is unusual to read aloud prewritten text. Academic texts are still commonly revised for language by native speakers before publication, and the process erases much of their original form. The Internet is changing such practices with emerging new forms of immediate publication of research results, but speech on the whole is still more open to new forms, shows broader non-standard diversity, and is the first to accept change, therefore revealing much more about the first signs of change in progress. Thus, for getting a handle on practices and discourses in academia, analysing speaking ought to occupy a central place.

Speaking in academic environments was overlooked for a long time in research into English for specific purposes and its subfield English for academic purposes because EAP interests in its first couple of decades were seen to lie mainly in improving and securing non-native students' and professionals' understanding of English-language textbooks and scientific papers (clearly seen in Swales 1985 and Trimble 1985) as well as other professional texts (e.g. Pugh & Ulijn 1984). Writing was ushered in on a larger scale in the 1990s, with Swales's seminal *Genre Analysis* (1990) leading the way. Since then, textual rhetoric with its conventions and variations in writing dissertations, theses, and above all research articles, has been the principal concern of practitioners as well as researchers in EAP. The research article, the flagship of research genres, constitutes the making or undoing of careers, and therefore is the natural hub for upwardly mobile academics. It has been the subject of extensive research, with the general purpose of uncovering what ENL writers do so that their practices and preferences can best be taken as models for learners and second-language users to emulate (see also Mauranen 2011).

There is thus a gap to be filled in investigating academic speaking, which has taken far longer to get off the ground than research into academic writing. There are now databases of academic speech in existence, some even freely accessible through the Internet, but this is still relatively recent. The compilation of the two American corpora, MICASE (http://quod.lib.umich.edu/m/micase/) and the T2K-SWAL (see e.g. Biber 2001, 2006), started in the late 1990s when there was virtually no research of speaking in academic contexts, and the British BASE (www2.warwick.ac.uk/fac/soc/al/research/collect/base/) followed soon in their tracks. This millennium has witnessed a sea change in EAP interest within speech, but the corpora are rather traditional in other ways, because they prioritise the ENL speaker, and research carried out on those databases reflects this. Although MICASE and BASE also include L2 speakers, the recordings are made in countries where English is the national language, the universities are run entirely in English, and native speakers are the majority. The research thus naturally revolves around the ways in which ENL is used in spoken university discourse.

None of this is to say that writing is unimportant in academia – quite the contrary – but investigating ENL academic writing does not seem to be in any immediate need of support, as it continues to be the main focus of research interest. Where we have not seen written corpora compiled yet is in ELF, but undoubtedly these will begin to appear in the near future. After all, academic publishing in English is increasingly done by writers whose first language is not English.

Speaking is, then, a vital part of academic life, but beyond that, it plays a special role for ELF research. A lingua franca can be likened to a language that has not been codified in writing: the linguistic vehicle used in communication is negotiated in interaction, as was already discussed in Chapter 2. Spoken interaction is the site of co-constructing shared understanding. As speakers engage in achieving intelligibility and managing the communicative situation, the full range of their linguistic and communicative repertoires comes into play more clearly than in written monologue. For assessing communicative success and effectiveness, dialogic data is particularly useful, as it is in real interaction that the effectiveness of communication comes out. Communicative turbulence, even breakdown, is immediately observable in participants' responses, and conversely, smoothly progressing discourse attests the adequacy of participants' contributions. Even though multi-party discussions obviously may include participants who do not follow everything that is being said, this is a much greater problem with monologues of any kind – capturing readers' or silent listeners' experience is notoriously hard. Dialogic events are the best authentic tests for speakers' ability to achieve communication, and they yield data with linguistic and social facets intertwined so that the analyst can focus on form, meaning, strategies, or processes.

The ELFA corpus is presented in the next section. It fills a gap in English research material on two fronts: first, it provides a large database of spoken English in a type of environment where English has been widely studied as an object of learning, but extremely seldom as a means of authentic communication. Secondly, it is the first database of academic English that opens the door to a new reality – beyond the Anglo-American context.

3.3 The ELFA corpus

The ELFA corpus was compiled between 2001 and 2007, its final form completed in 2008.[1] It consists of a million words of spoken language recorded in Finland, at two universities (Tampere and Helsinki) and two technological universities (Tampere and Helsinki). The original aim was to reflect the discourses of one university, along the lines of the American databases of academic speech (MICASE and T2K-SWAL) when the project started at Tampere, but the one-university approach was soon supplemented with technological data[2] (from the Tampere University of Technology), because the University of Tampere did not have much scientific discourse. The single-university idea was thus modified from the start, and after the project moved to Helsinki, the disciplinary domains were extended to science and forestry, with more technology from the Helsinki University of Technology. The result is a wide disciplinary coverage, with a more detailed breakdown given and discussed below (see Figure 3.2 on p. 77).

ELFA consists entirely of authentic speech in the sense that none of it has been elicited for research purposes. Events were recorded in ordinary university settings with speakers engaged in activities of their own concern. All recordings cover complete sessions in that the individual events have been recorded in their entire duration, without truncating them or sampling mere extracts. Sometimes the natural 'chaining' of academic speech events has been taken on board, and interlinked conference or seminar sessions are included.[3] Variation along the speakers' familiarity parameter can be captured by consulting the recording dates: the point of the term at which recordings have been made is a fairly reliable indicator of how long the group has been together.

3.3.1 Setting-related choices

The compilation of the corpus was generally based on 'external' criteria (cf. Sinclair 2005), that is, not linguistic ones but criteria that reflect relevant social uses of language. For ELFA, the prominent genres or discourse types were identified in the university community, and samples recorded from these, without considering the kind of language – whether 'formal', 'good', or something else – being used. In this way, the data-gathering was informed by 'local knowledge' (Geertz 1983) as far as possible, as gathered from members of the institutions and communities such as faculties, departments, or conference organisers and their public material about themselves. In effect, this meant grounding the speech event types on 'folk genres', that is, adopting event labels and definitions that were used by the members of the speech community themselves, rather than devising new ones. Many of the resulting event labels like 'seminar', 'lecture', 'symposium', and 'thesis defence' were used across institutions. A broad coverage was aimed at, and prominence was given to those shared and recognised widely and regarded as the prototypical academic speech genres.

The basic unit of sampling is what we call the 'speech event type', along the lines of MICASE. This is a looser term than 'genre', and therefore preferable for a corpus of this kind because the discourses represent a variety of events, some of which are more firmly established as genres (e.g. lectures) than others (e.g. panel discussions). Thus, even though many of the widely recognised event types are indeed genres, 'event type' is a useful cover term.

Event types have been selected according to a few main criteria. One is their centrality or perceived importance: (1) typicality, or the extent to which event types are shared and named by many disciplines, for example lectures, seminars, thesis defences, conference presentations; (2) influence: events that affect a large number of participants, for example introductory lecture courses; (3) prestige: event types

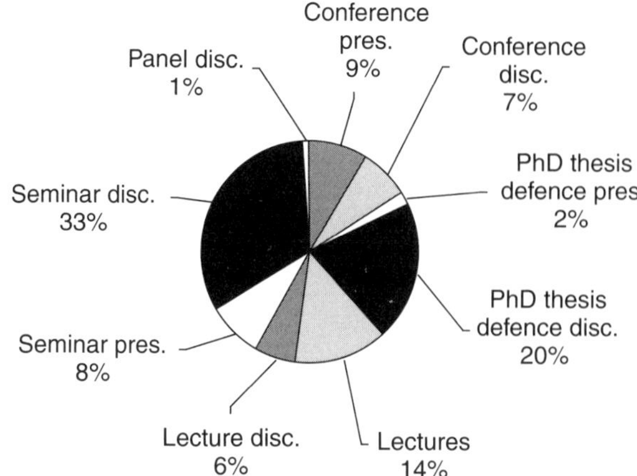

Figure 3.1 Distribution of event types in the ELFA corpus. Abbreviations: pres. = presentations, disc. = discussions. From Mauranen et al. 2010.

with high status in the discourse community, such as guest lectures or plenary conference talks. Clearly, conference presentations and discussions are more relevant to academic staff than to students, but given the dual role of universities as sites of education *and* research, both perspectives were regarded as valid. Event types were selected along these lines, with typical university-internal discourses and international programmes in the majority, as seen in Figure 3.1.

Many of the event-type labels ('seminar', 'lecture') probably have a familiar look to most readers. Nevertheless, it is worth keeping in mind that genres are context-dependent and academic genres can be surprisingly local. For example, in some countries 'seminar' implies a series of meetings discussing students' written papers, in others they may be linked to lecture series, with or without students' oral presentations – what they seem to have in common seems to be prepared discussion around a given topic in relatively small groups (Mauranen 1994). Thus the interpretations of these labels are culture-bound and the event types occupy different positions in relation to other genres and speech events in their contexts. Moreover, universities have different profiles and offer different ranges of disciplines; the selection and balance is unique to particular institutions even within countries, let alone across them. In environments where English is not the main language of the university, the choices are narrowed further: even where English-medium programmes are offered in all major disciplinary domains, they tend to be limited to certain departments or levels of study. For example, only graduate programmes are available in English in Finland (and many other European countries), which alone means a different scene from English-speaking environments.

It is also perhaps useful to remember that as a corpus of ELF, ELFA does not include ELT classes, where English is the object of study. A consistent ELF corpus must of course represent English as an authentic contact language. In contrast, learner corpora (see http://cecl.fltr.ucl.ac.be/Cecl-Projects/Icle/icle.htm) are compiled from the language of students of English.

Disciplines constitute important dividing lines and territorial boundaries in academia, and must somehow be taken on board in a corpus. It is not unproblematic to capture the right balance between them, and it may well not even be worth trying, in view of their divergences across universities. In a single-university approach, achieving a representative sample is a feasible task, because we can list all its departments, for example, but even there its benefits might not be very high, given that universities have their local profiles. The findings from a corpus that is perfectly representative of a particular university in terms of disciplinary distribution may not be valid or interesting more widely. What we can seek to cover is as diverse a selection of disciplines as possible within the limits of real-world constraints.

This is obviously a compromise between the reality of given institutions and some conceivable ideal balance of disciplines, if indeed such an ideal can be specified. To aggravate matters, identical departmental labels do not reflect identical divisions into disciplines or subdisciplines (Mauranen 2006c). Thus even if aggregate information of the disciplinary distributions of all the world's universities were available, it might not be a reliable guide to the kinds of academic activities actually being carried out. ELFA opted for as much diversity as was feasible, and rounded out the corpus to include a wider selection of disciplines than one or two universities would have yielded on their own. In this way, the disciplinary selection followed the approach in large reference corpora of including something of every major domain. It follows that caution needs to be exercised in inter-generic and inter-disciplinary comparisons – the data represents academic discourse as a large aggregate body, while its individual components do not claim to represent that particular discipline or genre in a balanced way.[4]

Disciplines can be divided up in several ways, and considered at different levels: as a broad disciplinary domain ('arts', 'technology'), or a single discipline ('political history', 'electrical engineering'), and subdiscipline ('organic chemistry', 'educational psychology'). With the smallish databases that spoken corpora are, selection is most usefully guided by the highest-level disciplinary domain. More

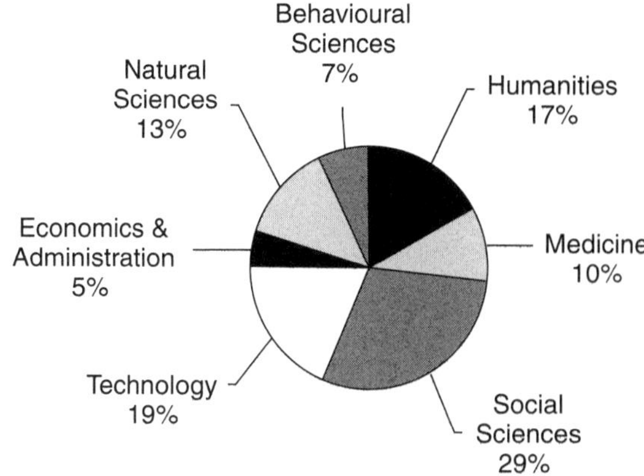

Figure 3.2 Distribution of disciplinary domains in the ELFA corpus. From Mauranen et al. 2010.

fine-grained categorisation can easily lead to too few cases of each kind to be of interest.[5]

Broad domains also give a clear picture of the overall balance of the corpus, even though it could be argued that it simultaneously hides some differences at lower levels – for example, the subdisciplinary orientations of universities. As can be seen in Figure 3.2, the ELFA boasts a wide spread of disciplines.

Questions of register use in a second language, mainly in the form of distinguishing levels of formality or casualness and maintaining such distinctions consistently, have arisen with regard to learner language. Some researchers have found traces of 'conversational' features in learners' written output in an academic context (Gilquin & Paquot 2008). The possibility that ELF discourse shows similar features of casual registers in fairly formal contexts opens intriguing issues – is there little or no differentiation? Do registers mix in a new way? Is there a consistent preference for conversational styles? and so on. Unfortunately, there is little suitable data of ELF so far for answering questions about register, because there is no large enough reference corpus of 'general ELF' (i.e. not limited to academic language)[6] available as yet, which could be used as a point of comparison. Neither is there a directly comparable description of an 'academic speech' register available in ENL, even though Biber's (2006) study on university registers comes fairly close. It gives an illuminating overall picture of registers in the American university environment, which covers a broad range of discourses from a student's perspective: the genres or registers are those that a new student will have to come to terms with, and in time, master. Biber paints a broad picture of the kind of language that universities use in their everyday activities. However, the data is only a partial match to ELFA, being in some respects narrower, in not having, for example, conferences and thesis defences, but in others broader, covering events like office hours, study groups, and service encounters. Despite this, Biber's findings make a useful point of comparison on some register features, which will be taken up in Chapter 5.

3.3.2 Speaker-related choices

Although ELFA was compiled on the basis of external, or non-linguistic, criteria as pointed out above, language also mattered. Two language-based dimensions were observed: speaker's first language and whether an event was monologic or dialogic. In the spirit of external selection criteria, these aspects of language were observed on an essentially external basis – by asking the subjects to report their first languages, and by taking note of the number of actively participating speakers.

In taking speakers' background language into account, the purpose was to ensure a maximal range of languages, and to keep the number of Finnish native speakers in check. Speakers of the local language easily dominate in sheer numbers, if their number is not kept track of. This monitoring paid off, because in the end the proportion of speech by Finnish speakers was only a little more than a quarter (28.5%) of the entire database. The general spread of language backgrounds shows considerable typological diversity: there are speakers of 51 different first languages ranging from African languages (e.g. Akan, Dagbani, Igbo, Kikuyu, Kihaya, Somali, Swahili), to Middle Eastern (e.g. Arabic, Persian, Turkish), Asian (e.g. Bengali, Chinese, Hindi, Japanese, Uzbek), and European languages (e.g. Czech, Dutch, French, German, Italian, Lithuanian, Polish, Portuguese, Russian, Swedish). Complete lists can be seen on the ELFA homepage (www.helsinki.fi/elfa).

Native English speakers account for 5% of the data. They were not kept away from the material, because their presence is a normal part of ELF. However, since the primary objective was to uncover ELF interaction, ENL speakers were not recorded in roles where they would give long monologues such as lectures or conference presentations. Neither were they included in doctoral defences in principal examiner's roles, because that would have come too close to dyadic L1–L2 communication, a borderline case for investigating ELF, as already discussed in the Introduction. The rule established in the

VOICE corpus (www.univie.ac.at/voice) of only including situations with ELF speakers in the majority was adopted here as well.

It is important to note that ELFA differs radically from learner corpora in not taking note of speaker proficiency (which would of course be a language-internal criterion). It is obvious that speakers' proficiency levels vary, but no attempt was made to control, measure, or code this. Since it is a normal part of lingua franca encounters that speaker proficiencies differ in the contact language, it is important to reflect this in research material. The purpose was not to look for successful or model speakers of ELF, but to capture speakers in their real diversity.

First language served as a criterion for excluding sessions where speakers all share an L1. This distinguishes ELF from CLIL (Content and Language Integrated Learning), where the normal case is a shared L1 among the students. ELF material is thus clearly distinct from both CLIL settings, where speakers typically share a first language, and learner data, which control proficiency levels.

Cross-language influence is ubiquitous, as was discussed in Chapter 2. The various first languages in ELFA can be expected to make their mark on speakers' idiolects, or cause transfer, and the resulting similects could in principle be grouped according to first language. However, the corpus is not suitable for comparisons across L1s, because it was not compiled with representative samples from all 51 first-language backgrounds in mind. The purpose was to ensure as much variety in the backgrounds as possible so as to minimise transfer effects, or excessive similect effects in the findings. The fact that many speakers are multilingual further reduces the feasibility of L1 comparisons and encourages the use of the corpus as a repository of ELF, with speakers from a mixture of first languages coming together. Speakers' first languages are nevertheless coded, which makes it easier to check that findings are not limited to a single similect. In addition to language background, speaker attributes coded in the files are gender, age group, and institutional position.

Even though the speakers in ELFA are never in the role of learners, formal learning of English is part of everyone's educational background. All speakers have a high level of education, with at least one university degree already, since there are no undergraduate programmes in the material.

The other language-related sampling criterion concerns monologue vs. dialogue. A deliberate choice was made to secure as much dialogue as possible. This bias was built in because it is in dialogic interaction that language primarily and most naturally takes shape. More precisely, the events were usually polylogic, or multi-party discussions, where the number of speakers ranged from three to a dozen, and could include silent participants in addition to active speakers. In practical terms this meant seeking out seminars, conference discussions and thesis defences. As was seen above (Figure 3.1), seminar discussions and thesis defences are proportionally the largest categories, in addition to which nearly as much conference discussion has been gathered as presentations, even though most conferences are structured along the typical 10- or 20-minute talk followed by five minutes' discussion section. In all, about two-thirds of the data (67%) are from dialogic, multi-party discussions. To facilitate researchers' focus on either dialogue, monologue, or comparing the two, the files were divided into monologic (presentations, lectures) and dialogues (discussions) and marked accordingly. This was done mechanically by observing the ends of presentations or lectures, even though occasionally lectures were interrupted by question-and-answer sequences. If the intervening discussion sequences were substantial, this was noted in the general background information provided for each speech event, i.e. the file headers. The interconnections between presentations or lectures and the ensuing discussions are easy to recover from the headers, and usually even from the transparent filenames.

In analysing the data I will be talking about dialogue even in the case of more than two speakers participating (polylogues), unless the distinction is particularly relevant in a given case. Commonly used terminologies are not satisfactory as regards dialogic or interactive language: a good case can be made for seeing all language use as dialogic and interactive, because linguistic communication is forever responding to earlier discourses and anticipating later ones, and it is always addressed to recipients, whether they are present or not. On the other hand, it is a convenient shorthand to talk about monologue and dialogue according to the primary mode adopted and – as the case may be – expected in the situation.

3.3.3 *Other choices*

Whenever speech recordings are transcribed, important choices need to be made concerning the amount of detail noted down from the soundtrack. Broad transcriptions, which are closer to standard orthography, miss out on much detail of the original sound, while very narrow kinds, incorporating symbols for details of voice or breathing alterations, highly precise accounts of pauses, and so on, tend to become illegible to the uninitiated. ELFA transcription is broad, with spelling normalised to Standard (British) English as far as possible, to facilitate reading and enable computer searches. To offset this lack of detail, the sound files are available to researchers who wish to consult them along with the corpus. This solution was felt expedient because corpus searches become not only cumbersome with several spelling variants, as is well known from historical corpora, but also potentially less reliable. Users would have a considerable learning load in mastering the spelling variants, and the risk and weight of transcriber error would have increased. A phonetic transcription following, say, the IPA system would also have been harder for a reader and for normally available computer search programs.

At this point the corpus does not have its own search interface that would allow searches on the basis of all the attributes distinguished in the background information (for instance age group, gender, or academic status). However, in corpora of this scale, many categories tend to remain small, and searches in such cases yield too few hits for useful results. The categories are therefore informative rather than classificatory. As with first languages or disciplines, the compilation did not seek to establish samples of each subcategory that would be representative of its class in its own right, but to ensure that all types would be included so that the whole would cover a sound mixture of background features deemed to be relevant. Moreover, subcorpora for individual researchers' interests are not laborious to establish.

3.4 A first glimpse: how does academic ELF compare to academic ENL?

The following chapters will delve into the ELF corpus from different perspectives and using different methodological approaches. Corpus research is best known for quantitative findings because the whole consists of a large mass of electronically held data, which can be searched for repeated patterns by corpus tools. What is often less obvious is that corpus data also lends itself readily to qualitative analyses of samples of the transcripts. We can, for example, take one or more transcripts of thesis defences and look into the detail of ongoing argumentation and debate in a traditional academic event type, analysing it by means of discourse analysis, argumentation analysis, or a dynamic grammatical analysis (Sinclair & Mauranen 2006), or some other kind of analytical method that proceeds from the original sequence of events as recorded and transcribed in the material.

Both quantitative and qualitative approaches can be alternately used on the same data, as has been done in this book, and we can argue that this alternation of perspectives can give us a holistic, well-rounded view of the kind of language use that we are interested in. New developments in databases will no doubt add new components to corpora as we know them, such as links to participant interviews, written, spoken, and visual material, but for the moment, a transcribed database gives us a firm handle on what happens when all the different kinds of Englishes resulting from first-order language contact come together.

When starting to talk about ELF, the first question that arises is what ELF looks like if it is just generally compared to ENL. Since it is hard to think of a simpler overview than a comparison between two wordlists, let us start with one before getting into more sophisticated analyses and comparisons. Below, in Table 3.1, the 50 most frequent words are listed in rank order from ELFA and the most closely comparable ENL corpus of academic speaking, MICASE.

Even a casual glance through the lists reveals that the two wordlists look remarkably similar. If we disregard certain differences in transcription practices[7] and the symbol 'xx', which denotes inaudible or unclear speech, we are left with 46 words, of which 38 appear on both lists; in other words, 83% of the words are shared. Because frequencies play significant roles in language use and in understanding how language works (see Chapters 2 and 4), this is an important fact about ELF, and good to bear in mind when considering its more non-standard manifestations. The basic building blocks in ELF are the same as in ENL, and their distribution is also very similar.

What we also see in this list is that there is most uniformity among the commonest words: the top ten words are almost identical, with just one exception. Among the next ten words five are in common, and as we go down the list, bifurcation continues (see the list of 200 most frequent words in Appendix 2). This follows a common pattern, where the most common items generally tend to be function words, which are recycled in the same form over and over again in speech and thus appear on top in any corpus, while lexical words disperse more. Interestingly, the one exception among the ten most frequent words indicates a difference between ELF and ENL speech that goes some way towards accounting for the fact that it is usually immediately obvious to a hearer, or even just a reader of a transcript with no access to pronunciation, that one is dealing with second language use: the frequent number of hesitations. The fact that *er* is the second most common item on an ELF wordlist is telling, even though hesitation markers are common enough in native speech as well. Table 3.1 shows that hesitation markers (*um* and *uh*) are high on the ENL rank scale. Evidence from longer sequences (Chapter 5) supports this; all speech contains hesitations, repeats, and other phenomena often known as 'dysfluencies', which play important roles in interactive

Table 3.1 Fifty most common words in academic English as a Lingua Franca (ELFA) and English as a native language (MICASE)

ELFA (1 m words)			MICASE (1.8 m words)	
N	Word	Freq.	Word	Freq.
1	THE	51,835	THE	77,672
2	ER	42,390	AND	47,110
3	AND	31,533	YOU	39,959
4	OF	26,884	OF	39,764
5	TO	23,023	THAT	39,075
6	IN	21,767	TO	37,476
7	THAT	18,995	A	37,390
8	I	18,342	I	36,852
9	IS	17,933	IN	26,772
10	YOU	17,553	IS	26,601
11	A	17,300	IT	25,429
12	THIS	12,446	SO	20,258
13	IT	12,281	THIS	19,536
14	SO	11,681	UM	17,819
15	HAVE	9,305	UH	16,675
16	WE	8,971	LIKE	14,159
17	BUT	8,802	HAVE	13,301
18	ARE	8,680	IT'S	13,241
19	FOR	7,966	WE	12,944
20	YEAH	7,791	WHAT	12,902
21	THEY	7,398	BUT	11,950
22	IT'S	7,359	KNOW	11,552
23	ERM	6,954	OKAY	10,825
24	MHM	6,890	FOR	10,523
25	OR	6,494	ONE	10,485
26	THERE	5,885	THEY	10,260
27	BE	5,750	BE	10,217
28	NOT	5,553	YEAH	10,100
29	WAS	5,552	ON	9,939
30	ON	5,499	ARE	9,671
31	WHAT	5,307	IF	9,643
32	AS	4,887	WAS	9,642
33	IF	4,876	JUST	9,404
34	XX	4,853	DO	8,893
35	#	4,826	OR	8,723
36	CAN	4,822	NOT	8,717
37	WITH	4,735	THAT'S	8,276
38	THINK	4,524	ABOUT	8,144
39	LIKE	4,469	RIGHT	8,009
40	THEN	4,388	WITH	7,834

Table 3.1 (Continued)

ELFA (1 m words)			MICASE (1.8 m words)	
41	VERY	4,272	CAN	7,387
42	ABOUT	4,219	AT	7,308
43	BECAUSE	4,093	AS	6,956
44	ONE	4,043	THINK	6,782
45	ALSO	3,994	THERE	6,725
46	WHICH	3,941	DON'T	6,723
47	SOME	3,906	THEN	6,299
48	FROM	3,826	ALL	6,033
49	THESE	3,353	TWO	5,567
50	AT	3,224	XX	5,335

discourse, but second language use tends to have more of these than first language use.

In all, the ELFA corpus fills a gap in academic English research material. It permits different research approaches, and covers a broad range of language backgrounds, genres, and disciplines. It complements other existing corpora. For academic speaking, the closest are MICASE, BASE, and the spoken part of T2K-SWAL (Biber 2001). For ELF, the only existing comparable database is the VOICE corpus in Vienna (www.univie.ac.at/voice), which is about the same size as ELFA, but not academically focused. Relevant comparisons can also be sought in the ICE corpus (http://ice-corpora.net/ice/index.htm) for New Englishes, even though much of the corpus consists of written material. In yet another direction, the learner corpora ICLE (www.uclouvain.be/cecl-icle.html) and LINDSEI (www.uclouvain.be/en-cecl-lindsei.html) provide fitting points of comparison, especially the spoken LINDSEI.

Material for comparison is thus already in existence, but which corpus is most relevant depends on the comparison at hand. For analysing contemporary academic English, MICASE is the best overall match for ELFA, and therefore mostly used in this book. More databases are being compiled in this fast-growing field, and it is to be hoped that as many of these as possible will be available to researchers, since ELF is an international phenomenon which benefits from widely shared research material and findings.

Notes

1. The ELFA corpus project was funded by the Academy of Finland 2004 –2007. Corpus compilation was part of the ELFA research project under the direction of Professor Anna Mauranen. The ELFA project investigates ELF-specific features in university discourses. Related projects at Helsinki are 'Studying in English as a Lingua Franca' (SELF), an ethnographically oriented investigation of discourses in university study and GlobE Helsinki, part of the GlobE Consortium: 'Global English (GlobE): contact-linguistic, typological, and second-language acquisition perspectives'.
2. From the Tampere University of Technology.
3. As academic events are often interlinked, and the idea of a 'whole' or 'complete' session in the case of one in a series of lectures or seminars could be questioned. Most recordings concern single events, but occasionally there are more sessions in a conference or a seminar series. Their mutual links are found in file headers.
4. This goes for all other academic corpora, and is perhaps worth keeping in mind when disciplinary comparisons are made or interpreted.
5. All the three levels mentioned here are coded in file headers, so the information is available to the interested researcher.
6. The only other appreciably large corpus so far (VOICE: www.univie.ac.at/voice) does not cover as broad a range of registers as one would normally expect of general reference corpora, and has a substantial share of higher education discourse.
7. Numbers are in digital form in ELFA, thus the symbol # ranks high, but small numbers spelt out in MICASE (explaining *two* being high on the list); hesitations are transcribed differently: ELF has *er* (# 2), *erm* (# 23), while MICASE uses *um* (# 14), *uh* (# 15).

References

Arnbjörnsdóttir, B. and Ingvarsdóttir, H. (forthcoming) 'ELF in academia: the effects of simultaneous parallel code use on students' learning'.

Biber, D. (2001) 'Dimensions of variation across university registers: an analysis based on the T2K-SWAL corpus', paper given at the Third North American Symposium on Corpus Linguistics and Language Teaching, University of Boston, 23–25 March 2001.

Biber, D. (2006) *University Language: A Corpus-Based Study of Spoken and Written Registers*, Amsterdam: John Benjamins.

Bjørge, A. K. (2007) 'Power distance in English lingua franca email communication', *International Journal of Applied Linguistics* 17 (1): 60–80.

Björkman, B. (2008a) '"So where we are": spoken lingua franca English at a Swedish technical university', *English Today* 24 (2): 11–17.

Björkman, B. (2008b) 'English as the lingua franca of engineering: the morphosyntax of academic speech events', *Nordic Journal of English Studies* 7 (3): 103–22.

Björkman, B. (2009) 'From code to discourse in spoken ELF', in Mauranen, A. and Ranta, E. (eds.) *English as a Lingua Franca: Studies and Findings*, Newcastle upon Tyne: Cambridge Scholars Publishing, 225–53.

Björkman, B. (2010) 'Spoken lingua franca English in tertiary education at a Swedish technical university: an investigation of form and communicative/pedagogical effectiveness', unpublished PhD thesis, University of Stockholm.

Bourdieu, P. and Passeron, J.-C. (1977) *Reproduction in Education, Society and Culture*, London: Sage.

Braine, G. (2002) 'Academic literacy and the nonnative speaker graduate student', *Journal of English for Academic Purposes* 1: 59–68.

Connor, U. (1996) *Contrastive Rhetoric: Cross-Cultural Aspects of Second-language Writing*, Cambridge: Cambridge University Press.

Dudley-Evans, T. (1998) *Developments in English for Specific Purposes: A Multi-Disciplinary Approach*, Cambridge: Cambridge University Press.

Geertz, C. (1983) *Local Knowledge: Further Essays in Interpretive Anthropology*, New York: Basic Books.

Giddens, A. (1984) *The Constitution of Society: An Outline of Structuration Theory*, Cambridge: Polity Press.

Gilquin, G. and Paquot, M. (2008) 'Too chatty: learner academic writing and register variation', *English Text Construction* 1 (1): 41–61.

Haberland, H., Mortensen, J., Fabricius, A., Preisler, B., Risager K. and Kjaerbeck, S. (eds.) (2008) *Higher Education in the Global Village*, Roskilde, Denmark: Department of Culture and Identity, Roskilde University.

Harder, P. (ed.) (2009) *English in Denmark: Language Policy, Internationalization and University Teaching*, vol. 9 of Angles on the English-Speaking World, Copenhagen: Museum Tusculanum Press.

Hewings, M. (2002) 'A history of ESP through English for Specific Purposes', *English for Specific Purposes World* 1 (3) (www.esp-world.info/Articles_3/Hewings_paper.htm).

Hutchinson, T. and Waters, A. (1987) *English for Specific Purposes: A Learner-Centered Approach*, Cambridge: Cambridge University Press.

Johns, A. M. and Dudley-Evans, T. (1991) 'English for Specific Purposes: international in scope, specific in purpose', *TESOL Quarterly* 25 (2): 297–314.

Koski, L. (1993) *Tieteen tahtomana, yliopiston tekemänä: Yliopiston sisäiset symboliset järjestykset*, Joensuu: University of Joensuu.

Louhiala-Salminen, L. and Kankaanranta, A. (2010) '"English? – Oh it's just work!" A study of BELF users perceptions', *English for Specific Purposes* 29 (3): 191–203.

Mäkinen, V. (2003) *Keskiajan aatehistoria: Näkökulmia tieteen, talouden ja yhteiskuntateorioiden kehitykseen 1100–1300-luvuilla*, Jyväskylä: Atena.

Mauranen, A. (1994) 'Two discourse worlds: study genres in Britain and Finland', *Finlance* 13: 1–40.

Mauranen, A. (2006c) 'Speaking the discipline', in Hyland, K. and Bondi, M. (eds.), *Academic Discourse Across Disciplines*, Bern: Peter Lang, 271–94.

Mauranen, A. (2011) 'Learners and users: who do we want corpus data from?', in Meunier, F., De Cock, S., Gilquin, G. and Paquot, M. (eds.) *A Taste for Corpora: A Tribute to Professor Sylviane Granger,* Amsterdam: John Benjamins, 155–72.

Mauranen, A., Hynninen, N. and Ranta, E. (2010) 'English as an academic lingua franca: the ELFA project', *English for Specific Purposes* 29 (3): 183–90.

Mortensen, J. (2010) 'Epistemic stance marking in the use of English as a lingua franca: a comparative study of the pragmatic functions of epistemic stance', PhD thesis, University of Roskilde.

Mortensen, J. and Haberland, H. (2009) 'Sprogvalg På danske universiteter i historisk perspektiv', *Sprogforum* 46: 8–13.

Owen, D. (2011) '"Native here and to the manner born" academic publishing and "proper" English', *English Text Construction* 4 (2): 279–302.

Pugh, A. K. and Ulijn, J. M. (eds.) (1984) *Reading for Professional Purposes: Studies and Practices in Native and Foreign Languages*, Guildford: Heinemann.

Shaw, P. (2008) 'Engelsk som lingua franca och som internationellt vetenskapsspråk', in Jansson, E. (ed.) *Vetenskapsengelska – med sensk kvalitet?* Stockholm: Språkrådet, 21–33.

Sinclair, J. (2005) 'Corpus and text: basic principles', in Wynne, M. (ed.) *Developing Linguistic Corpora: A Guide to Good Practice*, Oxford: Oxbow Books, 1–16 (http://ahds.ac.uk/linguistic-corpora/).

Sinclair, J. and Mauranen, A. (2006) *Linear Unit Grammar*, Amsterdam: John Benjamins.

Swales, J. M. (1985) *Episodes in ESP*, Oxford: Pergamon Press.

Swales, J. M. (1990) *Genre Analysis: English in Academic and Research Settings,* Cambridge: Cambridge University Press.

Trimble, L. (1985) *English for Science and Technology: A Discourse Approach*, New York: Cambridge University Press.

Väliverronen, E. (1992) 'Akateemiset puhetavat ja sisäänpääsyn esteet yliopistoyhteisössä', *Kasvatus* (1): 22–9.

Wächter, B. (2008) 'Teaching in English on the rise in European higher education', *International Higher Education* 52: 3–4 (www.bc.edu/bc_org/avp/soe/cihe/newsletter/ihe_pdf/ihe52.pdf).

Wenger E. (1998) *Communities of Practice: Learning, Meaning, and Identity,* Cambridge: Cambridge University Press.

Zamel, V. and Spack, R. (eds.) (1998) *Negotiating Academic Literacies: Teaching and Learning Across Languages and Cultures*, Mahwah: Lawrence Erlbaum.

4 *Vocabulary in speaking ELF*

Lexis is the most basic, most fundamental aspect of language, the sine qua non of communication. Words are what non-linguists are best aware of, and as scholars who work on vocabulary keep reminding us, there would be no communication without words. We might even conjecture that vocabulary is the most primitive domain of language, since speculation on the origins of language or assessment of the relative primitiveness or simplicity of languages rest largely on the kinds of vocabulary resources languages have, and the relationship between lexical and grammatical complexity. In cases where grammar may be reduced (as has recently been claimed for Piraha), or in extreme cases is virtually non-existent (rudimentary pidgins), we still use words. It is therefore a good starting point for exploring ELF.

Because words are so easy to notice, it is also easy to spot words in ELF use that diverge from Standard English. The frequency of lexical deviations may therefore easily get exaggerated; in reality, most lexical words are used in their ordinary Standard English forms, as we already saw in the previous chapter (Section 3.4; see also Appendix 2). In a wordlist ranked by frequency, one needs to go well below the 3,000 most common words before the first deviation from Standard English appears (*themself* ranks 3,514th with 17 occurrences). Any ELF text will also be sprinkled with items that are not English – mixing elements from other languages, proper names, and in academic speech particularly specialist terms that may be Latin- or Greek-based, although not established in general English.

This chapter looks into vocabulary in academic ELF. It makes use of data from the ELFA and MICASE corpora for primarily quantitative discussion before moving on to smaller-scale and closer views on the data. It starts out by looking at lexical phenomena in terms of frequencies (Section 4.1), and then widens out to approximations of form and meaning (Section 4.2). We then proceed to smaller-scale but more detailed evidence for processing and the units that might be involved in cognitive lexical operations (Section 4.3). The final section, 4.4, sums up briefly the findings from the first three, connecting them with relationships between forms and functions in lingua francas more generally.

4.1 Most common words in ELF and ENL

It has been known for a relatively long time in linguistics that word frequencies have a strong impact on what language is like. Highly frequent words are in many ways very different from less frequent ones (e.g. Bybee & Hopper 2001). The first statistical observation to bring this into general awareness was made by Zipf (1935) and is known as 'Zipf's Law', which basically states that a word's frequency and its rank order in a wordlist of a given language corpus are inversely related, the rank order roughly corresponding to 1/n, where *n* is the word's frequency rank in the corpus. In other words, a very few words occur very frequently whereas a large number of words occur very rarely. The vast majority of words thus occur rarely and rank low on wordlists. The most frequent word should appear twice as often as the second in rank, which in turn should be found roughly twice as often as the fourth and so on, the differences gradually diminishing as we move down the list. Very frequent words also tend to retain irregularity better than others (Francis & Kucera 1982) and show other kinds of idiosyncratic behaviour (Bybee 2008). Moreover, as noted in Chapter 2, a group of evolutionary biologists (Pagel et al. 2007) recently showed that most frequent words tend to evolve slowly and remain in use for very long periods of time, while less frequent words evolve faster and disappear sooner. From an individual language user's perspective, frequent words are faster to process, and speakers' accuracy in detecting and remembering them is greater than when they encounter rare words (Dabrowska 2004: 20).

With word frequencies relating to so many issues of interest in this book, it seemed worthwhile to cast a brief glance in their direction and get an overview of basic quantitative characteristics of ELF lexis as a backdrop to other questions of ELF vocabulary. The next two sections lay down some basic numerical facts concerning the distribution of the most common words in ELFA.

4.1.1 Distribution of common words

Zipf's Law (Zipf 1935, 1949) is a power law, which states that word frequencies and word rankings stand in a particular predictable relationship to each other. A well-known confirmation of it from the English language comes from one of the pioneering English corpora, the Brown corpus (www.archive.org/details/BrownCorpus), where the top-ranking word (*the*) accounts for about 7% of the data, and the second most frequent word slightly over 3.5% (see Table 4.1 below). The Brown corpus consists of a broad range of written text-types.

Table 4.1 Proportions of most common words in three corpora: Brown, ELFA, and MICASE

	Brown	ELFA	MICASE
#	%	%	%
1	6.90	5.10	4.46
2	3.60	4.17	2.70
3	2.85	3.10	2.29
4	2.59	2.64	2.28
5	2.32	2.26	2.24

It equals ELFA in size, with its roughly 1 million words. Yet ELFA does not follow the predicted pattern equally clearly. The most frequent word is the same (*the*), but it covers somewhat less of the corpus (5.10%). The second item on the list, however, is far above the expected value, with coverage of just over 4% of the data. It is not a word in the traditional sense but a hesitation marker (*er*), and it might be argued that it does not count for that reason. I would nevertheless not like to exclude it, because hesitation markers are a normal part of spoken language, and particularly common in ELF. And even if we look at the next item (*and*) on the rank list, its coverage is still somewhat higher than expected (over 3%), while it is only with the fourth-ranking item (*of*) that we get pretty close to half of the frequency of the first (2.64%).

Does this mean that ELF is deviant in terms of frequency, or could this imply that the difference lies in speech vs. writing? To get a clearer picture, I checked the values of top-ranking words for MICASE, and noticed that they deviated even more from the Brown corpus and from Zipf's Law (Table 4.1): it is only the fifth-ranking item whose coverage halves that of the top item, and although numbers 3, 4, and 5 all come very close to each other, the second most common item is clearly more frequent than any of them.

It would seem, then, that items in speech distribute differently from written text, which is what the Brown corpus consists of, like those that will have been available to Zipf in the 1930s. And if you remove the hesitation item *er* from the ELFA list, its distribution pattern resembles MICASE even more.

As Zipf's Law implies that the most frequent words cover a considerable part of the entire data, an interesting question arises with regard to a larger sample of the commonest words in relation to the whole corpus. For the Brown corpus, the 135 top-ranking words suffice

Table 4.2 Shares of the most frequent words in ELFA and MICASE

Words	ELFA %	MICASE %
Top 44	50.05	
Top 58		50.0
Top 200	68.7	68.0

to account for 50% of it. In other words, if we take these 135 most common types, or distinct items, they constitute 50% of the tokens, that is, of all the running words that make up the database. In view of this, what would we expect from ELF? A tendency towards lexical simplification has been noticed in both learner language (e.g. Granger 1998; Altenberg & Granger 2002; Granger et al. 2002) and translations (e.g. Laviosa-Braithwaite 1996; Nevalainen 2005; Tirkkonen-Condit 2005) that manifests itself in exceptionally frequent use of very frequent items. It seems reasonable to expect, then, that ELF might have proportionally fewer items to cover half of the corpus. What we find is a greatly reduced number of items: in ELFA,[1] 44 words (types) are enough to account for 50% of the data (tokens). The difference is indeed dramatic. Only a third of the number of distinct words reported for the Brown corpus (135) is required to cover half of the data.

Again, we might wonder to what extent this is a specialty of ELF, and how much could be ascribed to other factors such as the spoken mode, or the fact that ELFA consists of academic language only. To keep domain and genre as constant as possible, it is best to turn to MICASE again. What we see here is very similar to ELFA, even if somewhat less drastic (Table 4.2). MICASE requires 58 of the most common words to account for half of the corpus, which is well under a half (43%) of the number in Brown.

It seems, then, that speech looks radically different from writing from this perspective, too. This compares interestingly with Biber's findings on the grammatical differences between the spoken and written registers: spoken registers vary within a far narrower range than written registers (Biber 2009). He attributes this to processing factors: the possibilities of careful formulation and revision available to writing differ considerably from the real-time production circumstances of speech. What we need to keep in mind in respect of the present comparison is that the range of genre or register variation may be expected to be particularly narrow in ELFA and MICASE, which represent academic speaking only, not speaking in all its manifestations. In principle, it is possible that academic language is narrow in its vocabulary as a fair number of terms get used over and over again, and as subtechnical words, such as those in Coxhead's academic wordlist (2000), are shared across many fields. Nevertheless, one of the early questions asked in the compilation of the MICASE corpus – is academic speaking more like speaking or more like academic language? – received a clear answer from MICASE research saying it is essentially like any other speaking (see e.g. Lindemann & Mauranen 2001; Swales & Burke 2003; Mauranen 2004c).

On the other hand, academic language is lexically prolific in producing new terminology. This includes neologisms that may stay within one discipline or school of thought – so one may speak about *scientification* or *backdrivable* solutions in limited contexts where they make sense. Terms of this kind may gradually gain wider currency like many others that have spread beyond their academic origins, such as *empowerment* or *affordance*, or they may soon fall into oblivion, or never cross the boundaries of their narrow specialisations. The small communities of practice that these items get coined in regulate their term-formation along with their other activity, and it will perhaps never be possible for an outsider to decide whether a given item is acceptable or not. *Symbology* may be an error, a nonce item (word used only for the occasion), or a forerunner.

Moreover, we should make some allowance for the fact that the counts are based on exact repetitions of the items to the exclusion of approximate forms, which are fairly common in ELF. But even taking these considerations into account, a considerable difference remains between ELFA and MICASE: this is quite clear with the ELFA figure, which is a quarter (24%) lower than the MICASE figure in the number of tokens (different words) required to account for half of the data.

Therefore, we must conclude that ELF leads to notable lexical simplification. This is an important finding, not least because it agrees with results from other hybrid languages, such as translated language and learner language, as noted above. We can consider it in terms of the different perspectives discussed in Chapter 2. Simplification is common in language and dialect contact situations (Trudgill 1986; Thomason 2001; Winford 2003), although simplification in contact literature has tended to focus on grammatical structures, not lexis. Looking at it as a macro-level tendency, the robustness observed among the most common words in different languages (Pagel et al. 2007) could perhaps also hold for a hybrid form like ELF. From a cognitive perspective, this would seem to support the interpretation that the most common elements are best entrenched in speakers' minds and thereby most readily accessible for use (Dabrowska 2004).

However, counterevidence has also come up, at least in translations, suggesting that lexical simplification is not uniform across the board but varies with item types, and also in terms of collocational combinability (Mauranen 2000; Jantunen 2004a, 2004b). Further research is needed on the extent to which this holds for ELF – lexis comprises items which can be differentiated on many dimensions, such as closed vs. open classes, the degree of lexicality, general vs. specific scope, etc., and to understand how ELF lexis works we need to get much deeper into this.

In view of all the evidence presented here, it might tentatively be suggested, then, that language contact strengthens 'core' vocabulary at the expense of rarer words. By looking at distributions of individual words, we have covered an important aspect of lexical simplification, and we shall look into others later in this chapter (Section 4.2).

4.1.2 Which words are most common?

What are these words that cover so much of the use captured in corpora? What words get repeated time and time again in talk, and how much do they overlap in ELF and ENL? We already saw in Chapter 3 that many words among the most frequent 50 are the same in ELFA and MICASE. Let us now get a little more precise and instead of the top 50 focus on those items (types) that in each case account for half of all the words (tokens) in the corpus. In other words, let us look at the 44 most common words in ELFA and the 58 most common words in MICASE (with the whole lists ranked according to frequency down to the 200th word in Appendix 2).

Do the same words appear on both lists, or are they very different? In line with the earlier comparison of 50 words, the 50% lists are remarkably similar: 36 of the words appear on both lists, covering 82% of the ELFA list and 62% of MICASE. Even their rank ordering is highly similar. On the whole, then, roughly the same words are the most frequent even though there are more items on the MICASE list.

What words are the most frequent words, then? On the whole most can be identified as grammatical, closed-class words, such as articles, prepositions, auxiliaries, and pronouns, together with some hesitation and back-channelling noises (*er*, *erm*, *uh*, *uhm*, *mhm*). There are many ways in which we might classify these items, but let us begin by drawing some distinctions based on the way meaning is constructed.

A primary distinction can be drawn between items that contribute to the 'contents' of what gets said (*knowledge*, *little*, *always*) and those that indicate intended functions and organise the contents or the interaction (*as*, *or*, *yeah*, *does*). The division is rough, since language elements tend to be multifunctional and more than single words are involved in making meaning, but it serves as a point of departure. Content-oriented or **'content-constructing'** words are thus distinct from **'organising'** words. The division loosely resembles a standard distinction between lexical and grammatical words, but not very closely, since the organising type comprises much more than grammatical items.

Within the content-constructing category, we can again distinguish two types: those more or less independent in the meaning elements they contribute ('autonomous'), and those that depend primarily on the circumstances ('situational'). **Autonomous** words basically have plenty of independent meaning to contribute to the conversation; they are typical 'content words', which attract other items around them to set up meaningful units of communication (*said*, *work*, *important*).[2] They also carry the main weight in the information that speakers seek from each other, and play major roles when people summarise the import of a conversation. Words of this kind are usually nouns, adjectives, lexical verbs, and numbers as well as evaluative items like intensifiers (*really*) or mitigators (*somewhat*). Of these, nouns and adjectives are entirely absent from our sample of the 50 most frequent words, and lexical verbs all but missing: only *think* appeared in both corpora, and *know* in addition in MICASE. Both are only marginally full lexical verbs, because their most frequent uses are as parts of pragmatic elements: *I think* and *you know*. Two pragmatically evaluative elements were very common, an intensifier (*very*) in ELFA and a mitigator (*just*) in MICASE.

Words of the **situational** kind are those whose meaning depends heavily on the context of situation, such as referential pronouns and deictic items. An identical selection of pronouns (*I*, *you*, *we*, *they*, *it*) appears in both corpus samples, and deictic *this* and *that*.

The other major word type is the **organising** kind. This group comprises words that broadly indicate the function of utterances, their structural relations, and generally organise the text or speech ('textual'), or manage the interaction ('interactional'). The distinction is essentially between orientation to text (*however*, *because*, *also*) vs. orientation to the outward social situation, to the other participants (*let's*, *now*, *actually*).

Textual organisers are a large group in our sample. Among them we find items like local organisers within the sentence such as determiners (*the*, *a*), relative pronouns (*that*, *which*), syntactic organisers (*there*, *it's*), conjunctions (*and*, *so*, *but*, *if*, *or*) and prepositions (*of*, *to*, *in*, *for*, *on*, *with*, *about*, and *as*), one *wh*-word (*what*) and one 'sequencer' (*then*), an item type that organises longer stretches of discourse like narratives. Auxiliaries play important structural roles in addition to specifying things like tense, mood, and modality, and are therefore included among textual organisers: *have* and *can* are common in both corpora in addition to forms of BE (*is*, *are*, *be*, *was*). Determiners, which specify the status of the headword, featured in both samples (*the*, *a*), as did one negator (*not*).

Conjunctions and prepositions were large groups, accounting for a notable proportion of both lists: 34% of ELFA's top-frequency items and 26% of MICASE's, whereas not a single adjective appeared in either sample. Again, most of the conjunctions (*and*, *so*, *but*, *if*, *or*) and prepositions (*of*, *to*, *in*, *for*, *on*, *with*, *about*, *as*) were the same in ELFA and MICASE.

Interactional organisers appear as a very small group in the present account, where they are conservatively limited to those that serve purely interactional purposes. They are not always even words, but elements that indicate important pragmatic aspects of speaking, such as hesitation (e.g. Sacks et al. 1974, Laitinen et al. forthcoming) and listenership (e.g. McCarthy 2002; Warren 2006). They include hesitations (*er*, *erm*, *uh*, *like*) and back-channelling (*yeah*, *mhm*).

Some instances in the above categories raise the question of how much certainty there is in determining the function of an item by just looking at a wordlist. Items that are clearly very multifunctional were therefore given closer consideration. The multifunctional items included here all seemed to follow approximately an 80/20% distribution in ELFA: thus *there* mostly functioned as a syntactic organiser, not as a deictic pointer, *that* was principally used as a relative pronoun rather than a demonstrative, *as* was a preposition, and *then* mostly a temporal sequencer, although the logical function (*if–then*) accounted for nearly 20% of its use.

Some items were more problematic. One was *like*, which resists simple classification: its uses are distributed over a number of functions without any one of them being clearly dominant. Half of the time it is a preposition (49%), a quarter of its occurrences are hesitation markers (24%), nearly a fifth (18%) verbs, and some are conjunctions or other discourse organisers (12%). In the end, none of these uses alone would have been sufficient to place it among the top 44 words. Its high place on a scale is therefore an artifact of ranking by frequency of form. Another problem case was *it*, which seems to be fairly evenly divided between the pronoun and dummy subject roles. A reliably part-of-speech (POS) tagged corpus would be able to give more exact figures for some of these items, but neither ELFA nor MICASE have such tagging available, and some pragmatic and interactional items would fall through the net even so.

How similar were the corpus samples if we consider individual words in the four main categories outlined here? Since more types were involved in making up 50% of the tokens in MICASE, the expectation is that it has additional items compared to ELFA. This is indeed largely so: while ELFA had only three words that did not appear equally frequently in MICASE (*very*, *because*, and *also*), MICASE had some additional items in each category. Among content-constructing items were the autonomous *all*, *know*, and *just* and the situational *here*, and among organising items the textual kind included eight instances (*how*, *no*, *do/don't*, *would*, *get*, *at*, *an*) and the interactional type three: *okay*, *right*, and *well*. The rest of the mismatches resulted from different transcription conventions. If we look at the distributions of the words in the four categories, the corpora show a very similar picture: in both, textual organisers were overwhelmingly the largest group, followed by situational content-constructing words, and finally autonomous content-constructers and interactional organisers as equally small groups.

This quantitative overview of lexis shows that ELF vocabulary is very close to similar genres of ENL, with its most frequent items pretty much the same as in other comparable kinds of English speech.

4.1.3 Stability of common words

An intriguing study of the effects of word frequency on word stability was made recently by a group of evolutionary biologists, as already discussed briefly in Chapter 2. Their principal discovery was that certain types of high-frequency words remained remarkably stable over the languages and over thousands of years of language evolution. The Indo-European languages the group investigated included English, which makes an interesting point of comparison to contemporary ELF.

What Pagel et al. (2007) did was compare word frequencies in four contemporary languages,[3] showing that their present-day frequency predicted the rate at which they evolved over thousands of years of Indo-European language development. As they put it: 'In all four languages, the more a meaning is used today, the slower its rate of evolution has been throughout the 6,000- to 10,000-year history of Indo-European' (Pagel et al. 2007: 718). It is interesting, therefore, to see how far our small and specialised corpora of contemporary academic English match the common items that are reported to be the most stable. As we already saw in the previous section, ELFA and MICASE overlap strongly in their high-frequency items. A basic line of argument in Pagel's work rests on the centrality of the stable items in speech, which makes it particularly interesting in comparison with our spoken corpora: his team used databases largely drawn from written text, so what is the degree of similarity between their findings and the present data?

The comparison is not quite straightforward, because Pagel et al. do not list words but talk about 'meanings', which is understandable in view of their comparison of several languages. However, their categorisation in fact seems to follow a straightforward POS system: nouns, adjectives, verbs, pronouns, numbers, conjunctions, prepositions, and what they call 'special adverbs' (Pagel et al. 2007: 718). In other words, the categories of the 'meaning' groups are based on form and syntactic function. 'Special adverbs' make up the only class outside a standard grammar: *what*, *when*, *where*, *how*, *here*, *there*, *not*. This is thus a collection of interrogative words that also play other syntactic roles such as relativisation, two deictic items, and a negator.

These 'special adverbs' make up one of those categories that remained stable over millennia, along with numbers and pronouns. According to Pagel's team, such items were strongly selected for because they are crucial to spoken communication. The rapidly evolving ones may be less important, or as Pagel et al. put it, their 'exact forms may often be less important to conveying meaning' (2007: 719). While it is quite plausible that the slowly evolving items are vital to communication, the data that historical analyses operate on and reconstruct is not authentic speech. Claims about their centrality in spoken communication are therefore questionable. Despite this, the stable types are well represented at the level of word class in our speech corpora too: members of all three appeared in both ELFA and MICASE. As we already saw above, pronouns (*I*, *you*, *we*, *they*, and *it*), special adverbs (*what*, *there*, and *not*), and numbers all appear among the top-frequency items. If our lists appear shortish, it is partly because we are considering only around 50 items from each corpus, while Pagel and his colleagues operated with 200 of the most common meanings. We may thus safely say that the present data support the centrality of these item types.

The less stable, rapidly evolving types tell a slightly different story. Pagel's team reports conjunctions, prepositions, and adjectives as fast evolving. Of these, adjectives did not feature in our samples, but both conjunctions and prepositions were large groups. There was slightly more divergence between the corpora in these categories as compared to the stable ones, but not much. Conjunctions and prepositions, which indicate relationships between other elements of discourse, thus seem far more prominent in our data than in the evolutionary account.

While the general trends in this comparison show a reasonable match, the observations also give rise to new questions. First, to what extent can we assume that the items categorised according to POS types reliably represent 'meanings' that are supposedly essential to spoken communication? Secondly, what about item types that fall outside these lists? As to the first question, similar issues were already raised for wordlists in relation to polysemy and multifunctionality, showing that caution is needed in classifying items based on form. Even POS-tagged data may be unable to capture multifunctionality and context-sensitive meaning, with pragmatic and interactional items easily falling through the net. The POS-tagging used by the evolutionary biologists has categories that are not always transparent, or may not be appropriate: for instance their 'middle group', that is, items neither noticeably fast nor particularly slow evolvers, include the category 'verbs'. Presumably it covers auxiliaries as well as lexical verbs. It might nevertheless be preferable to separate auxiliaries from lexical verbs, as 'closed' word classes dominated both the most and the least stable categories, and thus appeared to behave differently from 'open' classes (which would include lexical verbs).

The second question concerning the adequacy of the categorisation and what it leaves out is more serious. Real speech seems to have elements that do not fit conventional POS categories, traditionally drawn from written data; that the items are essential to speech shows in their high frequencies, as was seen in the previous section. To understand better the relationship between evolutionary findings and contemporary speech data, let us look at the Pagel team results in view of the categories that were derived from the spoken corpora.

Among what were called content-constructing words above, we found instances of numerals and other quantifiers, which would go into the slowly evolving categories. A type of word that remains outside the evolutionary categories is the evaluative item; while adjectives, regarded as fast evolvers, did not appear among our high-ranking words, pragmatically evaluative elements like intensifiers (*very*) or mitigators (*just*) were high on the corpus lists. Such evaluative items would seem to be a potentially important candidate category to look for in accounting for language evolution; it is a plausible assumption that evaluation plays a crucial role in survival, enabling us to distinguish phenomena that are, for instance, dangerous, or desirable. Evaluation is ubiquitous in present-day language (e.g. Hunston & Thompson 2000), and therefore one would imagine it might play a role in language development.

Words of the situational kind included referential pronouns and deictic items. Pronouns are among evolutionary categories, but deixis is not, although personal pronouns and some of the special adverbs (*here*, *there*) are used for deictic functions. Both are slow evolvers, which suggests their 'coreness'. In the present corpora, *this* and *that* are deictic items that were not recognised by Pagel et al. (2007).

Textual organisers are the largest group in the corpus account above. This group is divided in respect of slow or rapid evolution: while *wh*-words and negators are slow, conjunctions and prepositions are fast. Insofar as auxiliaries may be included in the 'verb' class by Pagel's team, they are of intermediate speed. Determiners, relative pronouns, syntactic organisers, and sequencers remain outside the evolutionary categorisation. While *there* is also among the 'special adverbs', its main function in English is as a syntactic organiser, which is quite language-specific, unlike its deictic function.

Interactional items are an important group for real speech, which is rich in hesitations, back-channelling, and minimal response tokens. None of these features in the evolutionary account.

The broad categories outlined on the basis of the speech corpora thus draw attention to types missing from the evolutionary account. The absent groups include organisational and interactional, which means that words specialising in organising text, interaction, and even clause structure have not been considered, apart from some sentence structural organisers of which only conjunctions and prepositions were included. Another missing type is evaluative items, by which are meant not adjectives but pragmatically evaluative words, such as intensifiers and mitigators. It seems that the methods the evolutionary biologists used do not capture the realities of actual speech very well. Interactional features are of course less prominent in written text and presumably harder to reconstruct for older texts and at word level. Given that Pagel's (2007) group claim their findings reflect the centrality of the slowly evolving words in everyday conversation, the absence of interactional considerations is nevertheless problematic. Yet interactional exigencies penetrate grammatical choices – as in, for example, Fox's (1987) observation that choices of noun phrases vs. pronouns indicate a speaker's intention to either continue or end a sequence. Cognitive explanations did not feature much in the evolutionary approach, but the relative advantage of pronouns over open-class nouns would seem to go together very well with the claim made by Du Bois (2003) that lexical noun phrases reflect greater cognitive costs than pronouns to speakers and hearers alike.

The most stable categories, numbers, pronouns, and selected adverbs are not specific to speech but tend to be frequent in written text as well. It is also noteworthy that the slow and stable word types represent closed word classes, many of which are grammatical.

What can we make of these findings on very common words? First of all, the presence of stable, slowly evolving element categories supports the idea that these are central to language, and that they appear in actual contemporary speech data. They also suggest that core elements of language are not highly sensitive to genre limitations, as our two corpora represent academic speaking. Moreover, they seem to suggest that when it comes to fundamental vocabulary, first and second language use are highly similar; when we go further down the frequency scale, differentiation increases, as happens with any two corpora, but at the top end, a small set of very frequent items accounts for both first and second language use. This supports the notion of lingua franca use as focusing on what is most crucial to communication and most central to a language.

These observations illustrate very clearly the predominance of closed-class items, largely grammatical words, among the most frequent vocabulary. It is in some sense quite remarkable that half of all the words used in hundreds of hours of speech are so predominantly grammatical, because as speakers we tend not to notice this. In communicating meaning, content words are unquestionably central, but they are more variable and more dispersed among the texts or speech events that they appear in. To an extent the predominance of grammatical words in large masses of data comes to the fore because such words appear in fixed form across texts and speech events, while more variable items do not have the same statistical chances. Languages can nevertheless express the meanings incorporated in closed classes in alternative ways as well (e.g. Winter 1977), even though it is often convenient for speakers to resort to fixed, conventional forms. New expressions get grammaticalised over time but do not completely eliminate previous ones, or indeed other functions of the items involved (e.g. Hopper & Traugott 2003). An interesting point for frequency considerations is also that more general-sense words (such as *come*, *go*) than specific-sense words (*waddle*, *saunter*) are candidates for grammaticalisation processes (Bybee 2003); general-sense items tend to be far more common than specific ones.

It is also interesting from the perspective of language change that closed-class items feature so prominently among the stable categories, because with the exception of verbs, it is generally found to be the case that open-class items are the most readily borrowed between languages (e.g. Winford 2003). This would then explain the volatility of open-class items in the evolutionary account compared to structural items, which tend to resist change. Because morphological complexity associated with a lexical class makes it more resistant to change, verbs tend to be borrowed less than other open-class items (Winford 2003:

52). From the point of view of communicating meaning, content words are unquestionably important, but far more adaptable to circumstances – thereby also to changes brought about by time. Why some closed classes are less stable than others remains an intriguing question, to which some tentative answers will be suggested in the next chapter.

The quantitative overview thus shows some important things about ELF: within the categories of long-term development, it seemed to conform to the general mould of language. It is also very much in line with English on the whole, with its most frequent items pretty much the same as in other kinds of English, particularly speech. Analyses of long-term linguistic development promise deeper insights into the workings of language stripped of its most contingent and volatile aspects; yet such analyses would seem to need more innovative ways of breaking down linguistic categories before they can live up to this promise.

4.2 Variation in form and meaning

Wordlists yield fundamental information about vocabulary, but still paint only a fragment of the lexical picture, as we saw in the previous section. To flesh out this skeletal view, let us work our way towards individual vocabulary items while still maintaining the corpus-based view. Any vocabulary search or even a small stretch of a transcript in ELFA will throw up words that are unusual, unconventional, or unquestionably deviant. Although each instance occurs rarely, they fall into types. A first distinction can be drawn between form-based and meaning-based irregularities. While some items deviate from Standard English in form (4.1), others diverge in sense (4.2).

(4.1)

> ... our other basic industry paper and pulp it was *successing* as well so it's not totally the rise of information society ...

(4.2)

> ... they need and they they demand a power, that is *negated* to th- to them, at least in the secondary school ...

Form and sense distinctions can be extended inwards to parts of the orthographic word and outwards to its close contextual allies (discussed further in Chapter 5). In this section we start off with individual words, although we quickly come to the limits of treating words as self-standing units in isolation and without internal structure.

Looking at the two examples above, it is clear that neither conforms to Standard English, while at the same time it is not hard to see why they did not cause any observable communication breakdown when they were uttered in conversation. Both bear a strong resemblance to an element that would meet the requirements of convention in the context: *succeeding* in (4.1) and *denied* in (4.2). In the case of *successing*, we may surmise that it originates in the noun *success* turned into a verb, or as a blend of *successful* and *succeeding*. Clearly, it resembles the standard item in form. In contrast, *negated* in place of *denied* is based on semantic affinity: both can be used to signify that the speaker pronounces something to be untrue. They may therefore be conceptually linked in speakers' minds by virtue of shared semantic features. They also share an etymological origin in Latin (*de*)*negare* ('to say no, deny').

What the examples have in common is that both are *approximations* of a conventional English item. They are not quite what is expected in Standard English, but they are not arbitrary substitutions either; both have recognisable features in common with an item that would meet conventional expectations. Approximations are not unknown in learner language, and very likely to occur in interdialectal accommodation (cf. Trudgill 1986). It is thus not surprising that they appear in ELF.

The above examples were one-off occurrences, but there is ample evidence of similar approximations in ELFA. A few instances of each kind below illustrate formal and semantic approximation (examples 4.3 and 4.4 respectively, the standard forms following in square brackets).

(4.3)

(a) ... nothing is *guarantable,* the quest for theoretical certainty ... [*guaranteed*]
(b) ... *undoubtly* the whole work will be positively accepted ... [*undoubtedly*]
(c) ... they will not be *allowded* to have a ... [*allowed*]
(d) ... it's not accurately *assimilisation* and some way all these ... [*assimilation*]
(e) ... this *categoration* of both male and female ... [*categorisation*]

(4.4)

(a) ... social democrats in it was er *visioned* as er as a wicked political *strength* so ... [*envisaged/seen*; *power*]
(b) ... it's only eight per cent in slovakia they er they are *in front of* us as regards social and economic reforms [*ahead of*]

(c) ... we have a difficult tax system i think it's not so easy and also of course for the erm for the *normal* persons it's really hard to understand [*ordinary*]
(d) ... some people are afraid of the future because when these advantages will *finish* some of er of companies can move to the east to russia to ukraine [*stop/cease*]

As the cases in (4.3) show, often no context is needed to detect the simultaneous deviance and recognisability with respect to a standard form. Their immediate co-texts show that the items were not repaired by the speakers as if slips of the tongue, and none caused any noticeable reactions in their extended contexts, so it appears that they passed unnoticed by speakers and interlocutors alike. Occasionally form-based approximations need context to be detectable, if the speaker uses an existing but unsuitable word (*accepted it as a* ***base*** *of the con- connection of the two*) that sounds or looks similar to a word that fits the context (*accepted it as a* ***basis*** *of the connection*).

In contrast, semantic approximation cannot be detected out of context. Examples (4.4a–d) are all English words, and all have some semantic components that allow the intended meaning to be deciphered. Some are near-synonyms, distinguished by their contextual properties (for instance *strength – power*, *in front of – ahead of*, or *normal – ordinary*). In the European context some have the additional advantage of being related to a Latin origin, which would make the shared semantic components familiar via other languages that the speakers know.

A particular type of semantic approximation that is also found in translations and in SLA (e.g. Toury 1995; Altenberg & Granger 2002) is using general words instead of more specific ones (hyperonymic substitution), most often nouns or verbs. Examples in (4.5) illustrate this:

(4.5)

(a) <S7> there is typical autoimmune hepat- hepatitis which cause, which is *going* to cirrhosis in in women, primary biliary cirrhosis ... [*develops*]
(b) <S3> every leader beginning from president has to announce the amount of property he has before *you go into power* you have to say ... [*assume*]
(c) <S1> er okay before we go to the next topic, i i think that. in a way *the question <NAME> made* what made you study or be- become interested on this issue it is a relevant question cause this your topic leads us a bit further ... [*asked*]

(d) ... round the mhm original population so it had made *made* some er *problems* for er for er the area dominated by humans [*caused*]

(e) ... this er process is very similar this is the national assembly but the recent photo there women wanted *to get* er as erm *as members* [*be accepted*]

(f) ... there are a lot of erm people maybe the age of 50 who *get out of their job* because maybe erm the companies move to the east erm and erm these people are nearly unable to get a new job [*lose their job / are made redundant*]

Substituting more general items for specific ones can also be seen as kinds of lexical approximation. However, although we can find such cases in the data, the bigger picture does not confirm an overall preference for such substitution strategies in ELF. A wordlist comparison[4] shows that general nouns or verbs are not what best differentiates between ELF and ENL. Even though MAKE is one of the verbs Altenberg and Granger (2002) found to be excessively favoured by learners relative to native speakers, its overall frequency is actually lower in ELFA (1,555 pmw) than in MICASE (1,953 pmw). Along the same lines, GET turns out to be proportionally more common in MICASE, in fact one of the top differentiators for MICASE over ELFA.[5] Of nouns, both *stuff* (#44) and *thing* (#99) rank high in distinguishing MICASE from ELFA. As to the words that differentiate ELFA from MICASE, we only get some forms of BE and HAVE, and much of this is caused by register differences reflected in the transcripts: MICASE has mostly contracted forms like *we're*, *they've*, and frequently also *hafta*, while ELFA has proportionally fewer contractions. In brief, there is no support to the idea that general-sense verbs would be particularly typical of ELF. They are not even among the top-ranking words in ELFA, as seen in a simple frequency wordlist (Appendix 2): only some forms of *be* and *have* rank among the top 100, *get* is 102nd, and *make* 125th.

Overall lexical comparisons of two corpora are never straightforward for reasons already discussed in Chapter 3. In addition, some of what the comparisons throw up as distinguishing the two corpora at hand is based on differences in transcription or other linguistically trivial factors. Despite caveats, we can nevertheless gain a rough general overview of the lexical differences by looking at the differentiating items in ELFA and MICASE. In terms of register or style, the distinguishing features of ELFA tend to be more formal, such as *yes*, *have/has*, and the reverse is true of MICASE, where *yep*, *okay* (*mkay/kay*), *gonna*, and *lemme* show up. Apart from names of places and languages (*Europe*, *Russian*, *Tampere* in ELFA; *Roman*, *Michigan*, *Spanish* in MICASE), a good number of the best differentiating lexical words clearly relate to the topics at hand (*forest*, *education*, *democracy*, *policy* in ELFA; *temperature*, *drug*, *pornography*, *equilibrium* in MICASE). Some high-frequency ELFA differentiators appeared as parts of multi-word units. *Course* was one of the most frequent, and turned out to be almost exclusively part of the adverb phrase *of course*. *Case* also appeared in clusters – *in this/that case*, *in the case of*, etc. – as did *example* and *instance*, nearly always part of an exemplifying phrase. I shall return to phrases and multi-word units in Chapter 5.

Wordlist comparisons can generate further interesting observations in second-language vocabulary and lexical distributions. For instance, a comparison of the most frequent words in ELFA and MICASE[6] shows that many of the words that are particularly typical of ELFA and differentiate it from MICASE are among the commonest items in the wordlists. This might be interpreted as further evidence in support of the observation that the most common words are overrepresented in second language use, and thereby as lexical simplification. However, if we reverse the comparison, and look at the words particularly typical of the ENL corpus (MICASE) and compare them to the commonest words on the lists, it turns out that exactly the same thing happens. So it seems that some very common words serve to distinguish between databases of language more generally and that we should not read too much into one-way comparisons.

Wordlists give many other possibilities for delving deeper into vocabulary in second language use, but here I shall limit myself to one small exploration of one set of frequent words. As a point of departure, I chose an evaluative item, *important*, which is among the words that most clearly distinguish ELFA from MICASE, and which has been reported to get 'overused' by learners relative to native speakers (Granger 2009; Vetchinnikova 2010). I was also intrigued by Vetchinnikova's observation that her subjects used *important* almost always in predicative structures, but its near-synonyms like *significant* or *essential* in attributive positions. I therefore looked into all three of these words in ELFA, checking for their predicative vs. attributive uses. The results can be seen in Table 4.3, which shows that on the whole predicative uses were more common (60%) than attributive ones (40%). Table 4.3 also includes a division into dialogic and monologic speech, which shows that dialogue has a slightly stronger tendency to favour the predicative position.

It has been suggested that predicative and attributive uses of adjectives play different roles in spoken interaction, with predicative

Table 4.3 Attributive and predicative adjectives in ELFA
Boosting adjectives *important, essential,* and *significant* in attributive and predicative positions in ELFA monologue and dialogue.

	Attributive		Predicative		All
Dialogic speech					
Important	37%	(255)	63%	(444)	699
Essential	35%	(11)	65%	(20)	31
Significant	63%	(22)	37%	(13)	35
Total dialogic	38%	(288)	62%	(477)	765
Monologic speech					
Important	41%	(201)	59%	(284)	485
Essential	67%	(16)	33%	(8)	24
Significant	55%	(27)	45%	(22)	49
Total monologic	44%	(244)	56%	(314)	558
All	40%	(532)	60%	(791)	1323

adjectives doing more evaluative work (Thompson 1988) and being more common in conversations than formal situations or storytelling (Englebretson 1997). However, when we look more closely into the example adjectives, we can see that they each have their own profile: while *important* looks consistent in preferring the predicative position, and *significant* is equally consistently used more in the attributive position, *essential* shows a different pattern in dialogue (mostly predicative) and monologue (mostly attributive). The only adjective that acted according to Englebretson's prediction was thus *essential*, and no uniform pattern was discernible in ELFA across the dialogue–monologue divide. It looks like the preference depends on the actual adjective in question.

Alternatively, we might think ELF and generally SLU preferences differ from ENL. I examined non-natives' use in MICASE on *important* and found that it was in proportion to their number in the corpus, i.e. there is no indication of 'overuse' among this group. I then looked at the predicative vs. attributive use in MICASE, again separating monologue and dialogue (Table 4.4).

Here again we can see an overall preference for the predicative position (61% vs. 39%) in very similar proportions to ELFA, with

Table 4.4 Attributive and predicative adjectives in MICASE
Boosting adjectives *important*, *essential*, and *significant* in attributive and predicative positions in MICASE dialogue and monologue.

	Attributive		Predicative		All
Dialogic speech					
important	26%	(99)	74%	(288)	387
essential	50%	(3)	50%	(3)	6
significant	69%	(31)	31%	(14)	45
Total dialogic	30%	(133)	70%	(305)	438
Monologic speech					
important	46%	(139)	54%	(162)	301
essential	67%	(10)	33%	(5)	15
significant	57%	(26)	43%	(20)	46
Total monologic	48%	(175)	52%	(187)	362
All	39%	(308)	61%	(492)	800

the tendency stronger for dialogue than monologue. The distribution also essentially repeats that of ELFA: *important* (mostly predicative) and *significant* (mostly attributive) are consistent and in line with the ELFA pattern, with *essential* the odd one out, being divided equally in dialogue, but more often attributive in monologue. Again, it is only *essential* that supports Englebretson's hypothesis. The conclusion thus is that adjectives seem to behave differently in predicative vs. attributive uses, and that there is no evidence that this would differ between ELF and ENL speech. There is one distributional difference between ELF and ENL data here, and this is that each of these three adjectives had a far larger share in ELF than in ENL: *important* was three times, *essential* nearly five times, and *significant* around one and a half times more common in ELFA than in MICASE. While we might argue that *important* is a high-frequency item and therefore supports the 'overuse' findings from learner language, the other two are not particularly common, and some other explanation will be needed for their greater appearance in ELFA.

From the comparisons in this section, it seems, then, that ELF vocabulary is in many essential ways similar to ENL vocabulary and also fairly similarly distributed. While the overall reduction of the range of vocabulary that was noted in Section 4.1 is fairly clear, this is not a simple fact that would hold across the board, as we have seen in this section.

4.3 Approximation and processing

Let us shift our approach for a while from corpus-based overviews to the micro-scale of the speaker and look at speakers' moment-to-moment progression with words. We cannot observe speakers' lexical processes directly by any known methods, although various experimental methods or brain scanning can give interesting glimpses of some aspects of verbal learning and memory. It is particularly hard to capture speech processing when it goes on smoothly and untroubled, and most research methods resort to manipulating the input or otherwise focusing on the trouble spots. With our data of recorded authentic speech, the best places for accessing signs of processing trouble are the transcripts. One source of evidence we can access in this way are the signs of turbulence that are seen in hesitations, restarts, and rephrasing.

Much rephrasing is apparently prompted by speakers' desire to reformulate what they have just said as if to express it better or more accurately, or, as is usually assumed in connection with L2 speakers, to put it more correctly. Yet a good proportion of it looks involuntary and would seem to point to competing or conflicting item searches from memory to fit the context at hand. A particular strength of rephrasing and searching as evidence of possible lexical storage is that they indicate both initial stages, that is, search phases and trouble spots, and also the final stage, the result that satisfies the speaker well enough for him or her to proceed.

Repetition and rephrasing in their numerous interactional functions will be discussed more thoroughly in Chapter 7, but at this point we focus on things that specifically relate to the processing of words.

From the point of view of lexical processing, three kinds of evidence seem most relevant: lexical rephrases (***the quality of people the qualities** were inherited*), lexical searches (*and er **dif- diverse- diversity** in the other*), and 'echoing', or other-repetition (A: *well i asked the managers what they have is mainly **injuries*** B: ***injuries** yeah*).

4.3.1 Lexical rephrasing

To begin with lexical rephrases, the data seems to suggest that single words are subject to processing as independent units. This can be seen when speakers replace one word for another, as in (4.6), where the connection between the words is semantic – and in fact either word would seem to fit the context, where a group is attending to the same data reports.

(4.6)

> <S1> ... in this er prairie chicken the increase in population size doesn't *seem look* very strong also for adder this inc- er this er increase is ...

A very similar process seems to be involved in (4.7), where the relationship between the first output item (*the old*) and the replacement (*the former*) is semantic and fairly close – these items are used interchangeably in some contexts in many languages. Where (4.7) differs from (4.6) is that hesitation markers come between the two formulations, and that the replacement involves two words: the article is repeated in front of *former*, suggesting that the whole phrase *the... colonies* was the speaker's target unit.

(4.7)

> <S5> it goes on for example in france with *the old* er er *the former* colonies er we have the same situation in finland it is difficult to get n- there's always the language in er in the background

Both of these examples involve whole words and semantic rather than formal approximation. The same is true of the next two (4.8 and 4.9), both of which replace one lexical item, but in addition repeat more of the immediate co-text than the individual word.

(4.8)

> <S1> [in in es-] in tallinn <S4> yeah in tartu </S4> i've been ***investigating*** *this university* so **evaluating** *this universities* last spring </S1>

(4.9)

> <S2> ... property er er then er we would not respect the point *i* ***said*** *er earlier* that *i* ***made*** *earlier* that whenever there's a moral property there has to be ...

In (4.8), the speaker replaces *investigating* with *evaluating*, but repeats the whole verb phrase starting from the lexical verb: *investigating this university / evaluating this universities*. In (4.9), again, the relative clause *I said earlier* gets repeated with a verb replacement, *I made earlier*. Interestingly from a processing point of view, this speaker had already used the phrase *as I said earlier* in the same session. The recent activation may have made it a salient chunk, and therefore interfere with *the point … earlier*. Be that as it may, the rephrase points to larger chunks than individual words as a processing unit. This impression is further enhanced by straightforward repetitions with no rephrase or replacement at all, like the following (4.10):

(4.10)

<S2> … wanted to focus on tanzania because er it's one of the *poorest countries poorest countries* in the world …

What the last two instances seem to suggest, then, is that speakers operate not only with single-word units but also with larger chunks of language. Since self-rephrases can extend to quite sizeable entities, let us look at some clause-level rephrases while maintaining our focus on the individual word.

When speakers engage in self-rephrases, they often repeat more than just the individual item that they actually change. As we already saw, they can repeat one or more words preceding the original item, and put the replacement into that frame. Example (4.11) illustrates this in a clausal context. Here the repeated unit is a relative clause that gets interrupted after the first formulation, which is of the type usually known as a 'false start'. It is not utterance-initial, so not quite a 'start' in that sense, but because it recapitulates the relative clause after a self-interruption, it is very similar. 'False start' is not a good term, though, since these are real starts which get interrupted and followed by restarts. In this case the restart again involves a meaning-based connection between the original and the replacement.

(4.11)

<S7> for not all, the case that *i'm say- i'm talking about* is wood inhabiting fungi …

The restart thus involves a recapitulation of more than the item that is being replaced. A very typical recapitulation example is (4.12); as it replaces one item, the frame around it also gets repeated. The usual case is one where the immediately preceding frame is reproduced, as in (4.12) and (4.13):

(4.12)

<S9> i mean it's *it's not the **case** it's not the **factor*** for inbreeding so i mean just that what kind of factor factors [could] <S6> [mhm] </S6> could affect it </S9>

(4.13)

<S6> ... but a- at at least er *if we want to kind of* ***have*** *if we want to kind of* ***set*** *the stage* that er these are our species ...

As (4.13) shows, sometimes recapitulations can be quite long, and still involve a more or less verbatim repetition of the matrix unit that the replacement is embedded in.

4.3.2 Lexical searching

Moving on to the next type of evidence on what might be going on in online processing, we come to what looks like a lexical search (*the, er* ***designing*** *or* ***definite*** *factor*). Certain types seem to occur time and again. Example (4.14) shows a case where the speaker searches for a word to fit into the frame *there has been* which she has already begun. She first seems to hit upon an adjective, but is immediately aware that this is not the target item, so she continues without restarting the sequence, looking for an item that fits. As she hits upon it, she repeats it (*controversy about*) and then resumes her line of thought. Although here the target item seems to be a single word, the repeated unit includes the preposition that goes with it.

(4.14)

<S7> ... in florida there has been er *controversial er contro- controversy about er controversy about* er how successful ...

The search in (4.14) is based on form; the speaker first comes up with an approximate form and then the target form.

In (4.15), the form–meaning distinction begins to crumble. We see a search that appears to target two words as a single choice: both items are first incomplete, then completed at the next stage, as if parts of the same thing. The words are not parts of a compound, but neither are they entirely independent. They have a collocational bond: *empirical* collocates with words like *evidence*, *question*, *data*, and *study* in both our academic corpora. The speaker makes two consecutive restarts, one for each part of the collocation, before he utters the two together and proceeds to other things.

(4.15)

<S1> ... summarise the recent *empirica- stu- empirical studies* showing the ...

Collocational links between words are based neither on form nor on meaning in a simple way – they are, above all, attractions between the items themselves. A form-based explanation would not take us anywhere, but neither does meaning, because it is often collocational patterns that distinguish near-synonyms from each other (e.g. Jantunen 2004b). Another search with a collocate-based link is in (4.16) where the speaker seems to be looking for the best-fitting alternative among three acceptable and conventional possibilities.

(4.16)

<S1> ... today's four paper adder and the wolf bighorn sheep and panther and this er prairie chicken, so these are *the basic er main er key studies* that (survey) the rescue ...

In this case the choice appears to be between semantically related collocates to a noun, each with a good fit to the context; they come across as contextual near-synonyms, and the speaker seems to be running through them as if in search of the one that comes closest to the purpose of his utterance (its 'semantic prosody' in Sinclair's (2004) use of the term; see also Vetchinnikova forthcoming). In this he seems to act quite like a fluent native speaker, despite the obvious grammatical deviations he displays in the immediately preceding context (missing plural ending in *paper*, a list of animal terms, one with the definite article, one with a demonstrative, and three without either).

Some lexical searching seems to indicate that the 'same' items are stored several times in different ways, as single words, as parts of compounds, and probably as parts of strong collocations, supporting what research in frequency and psycholinguistics has suggested (Bybee & Hopper 2001; Wray 2002; Dabrowska 2004). Something of this complexity seems to be at stake in (4.17), where the search target is *fruit fly*, but the speaker first accesses the second part of the compound, *fly*, which is a meaningful and probably a fairly salient item in the context of insects, then a compound with likewise salient contextual associations (*butterfly*), and finally *fruit fly*, the target compound. The speaker seems to be consciously aware of his search in this case, in view of his apology for the unsuitable first candidates.

(4.17)

<S8> but of course you can induce also in lab er in lab in er animals like *fly butterf-* [er] <S6> [yeah] </S6> sorry *fruit flies* you can induce extremely different genomes

Lexical searching would appear to be a matter of an individual's cognition, something that speakers do within the confines of their own brains. However, there is an interactional facet to it as well, and an important one. I shall return to this in the next section, but at this point one aspect of it is particularly relevant. When speakers carry out lexical searching aloud, other participants become potentially more aware of their speech processes. Not only do hesitations and lexical searches give all participants more processing time, the current speaker as well as hearers, they also serve interactional purposes: lexical searching aloud helps the current speaker hold the floor and indicate that he or she has not finished yet, and it simultaneously alerts other speakers to the possibility that the speaker might need help. This may lead to collaborative completions (Chapter 2).

Example (4.18) illustrates a fairly common situation where the speaker searches for a word (on the basis of form), does not seem to be very successful, but by making several efforts finally hits the target and is immediately rewarded by a confirmation from another participant:

(4.18)

<S6> ... and well er how the regionalisation started in ASEAN er it started al- already in the 60s during the time of the cold war , and er it started from a common feeling of *ven- venera- ve-* @@ well they felt *vune- vulnerable* [you] </S6>
<SU> [*vul-*] yeah *vulnerable* @@ </SU>
<S6> *vulnerable* @@ five points erm well they had the @same enemy that's what i mean@ and ...

Following the fellow student's help, S6 repeats the item once again, cracks a joke about it (*five points*), and resumes the main thread of the discussion with *well*. This exchange, accompanied by laughter, suggests that the interactional consequences of making one's struggle with language open or public can be positive and work towards creating a friendly atmosphere, promoting solidarity and cooperation (see further discussion in Chapter 7).

4.3.3 Echoing

To work out what kinds of processing units of people might employ in active language performance, we can also glean evidence from interactional aspects of speaking. One thing that conversationalists engage in is what can be called 'echoing', repeating elements from the previous speaker's turn (also known as 'other-repetition' or 'allo-repetition'). Echoing applies to the immediately preceding context, because verbatim traces of speech dissolve fast, as new material comes in to fill the working memory. Later recycling of speech elements is better seen as a separate matter, 'topic resumption'. Echoing as an interactional phenomenon is discussed in more detail in Chapter 7, but here the focus is on what it can tell us about units of processing. As above, we see different kinds of units. In example (4.19) *outside* gets repeated after its first solitary appearance as an independent turn-constructing item, then repeated by BS7 in two different structures, and then confirmed once more by S10. S2 then uses the verb phrase *take care of themself*, which gets repeated by S5 – with just the slight modification of *themself* becoming *themselves*, as subtle other-correction.

(4.19)

<S2> ... where do they buy their occupational health service service i mean this kind of @place@ institute of occupational health </S2>
<S10> [*outside*] </S10>
<BS7> [they said] from *outside* <S2> yeah </S2> they said they buy from [*outside*] </BS7>
<S2> [yeah yeah] </S2>
<S10> [*outside*] yeah </S10>
<S2> that's true so they don't of course they don't *take care of themself* </S2>
<S5> i was thinking they would *take care of themselves* but </S5>
<S2> @@ yeah that's good but [no no] </S2>

The repeated sequence in (4.19) is a partly variable conventional unit, that is, while it overlaps with the highly formulaic *take care of yourself*, it is a form variant of that, and a case could be made for saying it is fully compositional. The degree of conventionalisation is apparently quite variable in expressions that get echoed, as can be seen in the following case (4.20), where a noun phrase is being recycled. The phrase is compositional, even though a fairly established and conventional one, especially in political language where the combination is a commonplace. Nevertheless, it is more likely to be an ad hoc combination here.

(4.20)

<S2> i didn't (remember) but is tanzania becoming a *real democracy* </S2>

<SU> mhm-hm (xx) a *real democracy* </SU>
<S2> er tanzania is not so *real democracy* so what do you think it <S3> mhm mhm [mhm] </S3> [it needs] to become *a real democracy* </S2>

In (4.21), a speaker begins her turn by echoing a prepositional phrase that the previous turn ended with. It looks as if S4 is trying to play for time in thinking of an answer to S1's question, as her *well* also indicates, and the prepositional phrase may serve the same purpose. It is not surprising that it is remembered in an unaltered form, since it was just uttered by S1. Conversationalists shadow each other's speech apparently quite closely, as suggested by the common phenomenon of collaborative completions, so the immediately preceding unit is still in the short-term memory for participants at this point.

(4.21)

<S1> and did you (got) some mhm research idea *from this paper* </S1>
<S4>*from this paper* well i've now...

As this example shows, the repeated unit need not always be a conventional or fixed structural expression. S4 echoes the immediately preceding co-text, that is, what S1 just said. This would seem to be a copy from working memory and have little to do with units as they may be stored in long-term memory. So allowance must be made for echoing as a property of working memory that provides useful material for the speaker to gain time and to align with the previous turn.

What the instances in this section seem to suggest, then, is that speakers operate with different kinds of elements as they go about producing speech. For some of the time, individual words seem to be at stake, but in other cases, larger units overstepping the boundaries of a word are more relevant. Individual word rephrases and searches seem to point to interconnections based on either form or sense, but when more than one word gets co-selected, the connection between the items seem either collocational or structural. This being so, it seems plausible that the 'same' items are stored in memory many times: as independent items, as collocates, and as part of conventionalised multi-word units. Such multiple storage has been postulated for native speakers (e.g. Bybee & Hopper 2001; Wray 2002; see also discussion in Chapter 2), and it seems that the same storage principles apply to second-language users.

There seems to be relatively little work on how compositional items are stored, but Dabrowska, at least, argues that there is no reason to assume that people do not also memorise fully compositional units such as *read a book, I am trying to* ..., or *brothers and sisters* (Dabrowska 2004: 19). Children acquire such units as chunks, and adults might store them along with their parts as they appear in their decomposed form. This multiple storage would help explain the deep entrenchment of very frequent items, which tend to appear as part of various combinations in addition to being accessible individually for constructing expressions from the start, or as following the "open choice" principle (Sinclair 1991).

Another major feature to note was lexical approximation, which appeared in many shapes. Individual word forms or item choices turned up in otherwise fluent contexts, and seemingly passed without further notice as representations of the items the speaker had in mind. On other occasions the going was less smooth, and approximations were made in rephrases and word searches. The speaker in these cases indicated awareness of missing the target in some way. Rephrases and searches displayed different bases for the approximations – the basis on which the item was sought was sometimes form, but in other cases there was a clear semantic link between the first attempt and the subsequent solution. Sense-based approximation strategies included the use of hyperonyms or general terms to stand for the more specific item that would have fitted the context better (similar phenomena in SLA literature are subsumed under 'communication strategies' (Oxford 1990; Cohen 1998). Unusual collocations could also be added to lexical approximations – since collocation is based on mutual attraction between lexical items, their unconventional selections do not reflect structural but lexical choices. They may be at the far end of the cline of speaker awareness of a norm breach; collocations are conventional co-occurrence tendencies, and for such co-occurrences to be firmly entrenched in a speaker's repertoire, extensive experience of repeated occasions would be required. This is obviously less true for most speakers when a foreign language is at stake, even if we may assume that field-specific collocations may be equally familiar to ELF-speaking and ENL-speaking academics. Collocations, however, are already on the borderlines between lexis and phraseology, which is the focus of the next chapter.

4.4 Summary

This chapter has looked into lexis from different angles: first in terms of frequencies, comparing ELF with ENL, then in use as revealed by co-text. The first corpus-based analyses indicated that ELF shows lexical simplification in similar manifestations to those observed in learner language and translations: the most frequent items tend to be even more frequent. At the same time, ELF speech turned out to be much closer to ENL speech in comparable circumstances than either was to written ENL. The principal difference therefore would seem to relate to mode, in other words, to obtain between speech and writing. The affinities among ELF lexical simplification, learner language, and translated language suggest that bilingual processing biases lexical choices towards the most frequent, presumably the most deeply entrenched, vocabulary. That translations show the same tendency means it is not just imperfect learning that is at stake.

Comparing present-day speaking to an evolutionary perspective was also revealing; it suggested that the types of most stable vocabulary discovered in analysing a large mass of data from different languages and a long historical perspective (Pagel et al. 2007) occupy core positions in speech. Moreover, it supported the idea that ELF incorporates those elements of language that are most stable and most vital to communication. The findings also seemed to fit in with Biber's (2009) suggestion based on academic speech corpora that speech may be less sensitive to register than writing. An important type of vocabulary that had been ignored in the large-scale evolutionary comparisons were what was called 'organising' vocabulary – words relating to organising discourse and interaction. The same was true of evaluative items. These categories are nevertheless fundamental to spoken communication and feature in ELF just as in ENL.

On the cognitive front, findings on lexical searching, repetition, and rephrasing lent support to the conception that items are multiply stored in the brain: the 'same' items appeared in different roles, as individual items and as components of larger units. As in the evolutionary comparison, distinctions between diverse word types seem more important than lexis as a unified phenomenon. There is lexis and lexis; frequency patterns, degrees of independent meaning and content versus organising orientations are among the fundamental divisions that need to be kept in mind when analysing vocabulary in SLU.

A major lexical process was approximation, which stemmed from connections between forms or meanings, and seemed to be a success strategy in most cases. Participants were apparently able to make sense of each other's approximations to target items, most likely because the mechanisms are shared, and the outcomes therefore comprehensible. Lexical phenomena that involved struggling with lexis also displayed an interactional facet; lexical searches, for example, not only indicated processing difficulties in speakers and conferred benefits to hearers as extra processing time, but also induced cooperative interaction and created space for the co-construction of conversational goals.

Lexical analyses thus viewed ELF from an interactional as well as a cognitive perspective, and adopted a wide macro-level viewpoint in comparing ELF to an evolutionary position. Integrative angles can also be found among grammatical structures and in the intermediate ground between lexis and grammar, and phraseology; these are the topics of the next chapter.

Notes

1. The actual words can be seen in Appendix 2, where the cut-off points for the types covering 50% of the tokens are marked with an asterisk for both ELFA and MICASE.
2. Not all of the examples illustrating the categories appear in our sample, but they are drawn from the 200 most common items in ELFA (Appendix 2). The findings from the sample originate in ELFA unless otherwise indicated.
3. English, Spanish, Russian, and Greek.
4. Using Keywords of Wordsmith Tools.
5. The forms rank as follows in MICASE: *get* is the 24th, *got* 36th, *getting* 103rd, *gets* 178th.
6. Using the Keyword Comparison function of Wordsmith Tools.

References

Altenberg, B. and Granger, S. (2002) 'The grammatical and lexical patterning of *make* in native and non-native student writing', *Applied Linguistics* 22 (2): 173–89.

Biber, D. (2001) 'Dimensions of variation across university registers: an analysis based on the T2K-SWAL corpus', paper given at the Third North American Symposium on Corpus Linguistics and Language Teaching, University of Boston, 23-25 March 2001.

Biber, D. (2009) 'Are there linguistic consequences of literacy? Comparing the potentials of language use in speech and writing', in Olson, D. R. and Torrance, N. (eds.) *Cambridge Handbook of Literacy*, Cambridge: Cambridge University Press, 75–91.

Bybee, J. L. (2003) 'Cognitive processes in grammaticalization', in Tomasello, M. (ed.), *The New Psychology of Language*, vol. II, Mahwah, NJ: Lawrence Erlbaum, 145–67.

Bybee, J. L. (2008) 'Usage-based grammar and second-language acquisition', in Robinson, P. and Ellis, N. C. (eds.) *Handbook of Cognitive Linguistics and Second Language Acquisition*, New York: Routledge.

Bybee, J. L. and Hopper, P. (2001) 'Introduction to frequency and the emergence of linguistic structure', in Bybee, J. and Hopper, P. (eds.) *Frequency and the Emergence of Linguistic Structure*, Amsterdam: John Benjamins, 1–2.

Cohen, A. D. (1998) *Strategies in Learning and Using a Second Language*, London: Longman.

Coxhead, A. (2000) 'A new academic word list', *TESOL Quarterly* 34: 213–38.

Dabrowska, E. (2004) *Language, Mind and Brain: Some Psychological and Neurological Constraints on Theories of Grammar*, Edinburgh: Edinburgh University Press.

Du Bois, J. W. (2003) 'Discourse and grammar', in Tomasello, M. (ed.) *The New Psychology of Language*, vol. II, Mahwah, NJ: Lawrence Erlbaum, 47–87.

Englebretson, R. (1997) 'Genre and grammar: predicative and attributive adjectives in spoken English', *Berkeley Linguistics Society* 23: 411–21.

Fox, B. A. (1987) *Anaphora and the Structure of Discourse*, Cambridge: Cambridge University Press.

Francis, W. and Kucera, H. (1982) *Frequency Analysis of English Usage*, New York: Houghton Mifflin.

Granger, S. (ed.) (1998) *Learner English on Computer*, London: Longman.

Granger, S. (2009) 'The contribution of learner corpora to second language acquisition and foreign language teaching: a critical evaluation', in Aijmer, K. (ed.) *Corpora and Language Teaching*, Amsterdam: John Benjamins, 13–32.

Granger, S., Hung, J. and Petch-Tyson, S. (eds.) (2002) *Computer Learner Corpora: Second Language Acquisition and Foreign Language Teaching*, Amsterdam: John Benjamins.

Hopper, P. and Traugott, E. (2003) *Grammaticalization* (2nd edn), Cambridge: Cambridge University Press.

Hunston, S. and Thompson, G. (eds.) (2000) *Evaluation in Text: Authorial Stance and the Construction of Discourse*, Oxford: Oxford University Press.

Jantunen, J. H. (2004a) *Synonymia ja käännössuomi*, Joensuu: University of Joensuu.

Jantunen, J. H. (2004b) 'Untypical patterns in translations: issues on corpus methodology and synonymity', in Mauranen, A. and Kujamäki, P. (eds.) *Translation Universals: Do They Exist?*, Amsterdam: John Benjamins, 101–26.

Laitinen, H., Mustajoki, A. and Mauranen, A. (forthcoming) 'Hesitation caused by competing intentions in Russian'.

Laviosa-Braithwaite, S. (1996) 'The English Comparable Corpus (ECC): a resource and a methodology for the empirical study of translation', unpublished PhD thesis, Centre for Translation and Intercultural Studies, UMIST.

Lindemann, S. and Mauranen, A. (2001) '"It's just real messy": the occurrence and function of *just* in a corpus of academic speech', *English for Specific Purposes* (1): 459–76.

Mauranen, A. (2000) 'Strange strings in translated language: a study on corpora', in Olohan, M. (ed.) *Intercultural Faultlines: Research Models in Translation Studies 1: Textual and Cognitive Aspects*, Manchester: St Jerome Publishing, 119–41.

Mauranen, A. (2004c) 'Speech corpora in the classroom', in Aston, G. Bernardini, S. and Stewart, D. (eds.) *Corpora and Language Learners*, Amsterdam: John Benjamins, 197–213.

McCarthy, M. (2002) 'Good listenership made plain: British and American non-minimal response tokens in everyday conversation', in Biber, D., Fitzpatrick, S. and Reppen, R. (eds.) *Using Corpora to Explore Linguistic Variation*, Amsterdam: John Benjamins, 49–71.

Nevalainen, S. (2005) 'Köyhtyykö kieli käännettäessä? – Mitä taajuuslistat kertovat suomennosten sanastosta', in Mauranen, A. and Jantunen, J. (eds.) *Käännössuomeksi. Tutkimuksia käännössuomen kielestä*, Tampere: Tampere University Press, 139–60.

Oxford, R. L. (1990) *Language Learning Strategies: What Every Teacher Should Know*, Boston: Heinle & Heinle.

Pagel, M., Atkinson, D. Q. and Meade, A. (2007) 'Frequency of word-use predicts rates of lexical evolution throughout Indo-European history', *Nature* 449 (11): 717–20.

Sacks, H., Schegloff, E. A. and Jefferson, G. (1974) 'A simplest systematics for the organization of turn-taking for conversation', *Language* 50 (4): 696–735.

Sinclair, J. McH. (1991) *Corpus Concordance Collocation*, Oxford: Oxford University Press.

Sinclair, J. McH. (ed.) (2004) *How to Use Corpora in Language Teaching*, Amsterdam: John Benjamins.

Swales, J. M. and Burke, A. (2003) '"It's really fascinating work": differences in evaluative adjectives across academic registers', in Meyer, C. and Leistyna, P. (eds.) *Corpus Analysis: Language Structure and Use*, Amsterdam: Rodopi, 1–18.

Thomason, S. G. (2001) *Language Contact*, Edinburgh: Edinburgh University Press.

Thompson, S. A. (1988) 'A discourse approach to the cross-linguistic category "adjective"', in Hawkins, J. A. (ed.) *Explaining Language Universals*, Oxford: Blackwell, 167–85.

Tirkkonen-Condit, S. (2005) 'Häviävätkö uniikkiainekset käännössuomesta?', in Mauranen, A. and Jantunen, J. (eds.) *Käännössuomeksi. Tutkimuksia käännössuomen* kielestä, Tampere: Tampere University Press, 123–37.

Toury, G. (1995) *Descriptive Translation Studies and Beyond*, Amsterdam: John Benjamins.

Trudgill, P. (1986) *Dialects in Contact*, Oxford: Blackwell.

Warren, M. (2006) *Features of Naturalness in Conversation*, Amsterdam: John Benjamins.

Vetchinnikova, S. (2010) 'EFL learners' lexical choices in context: is there evidence for the idiom principle?', paper presented at the Ninth TALC Conference, Brno, 30 June–3 July 2010.

Vetchinnikova, S. (forthcoming). 'Productive vocabulary acquisition: EFL users' lexical choices in context and the idiom principle', PhD thesis, University of Helsinki.

Winford, D. (2003) *An Introduction to Contact Linguistics*, Oxford: Blackwell.

Winter, E. (1977) 'A clause-relational approach to English texts', *Instructional Science* (Special issue) 6 (1): 1–92.

Wray, A. (2002) *Formulaic Language and the Lexicon*, Cambridge: Cambridge University Press.

Zipf, G. K. (1935) *The Psychobiology of Language*, Boston: Houghton-Mifflin.

Zipf, G. K. (1949) *Human Behavior and the Principle of Least-Effort*, New York: Addison-Wesley.

5 *Within and outside the word: lexis meets structure*

We do not speak by just stringing words together, one after another; we use them in a particular order, a particular form, and in particular combinations with other words so as to best express what we want to say. In other words, we intermesh words with structuring of different kinds, as a result of which lexical items are inescapably intertwined with structures, both internally and externally. Even though it is possible to take single words as the object of analysis (as in Chapter 4), we can think of vocabulary as a linguistic system, and for understanding any system, the best solution is to look into its internal components as well as into its connections outside itself.

We already saw in several instances in the previous chapter that speakers do not operate with single words but with larger chunks of language, as suggested by things like self-rephrasing, searching, and echoing. What we also saw were approximate forms of recognisable Standard English expressions; individual lexical items took unconventional shapes (*categoration*, *significally*, *unrespect*), and longer chunks showed unusual structural properties (*there is quite much problems*, *it's very much important*, *in accordance to*). In such unusual forms it is perhaps even easier to see than in perfectly standard ones how closely lexis is intertwined with grammar, which is what many branches of language study have emphasised in the last decade or two. We see structure inside the word in morphology and outside it in syntax, as already recognised in the oldest grammatical traditions, but it is also being noticed increasingly in phraseological units of various kinds. Studies in phraseology have been flourishing in recent years: not only are idioms and traditional phrases being investigated with a new zeal, but many kinds of fixed or semi-fixed sequences have been inspiring linguistic, cognitive, and psycholinguistic work. Expressions ranging from fairly loose collocational patterns to invariable sequences have been implicated in language processing and acquisition as well as second-language teaching, which makes it relevant to second language use like ELF. A focus on cognitive issues can be seen in recent work on multi-word expressions, but their role in language change can also be significant, which enhances the interest value to ELF study.

English is a comparatively analytic language, and codes grammatical meanings in separate items rather than in complex inflectional affixes like more synthetic languages. Much of what is incorporated in multi-word units in English is therefore coded in individual words in many other languages. We may assume that some issues of processing lexicogrammatical meanings have much in common irrespectively of whether they take place inside or outside word boundaries. It is therefore reasonable to look at phraseological and morphological questions in close adjacency. This chapter looks into the interface of structure and lexis; it starts out by a brief glance at some recurrent observations of structural features in ELF, dips inside the individual word, and then moves on to exploring phraseological, multi-word units.

5.1 Common features of grammatical structure

Structural deviations from the standard language are a default expectation when a second or additional language is at stake. They have been identified in learner language and studied intensely in SLA research for several decades as learner errors (see e.g. Doughty & Long 2003; Ellis 2008). Since Corder's (1973) work, learner errors have been seen not merely as mistakes to be eradicated, but also as indicators of the learner's progression towards the target language, which for learners is normally its standard variety. The idea of learners being at an 'interlanguage' stage on their way towards native-like proficiency was particularly developed by Selinker (1972). The concept of an interlanguage is not relevant to a lingua franca, which consists mainly in second language use (SLU), not a learner's progress. However, the idea that deviations from the standard language are indicative of a speaker's cognitive processes and communicative strategies holds for SLU as well as SLA. It needs to be added here, though, that it is not sufficient only to look at the deviations, the 'errors' as it were, as evidence of second-language processing and its progress; it is equally important to look at those aspects that are target-like in second-language speech.

Grammatical deviations from Standard English are a regular feature of English as a lingua franca. Along with non-standard accents and a high proportion of dysfluencies, non-standard core grammar is easy to notice and apparently influential in forming people's judgements on the linguistic ability of a speaker (see Hynninen 2010). A few recurrent features of non-standard grammar have been noted by many ELF scholars in a range of different data samples (see e.g. Seidlhofer 2004; Dewey 2006; Ranta 2006, 2009, Björkman 2008a,b,

2009; Hülmbauer 2009), and also by Dröschel (2011), even though she talks about 'Lingua Franca English' rather than ELF. We can therefore accept many as fairly clearly established features of ELF, and we find them well represented in ELFA as well.

What, then, makes the use of structures interesting in ELF, if second-language issues have been investigated from the structural point of view for decades? First of all, grammatical words are high-frequency items, and many of them are important differentiators of ELF use relative to comparable ENL use in the light of ELFA and MICASE corpora, as was illustrated in Chapter 4. They thus necessarily account for an important share of the differences we can expect to find between ELF and ENL. As we saw in the previous chapter, their stability vs. instability as language changes varies enormously according to category, but as high-frequency items they account for a large proportion of what communication via language is about. We cannot dismiss repeated findings of non-standard forms as arbitrary mistakes. Some of course are just passing slips of the tongue or idiosyncrasies, but even among hapaxes (words that occur only once) it is possible to discern patterns of instances that are similar, such as regularised past tenses, even if each individual case concerns a different verb.

Secondly, structural simplification has been found both in SLA and in language contact. ELF evidence differs in nature from SLA evidence (see Chapter 1 for discussion) and comes from novel kinds of contact environments. It can therefore shed light on the commonalities and differences in SLA and language contact and help check the robustness and accuracy of previous findings. Particularly relevant findings for comparison arise from second-language varieties, or 'New Englishes' (for an illuminating overview, see Kortmann & Szmrecsanyi 2004), and recent research looking into second-language varieties as well as learner language (papers in Mukherjee & Hundt 2011). Finally, structure plays a crucial role in fluency and comprehensibility – even though structural features also tolerate a good deal of turbulence without disrupting communication. A look into the detail of structures in use can throw light on the issues involved from cognitive, social, and also 'purely' language-internal perspectives.

5.1.1 Grammatical differences in ELF and ENL

To start with a brief look at the grammatical differentiators between ELFA and MICASE, we can find nine primarily grammatical ones among the best differentiating items,[1] that is, between those items that differ most in terms of how much they are used in the corpora.

Two are prepositions (*in*, *of*), two determiners (*the*, *some*), three connectors (*and*, *also*, *because*), one a relative pronoun (*which*), and another a dummy subject (*there*). Comparing these with the evolutionary categories posited by Pagel et al. (2007) that were discussed in Chapter 4, we can see that these are among his volatile, fast-evolving types or else neutral, neither fast nor slow. Only *there* might serve as a member of the more stable categories, but as already noted, this is problematic because apparently it is the deictic function that Pagel's team talks about, whereas it is in the presentative structure (*there is a continuum* ...) that *there* mostly appears in ELFA.

PREPOSITIONS

The structural items that are proportionally especially prominent in ELFA thus fall into types that are predicted as relatively likely to change. So what is going on here? Of the prepositions, it looks as if *of* is largely accounted for by just one very common phrase, *of course*, which, as pointed out in Chapter 4, is also the key to the very high frequency of *course* in ELFA. *In*, however, seems to be a kind of generalised preposition of time or place. The presence of a general indicator of temporal or local relationships suggests simplification in the system of prepositions. This interpretation is strengthened by the reverse differentiation of *at* in MICASE, which, compared to ELFA, is proportionally far more common; this would seem to suggest that one preposition stands for two in ELFA. Virtually every earlier ELF account that is concerned with structure tells us that prepositions are among the most commonly reported features that deviate from their conventional ENL uses. Typical examples from ELFA are those that make a non-standard choice (*obsession* ***in***; *insisted* ***for*** *full independence; the iron may accumulate* ***to*** *other organs*), use a preposition redundantly (*discuss* ***about***; *you study* ***about*** *the name*), or drop one (*we're dealing what is science*). This greater fluctuation than in standard language is interesting in comparison to the unexpectedly high frequency of one preposition in the data. Two simultaneous opposite tendencies seem to be in operation: wider variability and simplification. I shall return to these at the end of this section.

DETERMINERS

A similar case among the differentiating items is the definite article, in that article use is the most widely reported non-standard feature in ELF. Articles are often missing (*in Polish language*; *it was absolutely in spirit of the time*), superfluous (*not in* ***a*** *principle*; *of* ***the*** *Wilson's* *disease, as good as **the** own liver*), or just different from those expected in Standard English (*I have written down here **a** word chronic liver diseases*; *cause **an** deposition of iron*). Similar departures from Standard English use of articles as well as prepositions have been found in learner English (e.g. Jarvis & Odlin 2000), with article use remaining shaky even in near-native L2 learners (Ringbom 1993). On the other hand, ellipted articles are also a spoken language feature known in ENL (McCarthy 1998: 76). What we can see in comparing the ELFA and MICASE lists of differentiating keywords is that *the* ranks high in ELFA, while the indefinite article *a* ranks low and is among the differentiators of MICASE from ELFA.[2] Since there is this relationship, non-standard article use may not be best seen as a collection of random errors, but may reflect an ongoing reshuffle of article functions. The possible non-randomness of non-standard article use also relates to Dewey's (2006) finding that articles largely go missing in places where they are redundant, as in front of *same*. We can see this in an example from ELFA: ... *situation where rate is same all the time over millions of years* ... Clearly the article would add nothing essential to the speaker's message. Yet the figures for the fairly firmly fixed combination *the* + *same* in ELFA indicate that, in numerical terms, the standard form is overwhelmingly more common: *the same* N = 1,103; *same* N = 77, that is, only 6.5% of SAME.[3]

Apart from *the*, the other differentiating determiner *some* seems to contribute to a certain structural simplification. In this case the set of choices in a given structural function is shifted: *some* in relation to *few* / *a few* gains ground in ELF (as will be seen in Section 5.3). The relatively frequent use of the relative pronoun *which* in ELFA and a correspondingly higher proportion of *that* in MICASE would seem to support the anecdotal evidence of SLU tending towards 'bookish' language, but go against findings from both written learner language (Gilquin & Paquot 2008) and spoken ELF (Mauranen 2010) suggesting that less formal registers tend to be favoured. Even though in absolute terms[4] *that* is used more often than *which*, the proportional difference is clear: *that* is about five times as common as *which* in ELFA, but ten times as common in MICASE.

SUFFIXES

Some features that could be seen as lack of accuracy in grammatical detail include plural noun endings and third-person singular verb endings (*respect for **human right***; *she **live** in Tanzania*). These features resemble Dewey's (2006) findings on articles missing in regular environments where their anomaly can cause little disturbance to communication. Björkman (e.g. 2009) noted that it is quite common not to use plural endings after numerals in technological lectures in ELF. The third-person singular marker is well known to be missing from certain ENL dialects, with no loss to communicative clarity. This is not surprising, since it is an anomaly in Standard English.

5.1.2 Regularisation and productivity

In morphology, two major tendencies are discernible: regularisation of irregular inflectional forms (*teached*; *breaked*; *feeled*; *losed*) and the extension of productive derivational principles beyond their conventional boundaries (*undirectly*; *insuitable*; *permittable*; *proletariatic*; *standardisate*). We can also see regularisation underpinning the tendency to shift uncountable to countable nouns (*offsprings*, *informations*, *advices*, *knowledges*). Some regularised plurals appear repeatedly, such as *advices*, which together with its singular countable forms (*an/one advice*) accounts for 41% of the total occurrences of *advice*, *knowledges* (11 countable cases) and *researches*, which was found nine times (in seven different files, see Example 5.1).

(5.1)

1	for it and er for this many er many **researches** and for example world bank
2	research a- any kind of research **researches** metapopulation research to
3	side for educational science is that this **researches** were just only er researches
4	is that this researches were just only er **researches** from er business sides
5	also other thing erm they're making **researches** there so they also have to
6	er about NGOs and (xx) 1903 er did er **researches** on NGO exist before then
7	was] this statement of these er two **researches** that you mentioned before
8	had no opportunity to continue their **researches** and so on why i speak about
9	this library is orientated now er to the **researches** of the humanities because

The liberal extension of morphological productivity includes well-known ENL word-formation practices like 'back-formation', which in ELF leads to forms like *interpretate*, *introducted*, and *commentate*. A further similarity with ENL is that sometimes the division of labour between affixes does not get a clear resolution; for example, the endings *-ic* and *-ical* have fluctuated in their functional distribution over centuries and still do (Kaunisto 2004); there are words where both forms are in use, sometimes with a difference in meaning (*economic/al*), sometimes not (*symbolic/al*, *ethnic/al*, *asymmetric/al*). ELFA data shows a fairly distinct preference for the longer form where the shorter is the norm, as in *systematical*, *realistical*, or *scientifical*, although the reverse is also found occasionally (*theoretic*; *methodologic*). Unconventional coinages come in a variety of shapes, many of which seem to be based on analogies, applying principles that exist in the language but do not hold for the particular case on account of some conventional restriction.

Morphology tends to be potentially overproductive in natural languages. While convention and acquired preference keep it in check in stable language communities, its possibilities are liberally utilised by newcomers such as non-natives, as has been observed in learners. Scholars talk about 'overgeneralisation' (e.g. Master 1997) or 'elaborative simplification' (Meisel 1980). While some of the observed morphological processes can easily be seen as facets of simplification (like regularisation), they cannot all be comfortably thrown into that category (like overproductivity).[5]

LACK OF AGREEMENT

Syntactically, lack of concord or agreement is usual (*each sciences*; *the main ideas is*) as are, for example, non-standard word order in interrogative clauses (*so what kind of research you would like to do?*), embedded inversions, and the very high frequency of the *-ing* form of the verb, especially in its progressive use (Ranta 2006, 2010[6]). Such syntactic variation cannot readily be put down to an overarching tendency to simplify: there is nothing essentially simple in non-standard word order or lack of agreement, for example. Moreover, many of these features are observable widely in spoken Englishes all over the world, native, second-language, and learner varieties included. As Ranta (2009) shows, using *would* or *would have* in hypothetical *if*-clauses is one of such widespread features, as are embedded inversions (see also Kortmann & Szmrecsanyi 2004). Some of these features also appear in educated native English in the spoken mode. The use of the singular form of BE with plural nouns in existential constructions (*there is also many factors that you need to take in account*) is not only a well-recognised, non-standard feature in many ENL varieties, both present and historical (see e.g. Nevalainen 2009; Tagliamonte 2009), but also found in MICASE, that is, in educated ENL speech (Ranta 2009) as well as in ELFA. As Ranta further shows, embedded inversions are common in both ELFA (*I wonder where does that concept of knowledge come from*) and MICASE (*did you ask is Shannon done*). Some of the structural features in ELF are thus shared across many varieties of English, including ENL, and cannot be put down to an SLU effect alone. Even though proportions of such features are differently distributed within varieties, surprisingly many are shared.

CONNECTING DEVICES

Some items that clearly have structural import but do not always remain within the boundaries of clauses or sentences are connecting devices. On the list of differentiators of ELFA from MICASE, among the final set of items that carry structural significance we find three connectors: *and*, *also*, and *because*. These operate within and between clauses and utterances, whose dividing lines are more blurred in speech than in writing. These connectors organise ongoing discourse as text and as interaction (cf. Sinclair & Mauranen 2006): in individual cases the primary function can be gleaned from the co-text, but the shape of the item alone is only a very rough guide to its contextual use. Some general observations can nevertheless be made on the basis of distributional differences in the items. *And* is a general, flexible, multi-faceted connector that is highly adaptable and serves a very broad range of purposes. It is therefore an extremely useful device in SLU, ranging from a turn-initiator (*S1>* ***and*** *did you (got) some mhm research idea from this paper*) and placeholder (*general kind of concepts* ***and and, and*** *they er*) to a listing device (*plants* ***and*** *animals*) and clause connector (***and*** *then the process were monitored* ***and*** *there has been lots of controversy*). *Also* is more specifically additive and found as a general-purpose additive connector in written academic language of non-native writers (Ventola & Mauranen 1991). In ELFA, its greater specificity relative to *and* can be seen in their not infrequent co-occurrence (*this time we concentrate more on the genetic rescue or genetic restoration* ***and also*** *this time we er consider a new research project*). Presumably its frequency in L2 speaking has a utility value similar to written text – apart from frequency, there is no easily discernible difference in its use between ELFA and MICASE. *Because* looks like another general-purpose connector employed for a clear but broad function. Since causality is much discussed in academic discourse, this goes towards explaining why *because* is frequent, and its second function of introducing reasons (*this would be a very nice starting paper* ***because*** *this is really easy*) is particularly useful in argumentation (*this is not necessarily true* ***because*** *there are there are inferred pedigrees*). Again, the pattern is like *also* – the uses are essentially similar to ENL, but the preferred connector seems to carry a larger share of expressions for related functions in ELF than in ENL. Simplification in the sense of utilizing a smaller selection of expressions for a broad set of related functions seems to be at stake.

Before leaving the comparison of ELFA and MICASE, it is useful to take a look at those items that differentiate them in the reverse direction: what can we find considerably more of in MICASE than in ELFA? Articles were already mentioned above: *the* is represented particularly strongly in ELFA, while *a* is more prominent in MICASE in relative terms. Taken together with the article-dropping tendency in ELF, this may mean sliding towards a system where zero replaces *a(n)* – although it is far too early to make predictions about this. The second item type high on the ELFA differentiator list was *in*, potentially a multi-purpose preposition for relations of both time and place. The prepositions that conversely distinguished MICASE were *up*, *down,* and *at* – the last supporting the possibility that it is being substituted in ELF by *in* as a generic preposition of spatiotemporal positioning. *Up* and *down* of course also have adverb uses, but looking at their main occurrences in MICASE, they appear largely as particle-like elements in phrasal expressions (*bring up*, *finish up*, *write up*; *break down*, *cut down*, *pin down*), even though *down* seems slightly more adverbial and concrete (*the price went down*). Similarly in ELFA, *up* is mostly a particle, *come up with* and *end up* being the most frequent examples, and *set up*, *look up*, and *pick up* also common. *Down* is less common (250 instances vs. 831 of *up*), and distributed more evenly between adverb (*move up and down*, *slow down*) and particle (*narrow it down*, *write down*). The last category that reveals an appreciable difference between the corpora is the greater representation of DO (*do*, *does*, *did*), suggesting that there may be more direct questions in MICASE than there are in ELFA. Further support comes from *what* appearing among the differentiators, too.

The overview of structural features in ELFA suggests that simplification is taking place. At the same time, we find diversification, new coinages, and new item distribution. Some of the features and processes are similar to learner language, but also to those found in new or non-standard varieties of English, and others again are common to spoken English even among educated native speakers. What we see, then, is a complex picture of several simultaneous processes of variation and the potential for change.

5.2 Does structure matter?

The similarity of the above examples of recurrent lexicogrammatical ELF features to what are regarded as typical learner errors is clear. Such structural approximations to standard forms would seem to follow from speaking a second language. The similarity between learners (as in SLA) and L2 users (as in SLU) is most relevant in the domain of cognitive processes. They all use a linguistic repertoire where items tend to be less deeply entrenched than in an L1 repertoire. L2 processing may also involve online choices from competing systems. Such cognitive aspects of dealing with an L2 should cover much of the common ground between learners and users.

The variability of structure in use and the frequency of non-standard structural features would appear to call into question the significance of structure to successful communication. This might not be particularly surprising in rudimentary pidgin exchanges, or in routine tourist interaction, where communication is achieved chiefly by means of lexis and formulaic exchanges for non-abstract purposes. But in high-level academic communication, it is more puzzling: how much structural anomaly can language tolerate and still enable interactants to achieve discourse at a sophisticated level of argumentation?

5.2.1 Structural variability

Grammatical anomalies tend to be ignored by conversationalists in ELF, just as they are in L1 communication. Psycholinguists and cognitive linguists have noted that speakers – and this refers to L1 speech – are not always aware of their production trouble or errors, and that awareness is sensitive to context and fluctuates during an utterance (Levelt 1989). Levelt reports from his own experiments that speech errors are generally followed by editing in only 62% of cases, and repairs of appropriateness even less often, in 28% of cases (Levelt 1989: 483). People produce much that is ungrammatical in their first language, but it tends to pass unnoticed by hearers as well. As Dabrowska (2004: 13) notes: 'We know very little about how people process ill-formed sentences, although existing studies suggest that morphosyntactic anomalies present surprisingly little difficulty.' It is not the comprehensibility of the anomalies in itself, then, that is most in need of an ELF-specific explanation, but recurrent features in them. Some conform to more widely found tendencies. For example, regularisation of irregular forms serves both the principle of clarity and the principle of economy: using regular inflection is transparent and usually readily comprehensible even when it is unconventional. Regularised forms may well be less taxing on working memory capacity, and thus more likely to work better in communication for both hearers and speakers and thereby further strengthened.

Other features, again, must find different explanatory grounds. Derivational overproductivity, as already discussed in the previous section, seems to ensue from the prolific nature of morphology, which is held back by convention rather than rule. There are always unused possibilities that are compatible with the word-formation rules of a language, but simply not taken up. This productivity is much utilised in marketing and politics, where neologisms abound, as they do in academia. Academic language makes good use of morphological productivity in continually creating new terminology as well as satisfying ad hoc communicative needs. We tend to understand new formations by analogy – so, for example, *femininish* appeared in MICASE without any noticeable reaction from interlocutors, no doubt because *-ish* is a highly productive suffix. In SLU, we might surmise that since participants' repertoires are less entrenched than in first-language conversations, they might not recognise anomalies for what they are, but engage in fuzzier processing both as speakers and also as hearers. Morphological overproductivity might not cause great disturbance under circumstances where participants make less precise predictions of form, that is, where they are ready to accept variability.

While regularisation (*breaked*, *striked*, *staffs*) can be seen as simplification from the viewpoint of the language as well as a speaker's cognitive and communicative strategies, derivational productivity (*unproportional*, *couraged, intentiously*, *assaultment*) cannot. Derivational productivity may be communicatively efficient because it produces neologisms that are comprehensible on analogical grounds, i.e. on account of being rooted in normal word-formation rules. It may thus lighten the speaker's cognitive load by making use of rule-like regularity. Yet despite being possibly easier for speakers, the outcome for the language, seen either as text or as system, is greater complexity, as it brings in additional and alternative expressions for already existing ones and alters the categories of regular and irregular forms. As most such novel formations will be short-lived, such excessive productivity is not more likely to get out of hand than in communities of native speakers, but it is important in principle to note that the process leads to greater, not reduced, complexity in the forms present in real-time use.

It would seem reasonable to assume that if a particular linguistic feature does not hamper communication, it is less likely to be eradicated from a speaker's repertoire than something that does. In the absence of negative feedback, there is no reason to look for alternative expressions. Other factors may intervene in the continued use of a non-standard form, for instance accommodation to other speakers' usage, or other considerations inducing more standard-like use through social conformity. Even awareness of an external authority imposing grammatical norms may overrule the tendency to continue an established habit, but other things being equal, features that do not prevent speakers from successfully achieving conversation are likely to live on in their repertoires.

5.2.2 Structure and fluency

It seems, then, that many converging factors help explain why non-standard structural features do not seriously obstruct communication. The question thus arises as to why speakers bother with it at all. Is there any beneficial role for structure to make it worth the trouble?

Structure plays a crucial role in limiting the selection of elements that can combine in ongoing discourse. Only a very small proportion of the theoretically possible combinations ever occur, revealing the critical presence of structure: it reduces uncertainty. It helps reduce the indeterminacy of text, which is accentuated when speakers' language varies notably (cf. Sinclair & Mauranen 2006). Language varies between individuals in any case, but in a lingua franca environment variability at all levels is a particularly central aspect of the communication.

The two fundamental uses of structure in interpreting talk as it unfolds are (1) that it helps identify components, and (2) that it allows the hearer to prospect ahead and make informed guesses about what is to come (see also Sinclair 1992/2004). Prospection does not always imply an exact set of predictions, but it is more likely to provide a heuristic device for quick, efficient interpretation. It helps anticipate which elements are likely to follow the one that is being currently processed. Prospection also helps foresee likely points of unit completion, and to expect that more is to come at junctures where structures are felt to be incomplete. We may expect language users to be quite sensitive to structural possibilities at various places as discourse unfolds.

As hearers make prospections, anticipating things to come in terms of a few options, their task of making sense of what they hear is facilitated by these prospections: they mostly just need to confirm that their expectations were fulfilled. Listeners do not need to pay close attention to the stream of sound all the time as long as the signals they hear mostly confirm their guesses. It follows that it is possible to interpret sound that in itself is not very informative, as in situations where it is hard to hear, such as poor phone signal strength. More relevant to the present purpose, prospection also means that the more predictable a component is, the less it matters how exactly it is pronounced, or how exact its grammatical felicity.

As structure plays its important role in reducing uncertainty and enabling hearers to prospect ahead, it contributes to fluency. Speakers can be allowed to take more risks in their pronunciation or in the precise shape of what they are saying if structure carries the discourse along with sufficient support to the hearer. Hearers in turn can take shortcuts in interpreting the ongoing speech stream without having to spend too many of their attentional resources in detailed parsing before arriving at an interpretation. Speakers and hearers can thus achieve fluent communication by their joint efforts and be helped along by their shared structural knowledge of the language. It would seem, then, that while structure is an indispensable aid to fluent processing, relatively fuzzy processing such as prospection gets support from ELF evidence while exact prediction seems unnecessary to communicative success.

ENTRENCHMENT AND PROCESSING

We already saw in Chapter 4 how lexical and phraseological repeats, restarts, and hesitations are likely to illuminate speakers' ongoing processing. The focus there was on the kinds of units involved, but from another angle the same behaviour can throw light on the strength of entrenchment of elements in speakers' repertoires. Frequency plays an important role: more frequent items have been shown to be better entrenched and accessed more quickly and reliably than low-frequency items (e.g. Dabrowska 2004). The frequency with which linguistic elements, be they lexical items or structural schemata, have been encountered go a long way in accounting for their accessibility to the speaker. Many researchers (e.g. Levelt 1989; Ellis 2002; Du Bois 2003; Ford et al. 2003) talk about the aggregate lifetime experience that speakers have of linguistic elements. Frequently encountered units and their components become more entrenched as stored elements, more accessible to speakers for potential use. While deep entrenchment is hardly the sole factor accounting for element accessibility, it is a major one, and since it is a function of frequency, it is clear that speakers on average have less experience of their later acquired languages than their first. It is therefore quite predictable that ELF speech shows less entrenched structures than ENL speech.

One indicator of relatively weak structure entrenchment is fluctuation in a speaker's production; along with self-repairs, fluctuating usage shows that SLU does not have the level of stability that we normally expect from L1 speech – even if that, too, is less consistent than ideal models presented in reference grammars would suggest. Article use is not only often non-standard in ELF, but one speaker may use articles inconsistently in one turn (Examples 5.2 and 5.3).

(5.2)

<S1> ... the first moves in finnish foreign policy on the way back *to west* that was the beginning of of this long road rocky road *to west* and the final thing what's is still missing and we've been discussing here is the n- membership in the NATO then we are really *in the west* belong to the western community and have said goodbye to *the east* though we still have some orthodox people in finland its orthodox church belongs *to the east*, so we shouldn't be that happy to belong *to the west* we have also in our tradition *the east* ...

(5.3)

<S11> yeah but i think it's the same with *moon* and *the sun* it's er always like *the sun* is male and *the moon* is female but in german ...

In both examples, the speaker first omits the article, but in later mentions uses it. Similar sequences were found many times. Sometimes it is as if the initial reference functioned in a presentative manner, but later references to the same entity used the definite article. A clear case is Example (5.4).

(5.4)

<S7> yes this is *pancreas* which is swollen and this picture is very good, there's two big necrosis spots in ***the** pancreas*, that's swollen and this is necrotising pancreatitis, it's *typical picture*, and when ***the** picture* comes down, further ***the** pancreas* disappears (xx) this is the be- best this is very typical. okay you are the chairman of of the next case @our last case@ </S7>

Here the speaker first introduces both *pancreas* and *picture* without an article, but uses the article at second mention. This may result from the greater planning pressure that is often associated with the initial stages of an utterance. It is nevertheless a faithful reflection of the contrast between presenting and presuming reference in the standard article system, with only a small modification – the omission of the indefinite article. This would seem an expedient simplification, since one type of article suffices to maintain the contrast. This would also seem to offer a tentative basis for explaining why the indefinite article was so much rarer in ELF than in ENL.

Other grammatical elements show similar tendencies to fluctuate, thereby supporting the idea of weak entrenchment, as we can see in the next example (5.5) with the complementation pattern of APOLOGISE and in (5.6) with count noun vs. uncount noun (*offspring*).

(5.5)

<S1> ... we had on our list er er more people who couldn't come and they er *apologise us* er we have er one more ... first of all i have to also *apologise that* according to program we are ... and we have to also *apologise for* there will be no russian perspective @@

(5.6)

<S5> [these] lions they don't eat each other but certainly do kill each other like for example male lions are killing s- the er *offsprings* that are not from a certain er par- particular male lion's *offspring* </S5>

Even though we have seen in this section once more how frequencies surface in accounting for some perceptible characteristics of ELF speech, it is useful to remind ourselves of the scale of such divergence from Standard English: the items that are the most frequent in language, those that turn up at the top of frequency lists are probably so common that they may be relatively similar in ELF and ENL. These are encountered so often by anyone using English that the differences should be minimised between first and second language use. Although structural frequencies are hard to assess across corpora reliably, we saw in the previous chapter that the expectation was borne out by the simple item frequency lists of ELFA and MICASE. A notable proportion of the most frequent items, that is those that accounted for 50% of the corpora, were the same; well over a half of them were identical, remarkably often appearing in the same rank order as well. With less frequent elements, bifurcation between the speaker groups should get stronger, and this is again what we see going further down the lists. This deepens the picture sketched out by the case of *same* vs. *the same* above: although there is a clearly discernible tendency to depart from standard language in a consistent manner, it leaves the majority of instances intact.

Weakly entrenched structures should also show in a greater proportion of overtly observable processing difficulties. One source of evidence readily available from the corpus in simple trigrams (repeated sequences of three consecutive words) supports the intuitive observation that ELF has a large number of what are generally known as 'dysfluencies' – hesitations, repeats, and false starts. Although they are characteristic of normal speech, an enormous difference can be seen in their proportional share in ELF: hesitation markers (*uh*, *um*, *er*) and repeats (*the the the*, *of of of*) in the top 100 trigrams in ELFA and MICASE show that ELFA has nine times as many of those as MICASE. While this seems an unquestionable indication of uncertainty and harder work at production, it may not mean greater difficulty for the listener: frequent hesitations may provide them with more processing time and more breathing space.

SPEAKERS AND HEARERS

Weaker entrenchment of English structures thus applies to ELF interactants in their roles both as listeners and as speakers, although with different consequences to the roles. Speaker and hearer roles alternate constantly in conversation. From a discourse or textual point of view, there are only two roles: the *I* and the *you*, which real participants take turns to occupy, sometimes in rapid succession (cf. Sinclair & Mauranen 2006). From the point of view of processing, speakers' fluent and adept handling of this suggests that something in the processes must be closely parallel. There seems to be some support for such an interpretation in the psycholinguistic literature. According to Levelt (1989), speaker's and hearer's attention is differently occupied, but he also notes that speakers can monitor their own speech with much the same mechanisms as hearers can. Attention to one's own speech fluctuates, though, which is one of the reasons why much of what is not quite correct or appropriate passes unnoticed. For both speakers and hearers, processing mechanisms also appear to be relatively shallow, as suggested by Dabrowska (2004), and consist in piecing together different elements such as prefabricated chunks and individual words. In a speaker role, language users must attend to the relationships of the units to maintain grammaticality, while the listener's task seems to be making use of salient lexical items, some grammatical cues, and contextual information without fully parsing the sentence (Dabrowska 2004: 23). While dysfluencies and slow delivery may be more of a help than a hindrance to the listener, lack of stability in the use of structures reduces predictability and consequently the heuristic value of structures. Structural instability may add to the listener's processing load.

Since structures are less firmly entrenched in ELF repertoires, hearers have less use for them as scaffolding for their predictions. Their usefulness is not directly a function of their grammaticality, though, because grammaticality is probably less precise for speakers and hearers alike. Thus the potential communicative problems that may ensue from grammatical ELF features are not so much to do with the non-standardness of structures as the lack of stability in their use. This may mean fuzzier processing overall, as suggested already above, and favouring forms that are less taxing on working-memory capacity, such as regularised forms, and probably increased reliance on explicitation devices such as paraphrases (more on this in Chapter 7).

DIVERGENCES WITH DIRECTION

An interesting facet of divergences from Standard English is their apparent non-random directionality. For instance, *-ing* forms occur where they would not be used in standard language, but the reverse does not seem to be found, that is missing *-ing* forms where standard language would require their use. Similarly, existential constructions of *there's* or *there is* with a plural noun are quite common, in fact *there's* + plural noun is more common in MICASE than in ELFA (Ranta 2009). But comparing *there is* + plural noun and *there are* + a singular noun complement, we find an asymmetry: Ranta (2009) found 6.5% of *there's* + plural in her ELFA sample, whereas I found *there are* + a singular noun (*so there are a risk*) in 3.7% of all cases of *there are* in ELFA. In a similar vein, testifying to non-random structural variability in ELF, is Cogo and Dewey's (2006) finding that third-person singular *-s* was far more commonly used with auxiliaries than with main verbs. Since present tense verb inflection in one person only is something of a typological anomaly in English, there is no communicative efficiency attached to its use that would be lost in its zero realisations. We might nevertheless assume that its proportionally more common use with auxiliaries probably relates to auxiliaries constituting a closed class. As members of a closed class, auxiliaries are frequent and easy to memorise individually. Their syntactic roles are also well defined and salient in communication, and as we saw in Chapter 4, they rank high in both ELFA and MICASE.

The emerging picture of structure in ELF is that most of the time speakers in our academic data follow the general lines of standard grammar. Nevertheless, divergence from the standard is also found in almost every conversational turn. It does not seem reasonable to dismiss the divergences as arbitrary mistakes, even though some of course are just passing slips of the tongue or idiosyncrasies. Many structural features found here have also been observed in other studies on ELF, and the deviations tend to fall into types, as can be ascertained with corpus data.

There is no general consensus among scholars concerning the extent to which different aspects of change result from language contact. Yet on the whole, simplification is taken to be the general trend (Thomason 2001), with morphology and syntax as the structural domains most likely to resist change (Sankoff 2002). What we see from the present data, that is, from second-order contact, is that there is no straightforward, overarching tendency towards structural simplification. Phenomena such as non-standard word order or lack of agreement are not essentially simpler than their standard counterparts. Yet there are aspects where simplification can be discerned: regularisation of verbs and nominal plurals, for example. At the same time, such developments lead to increased structural variability, sometimes giving rise to novel forms that appear on independent occasions and may even become preferred forms with time. The next section takes this discussion forward by focusing on patterning at the intersection of lexis and structure: phraseological sequences.

5.3 Beyond the word: multi-word wholes

As we saw in the preceding section, listeners are adept at making prospections in discourse on the basis of structure. In addition to clause structure, prospection may also be informed by phraseological patterns. These are larger wholes than individual words (*the thing is*; *if you like*; *one of the*; *and I said*; *you just have to*; *in this day and age*), but they do not always conform to the types and boundaries of generally recognised structural units (group/phrase, clause, sentence). Yet they share a property with structure: extending over more than one lexical item. In this way they enable similar prospections to be made about what is to come. For the speaker, they conversely facilitate the production of utterances by providing useful routines. Handling units of an optimal size for the purposes of ongoing processing enables interactants who alternate in speaker and listener roles to manage contributions to the accumulating shared knowledge.

Recently multi-word sequences have captured the imagination of many researchers. We already saw traces of their potential role as units of processing in Chapter 4. In this section, we return to phraseological sequences to bridge the gap between lexis and structure. Multi-word units of various kinds, including traditional idioms (*get on one's high horse*; *hook, line and sinker*) and phraseological units (*at a stroke*; *you name it*), fixed expressions (Moon 1998), lexical bundles (Biber et al. 1999), grammatical patterns (Hunston & Francis 2000), prefabs (Erman & Warren 2000), formulaic sequences (Wray 2002) and constructions (Fillmore et al. 1988; Östman & Fried 2005), have been observed in important functions in language use and processing. They go under different names and diverse definitions, but most of them have in common the observation not only that words tend to keep company as in collocations, but also that there is a myriad of schematic language units where certain structural and lexical properties integrate into meaningful wholes without mapping onto the traditional division of words, phrases, and clauses.

As bridges between the lexical and the structural, such units are also involved in contact-induced language change. Structural borrowing, is mediated by lexical borrowing of open-class items: at the centre we have 'lexico-syntactic calquing' (Silva-Corvalan 1998), where lexical and pragmatic borrowing carry along their structural baggage, which then gets adopted into the borrowing language along with the lexis. Ellis (1996, 2002) argues that much of second language acquisition is sequence learning. If this is so, it could provide a link between language contact, language learning, and language change. But languages are also in contact in other ways that involve bilingual processing, such as translation and interpreting. Influence from lexico-syntactic calquing can be seen in translations (Gellerstam 1996; Mauranen 2000), which seem to bring structural properties into target texts also in pragmatic expressions.

There is a long tradition of research into idioms and conventional phraseology, but what seemed to spark off a renewed interest in units of meaning larger than the individual word were the possibilities that corpus linguistics opened up for such research. John Sinclair's seminal 'idiom principle' (1991) drew on his work on corpora and lexicography, and his insights turned a new page in understanding units of meaning (see also Sinclair 2004a).

Despite a shared interest in multi-word units, linguistic modelling of these sequences encompasses a broad range of approaches. They can roughly be divided up according to a primary emphasis either on lexical units, like collocations or lexical bundles, or on grammatical units like constructions, patterns, or frames. What seems shared is the awareness that the associated patterning is neither solely lexical nor completely structural, but a combination of elements from both. Stubbs (1996) describes such items as being 'between a word and a group', but even that is too restrictive, as they come in very many shapes and sizes. The weak spot in many accounts of these sequences is that very little if anything is said about meaning. Yet without anchorage in meaning, multi-word units could hardly occupy such a central position in language use. The firmest basis for treating them as one category is that they constitute recognisable units of meaning.

In addition to being recognisable through a meaning, three aspects in the conceptualisation of multi-word strings are important: (1) such units reflect holistic language processing, (2) they are to a large degree idiomatic or conventionalised but not completely fixed, and (3) they are complex in that they contain elements of different categories, such as grammar and lexis. The first two points are captured in Sinclair's formulation of the 'idiom principle': 'The principle of idiom is that a language user has available to him or her a large number of semi-preconstructed phrases that constitute single choices, even though they might appear to be analysable into segments' (Sinclair 1991: 110). Talking about multi-word units of meaning as semi-preconstructed, prefabricated, or formulaic acknowledges their conventionalised nature: these reflect speakers' preferred use over and above that which is theoretically possible in the language. Preferences are relatively easy to spot on account of their frequency by analysing large corpora, even though fully fixed sequences are so much more readily detectable that they tend to eclipse variability, which may be equally important.

Holistic processing is centrally involved in psycholinguistic approaches, as in Wray's (2002: 9) definition of formulaic sequences: 'a sequence, continuous or discontinuous, of words or other elements, which is, or appears to be, prefabricated: that is, stored and retrieved whole from memory at the time of use, rather than being subject to generation or analysis by the language grammar'. A corollary of holistic processing appears to be multiple storage of the 'same' items, that is items can appear as components of one or more multi-word units (TAKE *place*, TAKE *off*, TAKE *apart*) and can also be independent units in themselves (TAKE as an independent verb). As Bybee and Hopper (2001: 9) put it: 'even though complex units (such as *I don't*) are stored and accessed, their component parts are also identified in the categorization and storage process'. Similar views have been expressed in studies of L2 learning (e.g. Aston 1995; Myles & Mitchell 2004) and in psycholinguistic studies such as Wray (2002). Arguably the items that appear both as independent units of meaning and as components of phraseological sequences with their own meaning are not really cases of the 'same' item, because the contribution to utterance meaning is not identical and takes place at different levels: as a constituent of an utterance, or as a component of a constituent.

In our data frequent items appeared both as independent units and as components of phraseological sequences, as already discussed above. For example, some high-frequency differentiators occurred largely as components of multi-word units. *Course* was one of the most frequent and turned out to be almost exclusively part of the adverb phrase *of course*, and *case*[7] appeared also frequently in clusters – the most frequent instances were *in this case* and *in the case of, in that case, in your case, in any case, in case of. Example* and *instance* were nearly always components of an exemplifying phrase.

A working definition at this stage could be that a phraseological sequence is a recurrent unit of language which is associated with a recognisable meaning and includes more than one element; it includes grammatical as well as lexical components, of which some are fixed and some may be variable.

It would seem clear that although it is difficult to obtain direct evidence of phraseological units as units of processing without access to brain scans (and some innovative method of investigating them), we have access to reasonably informative sources of evidence from transcripts by looking at three things: recapitulations, echoing, and n-grams. If speakers recapitulate sequences of more than one word from their own immediately preceding speech when they engage in restarts, or echo their interlocutors' speech in units that include meaningful multi-word units, it would certainly seem to point to processing speech in bigger chunks than individual words or lemmas. This is what we already saw in Chapter 4. Likewise, if a large number of speakers use the same formulation involving the same three or four words over and over again, this certainly suggests that such repeated sequences are very good candidates for being speakers' processing units. Biber et al. (1999) talk about repeated three-word combinations, trigrams ('lexical bundles' in their terminology), being used as discourse building blocks. In this chapter we move the focus towards evidence obtainable through corpus methods, and include also these latter kinds of items.

5.3.1 Multi-word units and second language use

Phraseological sequences have been held up as the ultimate hurdle for the language learner, since it has become generally accepted that L2 users get these wrong even at very high proficiency levels (e.g. Pawley & Syder 1983; Nattinger & de Carrico 1992). Findings from learner language corpora compiled in the Centre for English Corpus Linguistics (CECL) in Louvain (e.g. papers in Meunier & Granger 2008) lend support to this view, as does research on collocations in learner language (Nesselhauf 2005). It seems, then, that the kinds of conventional turns of phrase, expressions, combinations, and collocations which native speakers prefer instead of equally grammatical alternatives may not be available for foreign-language speakers even when they are proficient enough not to make immediately obvious lexicogrammatical errors.

On the basis of such evidence from SLA studies, Wray (2002) has posited two processing mechanisms for the native language and other, later learned, languages. Native speakers, on this account, have two language-processing mechanisms available to them: one holistic, which operates with phraseological sequences, in Wray's terms 'formulaic sequences', and which chiefly accounts for fluency and easy execution of speech. The other mechanism is analytic or compositional. It operates with small components and allows for flexibility and novelty in language use. In contrast to native speakers, non-native speakers are not supposed to have the first type, holistic processing, available to them any longer. According to Wray, they apply compositional processing to everything in the foreign language, breaking it down to its smallest elements (Wray actually means individual words, not morphemes). In this way, L2 users must construct all their expressions from scratch. Such a process is clearly more error-prone than one that can utilise larger phraseological sequences; if no convenient formulae are readily at hand to reduce processing load, a good deal of faltering is to be expected. Two separate mechanisms can of course explain the difference in L1 and L2 speech in terms of conformity to certain sequences over others. Wray's claim may nevertheless be incorrect, because it would entail that conventionalised sequences are not used as single wholes at all by L2 speakers; if on the other hand they are, the production mechanisms cannot be entirely separate.

Looking at stretches of ELF discourse, we quickly notice that they vary very much in their fluency and conformity to ENL usage. In Example (5.7), the speaker's turn consists of very conventional sequences (*what did you suggest*; *you said something about*; *when we were talking earlier*; *it sounded really interesting*) even though there are no phraseological units of the kind usually associated with idioms. Even the incomplete units follow each other in fluent succession here.

(5.7)

<S4> but what did you suggest you said something about when we were talking earlier and it sounded really interesting like comparing not like for example two populations but instead like comparing </S4>

The next extract (5.8) is much less fluent, but speakers employ highly conventional units in pragmatic functions to show positive evaluation (*good timing*), polite disagreement (*not exactly*), and considerate discourse management (*if you don't mind*). Speaker 8 also uses a perfectly standard temporal expression (*at the end*) and an approximately standard phrase (*among yourself*); these two look like examples of a more and a less frequent and therefore a more and a less entrenched expression.

(5.8)

<S8> i know, <S1> okay yeah </S1> so, yeah *good timing* so was the idea to propose also, do you have a topic you you would like to start discussing, (critically), could be erm your interest in a research proposal out of the papers you've read </S8>
<S6> well mhm, <S8> or </S8> *not exactly* no but er my er i think i would personally be more interested in these natural population settings </S6>
<SS> mhm </SS>
<S8> erm *if you don't mind* i will write it down so *at the end* you will have the list of preferences but then you have to discuss among yourself what to choose ...

Example (5.9) shows more approximations than the previous two examples, in each case with some grammatical glitch in a unit that is otherwise recognisable in its meaning and used for the kind of purpose that matches that of standard language (*discuss together*, *discuss on*, *in a way that*), even though their forms are not entirely standard-like in their contexts.

(5.9)

<S8> yeah ***discuss together*** *come up with* a not the final but at least a draft plan <SS> mhm </SS> so basically what is your reasoning one sentence what animal and why or what plant and why and what you think is the method you will apply and what you expect it means less than a page just four sentences but then ***we will discuss on that*** and it means also that you have to meet before the next time and we planned this *in **a** way that* you have to work together because one important aspect of research is collaboration so you have to learn to become a group </S8>

Moving on to a sample of what look like phraseological sequences from the corpus, we can see in Example (5.10) that they are fairly similar to findings from learner language studies (e.g. papers in Schmitt 2004), notably in the corpora compiled in the CECL in Louvain (e.g. papers in Meunier & Granger 2008). Many of these examples have a preposition or article different from the typical ENL phrase, and also lexical and structural substitutions occur. More importantly, however, although they all fall short of a conventionalised sequence in the standard language, they are all recognisable as units of meaning in their contexts. Furthermore, these meanings match a conventional turn of phrase, because they seem to fall within an acceptable range of variability to be recognised and understood (*take a closer look at*; *put an end to*; *at its worst* ...). They are thus not random efforts at constructing expressions from the smallest possible components, but approximate versions of schematic wholes that to all intents look like being stored and processed as single wholes.

(5.10)

... take closer look to the world
... how to put the end on it
... it's on the worst during the first week
... so does it make any different where the fat is
... but then from other point of view
... behind the lines you could very well read
... i will tell you a few words about the hungarian political system
... you said a lot of er good points
... we'll build up from that

We can thus see a richer picture than Wray paints. SLU shows conventional sequences interspersed with stretches of discourse that look like following the Sinclairian 'open choice' principle, and furthermore, speakers use sequences which approximate conventionalised, phraseological units, but in ways that do not quite match the target. As we know from psycholinguistic research (e.g. Field 2003) and as we saw in Chapter 2, fluent and less fluent stretches tend to alternate in normal speech. What is thus worth noticing about these units is not only that ELF speakers tend to get them slightly wrong, but perhaps more importantly that they not only use them but also get them approximately right. That we find them outside environments of language pedagogy is important for efforts to understand their significance to SLU. Pedagogical settings may reward learners for their correct use and penalise them for minor deviations, whereas in real-life SLU such as lingua franca communication their use must be discussed in other terms.

We may postulate at this stage that phraseological sequences account for:

1. normal processing and processing fluency for both speakers and hearers and for L1 and SLU alike;
2. comprehensibility of a number of non-standard details that get embedded in the larger schematic unit, which is sufficiently conventionalised to be recognisable as a unit in a given function. The units must be frequent to serve this purpose.

5.3.2 Phraseological sequences in ELFA

The discourse samples above suggested that conventional sequences are used in SLU in much the same way as in ENL. How do they look in a quantitative perspective? There is no simple way of capturing the kinds of units that were considered in examples (5.7) to (5.10) in plain quantitative terms because they are often discontinuous and their variability is not systematic in form in a way that could be defined for computer searches. The variation is linguistically not random or arbitrary, but it is not related to form in a simple way. For instance *does it make any different* can be interpreted as an approximation of MAKE *a difference* in its context, but it is a unique occurrence in ELFA. A couple of instances of *make the difference* can also be found, and one *make difference*. The rest of the 60 occurrences found with MAKE + *differ** conform to the standard. This combination then mostly takes the standard form, and works as a unit of meaning in its contexts, but shows some vacillation reflecting less firm entrenchment.

By looking at the repeated forms, we can get a glimpse of the kinds of building blocks that speakers use repeatedly, which can be taken as reasonable evidence of their processing. Fully fixed phraseological sequences can be extracted by simply searching for multi-word sequences (n-grams) in a corpus. These show uninterrupted combinations in exactly the same form. Three-word combinations (trigrams) are particularly common, and as Biber et al. (1999: 991–2) point out, many of them are incomplete structural units, which can be considered as discourse building blocks. Comparing ELF and ENL data should give an idea of the degree of similarity between them.

Corpus frequency lists are 'top-heavy' in that the most frequent items cover very high proportions of running text. We already saw in Chapter 4 that spoken language seems to be even more sharply bounded in this way than written. Trigrams show similar patterns. Table 5.1 gives us a good overview of common combinations in ELF and ENL usage by showing the ten most frequent trigrams in ELFA and MICASE.[8]

The lists are strikingly similar. More than half of the trigrams are identical (bolded in Table 5.1). The similarity continues when we move further down the list, with the lists gradually bifurcating as they get towards less common expressions. Thus, four of the top five are identical on the two lists; six of the top ten, and twelve of the top 25. What is more, the trigrams are 'regular', that is, conform to Standard English. This holds for the vast majority of those further down frequency lists, and we have to look very far for the occasional deviation. It is quite clear that trigrams are exactly like those in ENL in the overwhelming majority of cases. The same phenomenon is observable

Table 5.1 Top trigrams from academic speaking

	ELF (ELFA)	ENL (MICASE)
1.	**I don't know**	**I don't know**
2.	**a lot of**	**a lot of**
3.	**I think that**	**one of the**
4.	**one of the**	**a little bit**
5.	and so on	**you have to**
6.	**you have to**	*this is the*
7.	*there is a*	*this is a*
8.	***I think it's***	in terms of
9.	the the the	***I don't think***
10.	**a little bit**	**I think that**

here as we already saw with individual lexical items: deviant forms are not very common, but the frequency distributions of items are different, for instance *in terms of* ranks 37th in ELFA, but 8th in MICASE. It looks as if it is above all statistical distributions of preference patterns that are different.

Features where ELF and ENL diverge on the lists are not very many but interesting. The most conspicuous, perhaps, is the repeated article (*the the the*). Such repetitions of single words, what Biber et al. (1999) call 'repeats', are characteristic of spontaneous speaking. Their presence is nevertheless much more pronounced in ELF than in ENL speech, which is particularly easy to see in n-grams of any length. N-grams also reveal that hesitation phenomena are far more common in ELF, because they make their way to a number of recurrent combinations. Examples from 4-grams (*and er and er*), 5-grams (*er I would like to*) are very common, whereas ENL speech had far fewer, and there was only one that was shared among the highest ranking n-grams: *in the in the in the*. This strengthens the impression that speaking a foreign language is comparatively taxing on the working memory. Repeats in processing will be discussed in Chapter 7 in relation to other kinds of repetition.

MORE OR LESS VAGUE?

A point of interest is also the vague expression *and so on*, which appeared only on the ELFA list. Could this mean that ELF speech has more vagueness? Vagueness in SLA has been variously claimed to be overused (Ringbom 1998), underused (Nikula 1996; De Cock et al. 1998), or used equally by L2 learners and ENL speakers (Cheng & Warren 2001). Channell (1994) and Cutting (2006) suggest that vague expressions be taught to learners, because vagueness is an integral part of language; they suggest that L2 speakers may sound less natural to L1 speakers on account of lacking vagueness. The researchers (with the exception of Cheng & Warren) also worry about the naturalness of L2 speech in ENL speakers' ears. When ENL sensibilities are not an issue, as in ELF, the question arises as to how necessary vague expressions are in language, and whether the benefits conferred to communication that Channell (1994) lays down hold true more widely than among native speakers. In principle, the communicative functions ought to be similar. Metsä-Ketelä (2006, 2008) finds in her studies on the ELFA corpus that their functions look much the same, but that the relative presence is clearly stronger in ELFA, and there are differences in distributions and preferred expressions. So, for example, *more or less* is used far more in ELF (Metsä-Ketelä 2006). The high rank of *and so on* noted above supports this.

For a glimpse on other phraseological sequences expressing vagueness, we could view the comparative lists slightly further, and include the 100 most common sequences. For central categories of vagueness markers, such as tags (*and so on*, *or something*), degree expressions (*a couple of*, *more or less*), detachers (*in some sense*, *in a way*), and classifiers (*some kind of*), a scan of the 100 most frequent trigrams in ELFA and MICASE reveals that ELFA has proportionally far more tokens (1657 vs. 974 pmw) of these expressions, and also more types (7 vs. 5), which means that there is more variation, too, and speakers are not merely repeating a very small selection over and over again. These figures certainly suggest that vagueness is amply expressed in ELF. Metsä-Ketelä's (forthcoming) findings on a wider range of vague expressions in a subsection of ELFA also indicate that there is more, not less, vagueness in ELF. In view of this, the fears concerning L2 speakers' underuse of vague expressions seem vastly exaggerated. At least in academic discourse vagueness appears to be in place. This throws some light again on some of the more general issues in relation to ELF: language phenomena that are vital to communication should be seen in lingua franca talk. We may therefore assume that expressing appropriate degrees of vagueness is fundamental to language use (as argued, for example, by Channell 1994).

It is also worth noticing how presentative structures differ on the trigram lists (Table 5.1 above). In ELFA, *there is a* is the most prominent, while *this is a* and *this is the* appear in MICASE. Since the *there*-structure has no direct equivalent in many languages, it is generally regarded as a translation problem (Mauranen 1999), and on this account we might not expect L2 speakers to use it more frequently than ENL speakers. Even though most research on *there* has focused on its clausal functions, those scholars who have looked at its discourse functions have noticed its tendency to present topics to the discourse (Lakoff 1987; Huckin & Pesante 1988), in other words, to bring something new to the hearer's awareness.

CHATTY OR BOOKISH?

As pointed out in Chapter 3, we cannot make statements about register because there is no suitable reference corpus of ELF as yet, and ENL analyses have not offered an overall description of an academic speech register with which to compare it. The closest description that we find is Biber's (2006) study on the language of university registers. His work offers some points of comparison, although his focus and data do not overlap enough with ELFA to allow the more direct comparisons that are possible between ELFA and MICASE.

A couple of interesting small things came out in the above ELFA–MICASE comparison nonetheless, when the trigram lists of both corpora were viewed against register features found by others. Biber et al. (1999) report a number of register attributes, some based on lexical bundles, from their work on some major English corpora. Two of their most often contrasted registers are 'conversation' and 'academic prose', both relevant to our interest in academic speaking. It was not at all clear whether academic speaking would turn out to be more like speech or more like academic prose when academic speech corpora were first being compiled. It turned out that academic speech is closer to spoken language than to academic prose (see e.g. Swales & Burke 2003; Biber et al. 2004; Mauranen 2004; Biber 2006; Biber & Gray 2010). With hindsight the conclusion might seem obvious, but it was far from it at the time, and the assumption that academic genres must be very similar independently of mode still appears to inform much teaching of academic language. Moreover, one of the surprising things that transpired from Biber et al. (2004) was that university teaching was not intermediate between conversation and academic prose in its use of lexical bundles, but in fact used a greater number of different bundles than either of the others.

If we now look at some of the very common lexical bundles that Biber et al. (1999) report and compare these to the lists of 25 most common trigrams[9] in ELFA and MICASE, we find that items which Biber's team found in 'conversation' occurred on both lists, although somewhat more frequently in MICASE. Apart from *I don't know*, which was the most common trigram in all three cases, only *you have to* appeared in both our corpora. In addition, MICASE also had *I don't think* and *I mean I*. As to academic prose, *one of the* was among the commonest Biber bundles, and on both of our lists. In addition, *there is a* appeared in ELFA, but not in MICASE. It would thus seem that both conversational and academic features are represented in the corpora, with a slight difference between them, suggesting that MICASE is the more conversational of the two.[10] This is very slight evidence in itself, even though backed up by a further detail: among four-word sequences, one in ELFA (*on the other hand*) was among Biber's academic prose bundles, and one MICASE 4-gram (*I don't know what*) among the conversational group. We might expect some degree of conversational bias in MICASE, because its speech events include some that are less academic than in ELFA, but these findings would seem to tally with the anecdotal evidence that non-natives speak in a more 'bookish' way (e.g. Sinclair 1991), which makes it more interesting. On the other hand, there is also evidence suggesting that in written text, L2 learners tend to overuse expressions from informal spoken mode (see e.g. Gilquin & Paquot 2008; Szmrecsanyi & Kortmann 2011).

In Biber's later analysis (2006), lexical bundles are all 4-grams, and although his analysis purports to integrate earlier work (Biber et al. 1999; Biber et al. 2004), the units are inevitably slightly different. Thus, for comparing ELFA and MICASE to Biber (2006), I turned to 4-grams, too. Biber deals with two main registers, 'classroom teaching' and 'textbooks', neither of which quite corresponds to ELFA (or MICASE), but should be close enough for a very rough outline. I looked at only the very common sequences and, as above, chose the top 25 from ELFA and MICASE, and correspondingly those with the highest occurrences in T2K-SWAL. The result was that ELFA had no items in common with textbooks at all, and only one (*if you want to*) with classroom teaching. MICASE in turn shared one item with textbooks (*at the end of*), and four with classroom teaching. What these comparisons seem to suggest is above all that we should not overlook the importance of methodological issues: differences in the composition of corpora give rise to different results. If we did not have two corpora of ENL speech from the USA, we might draw hasty conclusions about L1 and L2 use, or if we made comparisons with, say, the BASE corpus, about British and American speech. As it is, the lack of agreement between T2K-SWAL and MICASE indicates that corpora are indeed sensitive to register, and that normal variability in speech may be wider within genre clusters than we usually give credit for. In brief, then, the issue of bookishness vs. chattiness in ELF cannot be resolved at this stage, but some things are clear: first, although it is thinkable that ELF speakers may have a different, possibly more diffuse, notion of register from ENL speakers, it may not be so uniform among the latter either. Secondly, n-grams provide useful glimpses on language that are worth following up with other kinds of research tools. Finally, not only does ELF speech contain sequences of more than one word, but these tend to be very similar to those in ENL. Postulating separate underlying processing mechanisms for first and later languages does not seem warranted in the light of this evidence.

5.3.3 Special features of ELF phraseology

The trigrams and 4-grams showed a very uniform picture of ELF and ENL phraseology, in part on account of the immutable nature of n-grams. The commonalities were thus highlighted, which is important for maintaining a realistic perspective on the bigger picture: for the most part, ENL and ELF are quite similar. It is nevertheless the divergent aspects that are the most intriguing, because it is those that contain the seeds of things to come. Much in ELF phraseological sequences diverges from ENL, takes unorthodox and non-standard forms, and yet maintains comprehensibility. Some scholars have argued that ELF breaches of the standard show no pattern, and that deviations are irregular and idiosyncratic (e.g. Mollin 2006; Promodrou 2008). To examine this matter a little, I look at some cases of phraseological sequences in the ELFA corpus.

'LET ME SAY A FEW WORDS ...'

I start from an expression I stumbled upon in searching MICASE for metadiscoursal expressions (5.11):

(5.11)

> ***Let me say*** *a few words about the solution*

This is an ENL snippet that incorporates a very common pattern in academic discourse: *let me* with a verb of communication (*let me* + V_{comm}). It is discourse reflexive (see Chapter 6), a handy starting device (*let me begin by saying*), and commonly used at junctions and transitions; in monologues such as lectures it acts as an organiser looking ahead, making the speaker's intended continuation transparent (*let me deepen the issue a bit*), and thereby orienting hearers towards this intention. It would seem to be a fairly salient transition frame, which has parallels in other languages, and is certainly useful in helping speakers to keep their hearers following the thread of talk, to enable them to change tack (*let me change a bit my questions into different area*) and to shelve issues (*let me come back to that i won't answer it fully but i'll at least touch on that issue*), as well as to go back and forth in the presentation. Yet it is not limited to monologues, but serves in competing for the floor as well, often appearing turn-initially (*let me g- just one clarification*).

If we compare ELF and ENL use of this pattern (Table 5.2), the striking difference is quantitative: the overall use is two and a half times higher among ENLs (ELFA 103 vs. MICASE 256 pmw). Moreover, ENL preferences for certain verbs in the V slot have a somewhat broader selection before the frequencies drop more steeply. However, the most preferred verbs are largely the same, albeit in a different order.

As we can see in Table 5.2, each corpus has one clearly preferred verb, *go* (ELFA) and *tell* (MICASE) and all verbs except one in each corpus (*put* in ELFA and *give* in MICASE) appear on both lists. The ELF preference is for an unspecific verb; it shows a clear pattern with *back* as an ingredient in over half of the instances, so that the pattern can be summarized as *let me go back* (as in *let me go back to the methodology*).The ENL preferred verb is specifically a verb of communication, illustrated in *let me tell you what I'm driving at.* The communicative verb role is reversed with the second most common verbs, where the ENL one is unspecific *give*, and the ELF verb is communication-specific *say. Give* collocates strongly with *example*, as in *let me give you an example.* It was rare in ELF, where only two cases were found.

Table 5.2 ELF (ELFA) and ENL (MICASE) comparison on let me + V_{comm}

	ELFA		MICASE	
Occurrence / million words				
		103		256
Preferred verbs / million words				
	go (back/ to)	11	tell (you)	18
	say	7	give (you)	13
	ask	5	ask	11
	tell (you)	5	say	9
	put (it)	4	go (on/back/ through)	7

The pattern can be mitigated with *just*, which both use in similar ways, but the ENLs more often (15%) than ELFs (7%). This does not mean that ELFs mitigate it less, but that the expressions vary more: *let me* ***maybe*** *go back to*; *let me* ***quickly*** *go to*; *let me* ***maybe little just*** *add* ***a bit***. This points to a shallower entrenchment of the conventionalised pattern.

A random sample of concordance lines from ELFA (5.12) shows that most instances are mainstream, and in fact nearly all expressions in the variable verb slot found in ELFA were also found in MICASE. Not quite all, though.

(5.12) *let me* +V_{comm} **in ELFA**

questions to raise in the (xx) coming but **let me** first before we go into that even if
the durability of phenomena erm but erm **let me** well let me say one thing in defence of
of communication infrastructure , now **let me** qualify this statement i am not
that very very troublesome . because . **let me** give you one example . the thinking
some again some problems mhm-hm **let me** discuss it with er your erm one of the
want to know what is the nation's interest **let me** remind you f- of one more thing the end
if you if you only talking about er or **let me** correct myself not only but you are
countries (xx) that this one is not true but **let me** tell you the bases the bases are that the
villages where stations are located er **let me** point out also that not only in
i mean and the process is useful but **let me** just add er one thing here namely that

In (5.12), two concordance lines contain expressions not in MICASE: *let me qualify this statement* and *let me correct myself*. They are hapax legomenae, that is occur only once in the data. It would be unmotivated to treat them as 'errors', since there is nothing ungrammatical about either of them, nor are they in any way conspicuous. Neither is there any particular reason to hasten to label them 'innovations', since they simply appear to make use of the resources of English to meet a communicative need. One is tempted to think, rather, that if the corpus was large enough, they might turn up again. As it happens, neither was found in VOICE, but its genre distribution is different (see Chapter 3), so this was not surprising.

Turning to MICASE to see how ad hoc creativity works there, a good number of single occurrences were found, some of them quite imaginative. Concordance lines in (5.13) show a sample.

(5.13) **Single occurrences of** *let me* +V_{comm} **in MICASE**

hesitate, to, okay but let **let me** pick up on Edward Craig's very useful
people with your range of intelligence. **let me** summarize. uh, one, methodology, studying
which maximizes the total value. **let me** just stop you for a minute Rob mhm so, just
parenthesis parenthesis women. now **let me** stress, one, more, time. farm must always
um... assuming he's said enough um **let me** make my comment which is that in in
past, but also, this point which is, and **let me** illustrate it for you, Gregory the Seventh
for a sense of historical perspective, **let me** just give you a a forty-five second
okay so let me just, **let me** be episodic. i me- w- one of the
m detecting quiescence but you gotta **let me**, decommit because i'm not ready here.
then obviously basic biology failed **let me**, digress a little here. um, there is no

Like the ELF examples, most of these look perfectly inconspicuous, and it is easy to imagine that in a larger corpus or another same-genre corpus many of the instances could be repeated (*pick up on*, *summarise*, *stress*, *illustrate*, *digress*). Others, however, look rather unlikely to be found again, for instance the pragmatically slightly risky *let me stop you for a minute*, or those that seem ad hoc creations, like *let me be episodic*, *let me decommit*, or *let me just give you a forty-five second sketch of Einstein's early life*. These examples illustrate the inherent and ubiquitous variability that natural languages hold, and serve as a useful reminder that it may not be a good idea to abstract away from it in pedagogical applications: it is neither realistic nor desirable to convey a picture of target language speakers following endlessly intricate rules and practices of applying conventional expressions. Chapter 8 takes up this application issue more fully, while there is more to discover about patterning here that is relevant to applications, too. Both of our speaker groups seemed to be engaged in reproducing conventional expressions along with ad hoc creativity.

Our example (5.11), *let me say a few words about the solution*, is not exhausted yet. It harbours another multi-word unit, which is shown by the following concordance lines from MICASE (5.14):

(5.14)

um by the end of the day. just	**a few words about**	the planning committee um
so, i want to conclude with	**a, few words about**	Hilbert and his problems.
possibilities like this... let me say	**a few words about**	the solution. um... in my
geometric models, gonna say	**a few words about**	why this problem is difficult
problem is difficult to solve, and	**a few words about**	the solution, and then

These five examples of *words about* were all that were found in MICASE, and there was no variation at all, so that *a few words about* looks like a fixed cluster. Not so in ELFA. There were several times as many occurrences (25 pmw, vs. 2.8 pmw in MICASE), and there was not only one fixed cluster for the same function. Both *a few words about* (7) and *few words about* (6) were used, but the latter can be put down as common article dropping. *A couple of words about* occurred once. What was a bigger surprise, though, was that the most common pattern was *some words about* (5.15):

(5.15)

mentation process okay and the then	**some words about**	forest legislation and
brief way yeah most important then	**some words about**	app- theoretical
where i showed er some er	**some words about**	different methods of
er now er i'm at last i'm going to , say	**some words about**	the library information
positive influences of er the past , now	**some words about**	the problem (xx) and
[that] [yeah] you are you are . okay er	**some words about**	the state of the art in
are verified with experiments and	**some words about**	er the aspects the
you [have] [mhm] you have done , then	**some words about**	the thickness of the
okay , then if we open book and say	**some words about**	the , nomenclature

The pattern was found in five different files, so it is not just an idiosyncrasy. Just out of curiosity I looked for it in VOICE and found three instances. Two things seem clear from this: first, that ELF has brought variability into the pattern, and secondly, that there seems to be an emerging pattern that is ELF-specific. Variability was further enhanced by the discovery in both ELFA and VOICE of an adjectival modifier: *beautiful words about* and *nice words about*. The new pattern is not very easy to explain – why should it arise in several contexts in the same way? I presented this to a group of students, and the suggestion was raised that perhaps *some* is an 'easier' word for an L2 user than *a few*. I dug out the frequencies and found what is shown in Table 5.3.

In both cases, *some* is roughly ten times more common than *few / a few*, but between *few* and *a few* there is a notable difference: while they are equally common in ELF, *a few* is distinctly more frequent in ENL. Again, the latter can be put down to the article-dropping tendency, but the overwhelming frequency difference of *some* over *few / a few* may go a long way towards explaining why it has spread to this pattern.

Table 5.3 Some *and* few *in ELFA and MICASE*

		pmw
ELFA	some	3,906
	few/ a few	293
	a few	146
	few	147
MICASE	some	2,390
	few/ a few	234
	a few	172
	few	62

'REALISTICALLY SPEAKING'

The next case illustrates a fairly productive albeit restricted phraseological frame, ***-ly speaking***. ENL patterning of this frame shows a common distribution shape (Table 5.4) where one expression is clearly preferred (*generally speaking*), another a secondary option (*strictly speaking*), and the rest one-off appearances.

With 15 occurrences in MICASE, the expected number in ELFA would be 10. However, the real number that we find is 26. Can this be likened to 'overuse' typical of learner language?

In ELF, the distribution curve is distinctly shallower (Table 5.5): there is no clear favourite, and of the 18 types, seven are repeated, but only one occurs three times. The expressions are much more evenly distributed. The ENL preferred unit is not prominent at all, but one of a number of twice-occurring sequences. What is going on here is thus simultaneous 'overuse' and 'underuse' in relation to ENL: speakers use the frame more often and more freely than ENL speakers, and at the same time they use the most common, conventional expression less. In brief, they have taken the frame on board but do not share ENL preferences with regard to its use.

These instances are in accordance with Standard English in being fully grammatical, even though they do not comply with ENL conventional preferences. Such a divergence from ENL conventions can be likened to what has been extensively investigated with learner corpora (Granger 1998; Granger et al. 2002; Nesselhauf 2005; Gilquin et al. 2007) and seen as over- or underuse. Learners' subtle non-native-like uses that are grammatical but not the conventionally preferred native choices have become a target for improvement fairly recently, with the increasing utilisation of ENL corpora to inform pedagogical practices

Table 5.4 -ly speaking in MICASE

ENL (MICASE)		
	generally speaking	6
	strictly speaking	2
	morally speaking	1
	objectively speaking	1
	properly speaking	1
	relatively speaking	1
	roughly speaking	1
	simply speaking	1
	stylistically speaking	1
	Total	**15**

Table 5.5 -ly speaking *in ELFA*

ELF (ELFA)		
	historically speaking	3
	basically speaking	2
	formally speaking	2
	frankly speaking	2
	generally speaking	2
	honestly speaking	2
	relatively speaking	2
	comfortably speaking	1
	economically speaking	1
	largely speaking	1
	legally speaking	1
	linguistically speaking	1
	politically speaking	1
	realistically speaking	1
	seriously speaking	1
	socially speaking	1
	socio-economically speaking	1
	strictly speaking	1
	Total	**26**

(e.g. Johns & King 1991; Burnard & McEnery 2000; Aston et al. 2004; Römer 2005). This is one of the places where ELF parts company with learners. The distribution patterns of grammatical expressions may deviate from ENL in both cases, but this cannot of course be seen as a problem in ELF: if ENL preferences are not followed, this need not in itself cause problems in comprehensibility among lingua franca speakers, because clearly those preferences have not been internalised.

'IN MY POINT OF VIEW'

A different development is the next case, *point of view*. Looking at it in context first (Example 5.16), we can see that it is used in the sense of 'opinion', that is, framing the speaker's view of what he or she is about to say next. In terms of form it is a blend of *in my view* and *from my point of view*.

(5.16)

<S1> ... the conclusion we have where, *on my point of view* my humble point of view i would say, dystopia is where we're gonna end up ...

This is not an individual's idiosyncrasy, as the phraseological sequence recurs in ELFA (5.17).

(5.17)

there is no er specific in- , interest erm	**in my point of view**	in in this kind of usage
[perspective] [mhm] for example	**in my point of view**	daddies always cook
, is not something new globalisation	**in my point of view**	er but on the other
more time to do whatever yeah but i	**in my point of view**	that was really good
the globalisation intensifies , the world	**on my point of view**	if you want we can
of of united states actually practise	**on my point of view**	where here in europe
of for instance erm market regulation	**on my point of view**	are the third world
of united states , it can be said and er	**on my point of view**	er i will say that the
and the conclusion we have where ,	**on my point of view**	my humble point of

The sequence, with the minor variation of *on/in*, was uttered in five different speech events by speakers from four L1 backgrounds: Estonian, Flemish, French, and Somali. I also checked the VOICE corpus and found two instances of *in my point of view*, by one Swedish L1 speaker and one German, as well as one case of a German L1 speaker saying *in your point of view*. Further evidence was provided in extracts from an international business school 'reflective essay' coursework set as email group discussion (Karhukorpi 2006: 110), which we see in (5.18).[11] It is clear that this phrase crops up in the speech of people from different and typologically distant first languages. It is not very common, but it occurs repeatedly. It is thus a parallel development in speakers of a variety of backgrounds.

(5.18)

In my point of view, she should talk with him about her feelings ...
In my point of view the most important thing here is the good for the child ...

This expression was not found in MICASE at all. *From my point of view* can in ordinary ENL be used either in a 'perspective' meaning or in an 'opinion' meaning, the latter being equivalent to *in my view*. A closer look revealed that MICASE had a strong tendency to use it in the perspective sense and keep *in my view* for the opinion sense. In ELFA, *point of view* was used in both senses, including cases where it was used with the preposition *from*. Sheer quantities reveal that *in my view* is not much used in either ELFA or MICASE (5 and 6 occurrences respectively), but that *point of view* in various combinations in ELFA amounts to 185 pmw, far exceeding the frequency in MICASE (73 pmw). MICASE frequency is further reduced (to 37 pmw) if we remove one outlier event where the discussion topic was 'point of view', and mentioned 65 times. The frequency discrepancy is considerable between the two corpora whichever way the counting is done. The sequence *point of view* itself is mostly used as part of a unit of meaning, such as *the point of view of X* or *from the X point of view*. This is so among ELF and ENL speakers alike, but ELF has extended it far more towards use with possessive pronouns, particularly *my point of view* (33 vs. 3 instances pmw), which conveniently covers opinion meanings along with perspective meanings.

What seems to be going on with this sequence is the extension of a common element that participates in several salient phrases, and expands its potential to less frequently used but grammatical sequences. In one case, *in/on my point of view*, the conventional ENL frame is overstepped and a new extension begins to take shape. Simplification is not involved, at least not of form, since *in my view* would definitely look like the simpler option, and one already existing in the language.

In using a phrase like *in my point of view*, ELF speakers seem to exploit the less used potential of the language (the opinion sense of *from my point of view*), mixing it with elements from a related expression (*in my view*) in the manner of blends, and bending it slightly to serve a fundamental communicative need (expressing opinion or stance).

'AS A MATTER OF FACT'

The final case starts from ENL again and moves one step further from flexibility. This is a completely immutable expression, *as a matter of fact*. It is like a single big word, with a clear discourse function of signalling that the speaker is about to make some kind of change of tack: he or she may start an elaboration of the state of the discourse at that point, a specification, a side sequence, correction, or contradiction. It is therefore a very useful marker, especially in the kind of argumentative discourse that most academic discourses are. Example (5.19) shows the concordance lines in ELFA, in line with Standard English.

(5.19)

er my country as india is and er **as a matter of fact** i can er let you all in to a
globalisation today erm , no-one er **as a matter of fact** er can put mud on our
than . 50 absolutely unbelievable **as a matter of fact** it's really unbelievable .
soft consonant er opposition which **as a matter of fact** is not so obvious but let's
to be as well known as jakobson , **as a matter of fact** the- erm reading his
is essential in a language where at **as a matter of fact** the more precise the
we then need lifeboats i'm curious **as a matter of fact** . talking about that i'm
ons can we sit] [yeah yes] thank you **as a matter of fact** at the beginning of your

However, this is not the whole story. Example (5.20) shows that a new chink has appeared in the conventional sequence.

(5.20)

despite some difficulties that **as the matter of fact** they come across what
ever seen in finland , he invented **as the matter of fact** er many initiatives one
made a controversial er statements **as the matter of fact** er soviets were very
cambridge polity er 1998 er it's **as the matter of fact** erm . i appreciate him
ghetto er but there you have @ **as the matter of fact**@ i mean when you
don't have constitution but there is **as the matter of fact** in brussels there are
erm well he he wrote many books er **as the matter of fact** in , sociology and in in
21st century i mean erm , it's er it's **as the matter of fact** bad er . but terrorism
intensifies . it's not new phenomena **as the matter of fact** but . it has it has er er
er these ethical challenge er **as the matter of fact** very vital in order to
economically their economy is **as the matter of fact** very much scrambling
say something you know erm well **as the matter of fact** i i i agree with you er
but did they did they solve it no , **as the matter of fact** none none have been
is a phenomena in which we have to **as the matter of fact** embrace very much
the next session will which will be **as the matter of fact** next thursday erm i will
when i define globalisation erm i **as the matter of fact** pick internet revolution
and use empirical data erm and i did **as the matter of fact** erm i did lecture
functions well the democracy will **as the matter of fact** function well , well on
in this contest in this context erm is **as the matter of fact** indirectly proportional
nations er er i i i when i lecture **as the matter of fact** these topics i erm i'm a
lives and yet erm something that **as the matter of fact** er very bad erm and

The fracture is not as dramatic as it looks, since despite the large number, this expression appeared in only two speech events. What it helps illustrate is that even fully fixed expressions may be susceptible to reinterpretation in ELF discourse, especially where there is little danger of misunderstanding, as here. The article is a non-prominent syllable in any case, and not particularly noticeable on the whole.

What all the cases discussed in this section show is that ELF speech displays not only idiosyncratic errors but also incipient patterns that occur in the same form and sense on different occasions and are used by several speakers. ELF speech is thus converging on new preferences. The patterns we are observing do not seem primarily to have interactional origins but, rather, linguistic ones. Although they all have arisen in the academic ELF community at large, the site is more like a wide imagined community, consisting of several communities of practice that do not directly interact with each other. These patterns occur in interactional situations and work as valid components of communicative acts, but the instances are not from one community of speakers in direct contact with each other. They are therefore repeated parallel occurrences of the same or similar expressions that are emerging in ELF and may well spread given that they are communicatively functional and do not originate in one place, which might confine them to one 'local' community.

5.4 Summary

In this chapter, we have moved from lexis to structures. It is nevertheless essential to keep in mind that the cutting-off point is anything but determinate, and that lexis and grammar in actual use are inextricably intertwined. The discussion thus followed on from some of the central themes around lexis: the import of frequencies and processing units. Structural items tend to be highly frequent, play vital roles in communication, and yet diverge and fluctuate in contexts of second language use. They are not quite as uniform as has been traditionally thought in standard languages either, but variable, for example, in dialects. The fundamental role of structure in language is to keep combinations of elements under control; the fact that only a fraction of the theoretically possible combinations ever occur paves the way for fluency in communication. Speaking and making sense of what is heard are both facilitated by selectional limitations. These enable prospection, a facet of top-down processing. Yet the processes involved tolerate a considerable degree of fuzziness and variability. Ordinary speech among speakers of the same first language absorbs a good proportion of variation and anomaly, and SLU tolerates even more without a noticeable effect on comprehensibility. It is plausible that a number of processes converge in prospection, with structure as one of them.

Structural variability in ELF is more wide-reaching than in L1 environments, but not random. Most of the time the grammar nevertheless conforms to Standard English, with some non-standard features shared with ENL spoken use. Many similarities to non-standard dialect features can also be discerned, as can affinities with second-language varieties such as World Englishes or indigenised varieties. In brief, ELF is not far from other kinds of English, at least in its academic genres. Yet there are also distinguishing features. Findings on structures in ELFA suggest that simplification is taking place; for instance regularisation of verbs and nominal plurals, and utilizing a smaller selection of expressions for a broad set of related functions. Still there is no straightforward overarching tendency towards structural simplification. Non-standard structures are not always simple.

The bridge between structure and lexis, phraseology, is in line with the notion that ELF mostly conforms to Standard English patterns – deviations are fairly rare, and appear very far down the line on indicators like frequency-based n-gram lists. Just as with structures, there is more variability in conventional patterns than in L1, but that is not the whole story: the variability is not random, and there are signs of ELF-specific developments. We find incipient patterns that are shared across independent events and speakers. This is perhaps the most intriguing evidence on the linguistic processes that have begun to take shape in ELF. Phraseological sequences are a pivotal element in how language is organised, and in a key position to account for stability and change. Not only do they combine lexical and structural elements, but they also straddle the three perspectives that constitute the backbone of our exploration of ELF.

From one point of view, a phraseological sequence can be seen as a kind of extended word. In this interpretation the stability and frequency of phraseological sequences can be expected to be related in the same way as with words (cf. the discussion in Chapter 4). From a cognitive perspective they are inclined to destabilise in second-language users' repertoires. From a macrosocial perspective they tend to destabilise in social environments characterised by wide and variable networks where weak social ties predominate (as discussed in Chapter 2). Since they appear to function in interaction successfully, even if they are fairly approximate representations of the target standard item (microsocial perspective), their non-standard forms are fit enough to survive if employed for recognisable meanings; through repeated accommodation the items diffuse in ELF communities, which again reflects their role in a macrosocial frame of reference.

Notes

1. These are taken from the 50 best differentiators distinguishing ELFA from MICASE (see Appendix 3), using Wordsmith Tools Keywords. The comparison produces a rank-ordered list of the most frequent items, and shows which ones best differentiate one corpus from the other, that is, which items are proportionally more frequent in the 'primary' corpus compared to the reference corpus. These are thus the words that are significantly more frequent in ELFA than MICASE.
2. Even though the tendencies are not equally strong, so that the greater use of *the* in ELFA is the clearer tendency, it is helpful to see them as interrelated.
3. Small capitals stand for both forms *the same* and ø *same* i.e. the lemma.
4. *That* is the 7th most frequent word in ELFA (N= 18,995) but *which* the 46th (N= 3,941). In MICASE, *that* is the 5th (21,667 pmw), *which* the 75th (2,222 pmw).

5. Unless we adopt simplification as an overarching cover term in Meisel's (1980) way, and add modifiers like 'elaborative' to keep it alive. This, however, raises the question of how useful a concept is if it is stretched this far: if simplicity includes elaboration, it begins to lose some of its meaningfulness.
6. Note, however that Dröschel's (2011) study of Lingua Franca English among Swiss speakers found little non-native use of either the progressive or embedded questions.
7. The precise figures for *case* (817 hits altogether): *in this case* (182); *in the case of* (61); *in that case* (28); *in your case* (19); *in any case* (17); *in case of* (13).
8. The 25 most common trigrams of both corpora are listed in Appendix 4.
9. Listed in Appendix 4.
10. Of the conversational features, ELFA showed two against five in MICASE, whereas of the academic prose features ELFA had two, but MICASE only one.
11. Karhukorpi's data was so efficiently anonymised that it is impossible to tell the first language of the examples, but her group consisted of L1 speakers of Finnish, German, and Swedish, the speakers were not the same person, and the course was run using ELF.

References

Aston, G. (1995) 'Corpora in language pedagogy: matching theory and practice', in Cook, G. and Seidlhofer, B. (eds.) *Principle and Practice in Applied Linguistics: Studies in Honour of HG Widdowson*, Oxford: Oxford University Press, 257–70.

Aston, G., Bernardini, S. and Stewart, D. (eds.) (2004) *Corpora and Language Learners*, Amsterdam: John Benjamins.

Biber, D. (2006) *University Language: A Corpus-Based Study of Spoken and Written Registers*, Amsterdam: John Benjamins.

Biber, D. and Gray, B. (2010) 'Challenging stereotypes about academic writing: complexity, elaboration, explicitness', *Journal of English for Academic Purposes* 1 (19): 2–20.

Biber, D., Conrad, S. and Cortes, V. (2004) '*If you look at…*: lexical bundles in university teaching and textbooks', *Applied Linguistics* 25: 371–405.

Biber, D., Johansson, S., Leech, G., Conrad, S. and Finegan, E. (1999) *The Longman Grammar of Spoken and Written English*, London: Pearson.

Björkman, B. (2008a) '"So where we are": spoken lingua franca English at a Swedish technical university', *English Today* 24 (2): 11–17.

Björkman, B. (2008b) 'English as the lingua franca of engineering: the morphosyntax of academic speech events', *Nordic Journal of English Studies* 7 (3): 103–22.

Björkman, B. (2009) 'From code to discourse in spoken ELF', in Mauranen, A. and Ranta, E. (eds.) *English as a Lingua Franca: Studies and Findings*, Newcastle upon Tyne: Cambridge Scholars Publishing, 225–53.

Burnard, L. and McEnery, T. (eds.) (2000) *Rethinking Language Pedagogy from a Corpus Perspective*, Frankfurt: Peter Lang.

Bybee, J. L. and Hopper, P. (2001) 'Introduction to frequency and the emergence of linguistic structure', in Bybee, J. L. and Hopper, P. (eds.) *Frequency and the Emergence of Linguistic Structure*, Amsterdam: John Benjamins, 1–24.

Channell, J. (1994) *Vague Language*, Oxford: Oxford University Press.
Cheng, W. and Warren, M. (2001) 'The use of vague language in intercultural conversations in Hong Kong', *English World-Wide* 22: 81–104.
Corder, S. P. (1973) *Introducing Applied Linguistics*, Middlesex: Penguin.
Cutting, J. (2006) 'Spoken grammar: vague language and EAP', in Hughes, R. (ed.) *Spoken English, TESOL and Applied Linguistics*, New York: Palgrave Macmillan, 159–81.
Dabrowska, E. (2004) *Language, Mind and Brain: Some Psychological and Neurological Constraints on Theories of Grammar*, Edinburgh: Edinburgh University Press.
De Cock, S., Granger, S., Leech, G. and McEnery, T. (1998) 'An automated approach to the phrasicon of EFL learners', in Granger S. (ed.), *Learner English on Computer*, London: Longman, 67–79.
Dewey, M. (2006) 'English as a Lingua Franca: an empirical study of innovation in lexis and grammar', unpublished PhD thesis, King's College London.
Doughty, C. J. and Long, M. H. (eds.) (2003) *Handbook of Second Language Acquisition*, Oxford: Blackwell.
Dröschel, Y. (2011) *Lingua Franca English: The Role of Simplification and Transfer*, Bern: Peter Lang.
Du Bois, J. W. (2003) 'Discourse and grammar', in Tomasello, M. (ed.) *The New Psychology of Language*, vol. II, Mahwah, NJ: Lawrence Erlbaum, 47–87.
Ellis, N. C. (1996) 'Sequencing in SLA: phonological memory, chunking, and points of order', *SSLA* 18: 91–126.
Ellis, N. C. (2002) 'Frequency effects in language processing: a review with implications for theories of implicit and explicit language acquisition', *Studies in Second Language Acquisition* 24 (2): 143–88.
Ellis, R. (2008) *The Study of Second Language Acquisition* (2nd edn), Oxford: Oxford University Press.
Erman, B. and Warren, B. (2000) 'The idiom principle and the open choice principle', *Text* 20 (1): 87–120.
Field, J. (2003) *Psycholinguistics*, London: Routledge.
Fillmore, C. J., Kay, P. and O'Connor, M. (1988) 'Regularity and idiomaticity in grammatical constructions: the case of "let alone"', *Language* 64 (3): 501–38.
Ford, C. E., Fox, B. A. and Thompson, S. A. (2003) 'Social interaction and grammar', in Tomasello, M. (ed.) *The New Psychology of Language*, vol. II, Mahwah, NJ: Lawrence Erlbaum, 119–43.
Gellerstam, M. (1996) 'Translation as a source for cross-linguistic studies', in Aijmer, K., Altenberg, B. and Johansson, M. (eds.) *Languages in Contrast*, Lund: Studentlitteratur, 53–62.
Gilquin, G. and Paquot, M. (2008) 'Too chatty: learner academic writing and register variation', *English Text Construction* 1 (1): 41–61.
Gilquin G., Granger, S. and Paquot, M. (2007) 'Learner corpora: the missing link in EAP pedagogy', *Journal of English for Academic Purposes* 6 (4): 319–35.
Granger S. (ed.) (1998) *Learner English on Computer*, London: Longman.

Granger, S., Hung, J. and Petch-Tyson, S. (eds.) (2002) *Computer Learner Corpora, Second Language Acquisition and Foreign Language Teaching*, Amsterdam: John Benjamins.

Huckin, T. and Pesante, L. (1988) 'Existential *there', Written Communication* 5 (3): 368–91.

Hülmbauer, C. (2009) '"We don't take the right way. We just take the way we think you will understand" – the shifting relationship between correctness and effectiveness in ELF', in Mauranen, A. and Ranta, E. (eds.) *English as a Lingua Franca: Studies and Findings*, Newcastle upon Tyne: Cambridge Scholars Publishing, 323–47.

Hunston, S. and Francis, G. (2000) *Pattern Grammar: A Corpus-Driven Approach to the Lexical Grammar of English*, Amsterdam: John Benjamins.

Hynninen, N. (2010) '"We try to to to speak all the time in easy sentences" – student conceptions of ELF interaction', *English as a Lingua Franca*. Special issue of *Helsinki English Studies* (ed. A. Mauranen and N. Hynninen) 6: 29–43.

Jarvis, S. and Odlin, T. (2000) 'Morphological type, spatial reference, and language transfer', *Studies in Second Language Acquisition* 22: 535–56.

Johns, T. and King, P. (eds.) (1991) *Classroom Concordancing*, ELR Journal 4, University of Birmingham.

Karhukorpi, J. (2006) 'Negotiating opinions in lingua franca e-mail discussion groups: discourse structure, hedges and repair in online communication', unpublished licenciate thesis, University of Turku.

Kaunisto, M. (2004) 'Adjective Pairs Ending in -ic and -ical: A Study of Variation and Change Across Centuries', PhD thesis, University of Tampere.

Kortmann, B. and Szmrecsanyi, B. (2004) 'Global synopsis: morphological and syntactic variation in English', in Kortmann, B., Burridge, K., Mesthrie, R., Schneider, E. W. and Upton, C. (eds.) *A Handbook of Varieties of English*, Berlin: Mouton de Gruyter, 1122–82.

Lakoff, G. (1987) *Women, Fire, and Dangerous Things*, Chicago: University of Chicago Press.

Levelt, W. (1989) *Speaking*, Cambridge, MA: MIT.

Master, P. (1997) 'The English article system: acquisition, function, and pedagogy', *System* 25: 215–32.

Mauranen, A. (1999) 'What sort of theme is *there*? A translational perspective', *Languages in Contrast* 2 (1): 57–86.

Mauranen, A. (2000) 'Strange strings in translated language: a study on corpora', in Olohan, M. (ed.) *Intercultural Faultlines: Research Models in Translation Studies 1: Textual and Cognitive Aspects*, Manchester: St Jerome Publishing, 119–41.

Mauranen, A. (2004) 'Talking academic: a corpus approach to academic speech', in Aijmer, K. (ed.) *Dialogue Analysis VIII: Understanding and Misunderstanding in Dialogue*,Tübingen: Max Niemeyer, 201–17.

Mauranen, A. (2010) 'Discourse reflexivity: a discourse universal? The case of ELF', *Nordic Journal of English Studies*, 13–40.

Meisel, J. (1980) 'Linguistic simplification', in Felix, S. (ed.) *Second Language Development: Trends and Issues*, Tübingen: Gunter Narr, 13–40.

McCarthy, M. (1998) *Spoken Language and Applied Linguistics*, Cambridge: Cambridge University Press.

Metsä-Ketelä, M. (2006) '"Words are more or less superfluous": the case of *more or less* in academic lingua franca English', *English as a Lingua Franca*. Special issue of *The Nordic Journal of English Studies* (ed. A. Mauranen and M. Metsä-Ketelä) 5 (2): 117–43.

Metsä-Ketelä, M. (forthcoming) 'Vague expressions and their communicative functions in *Lingua Franca* English', PhD thesis, University of Tampere.

Mollin, S. (2006) 'English as a lingua franca: a new variety in the new Expanding Circle?', *English as a Lingua Franca*. Special Issue of *The Nordic Journal of English Studies* (ed. A. Mauranen and M. Metsä-Ketelä) 5 (2): 41–58.

Moon, R. (1998) *Fixed Expressions and Idioms in English*, Oxford: Clarendon.

Mukherjee, J. and Hundt, M. (eds.) (2011) *Exploring Second-Language Varieties of English and Learner Englishes*, Amsterdam: John Benjamins.

Myles, F. and Mitchell, R. (2004) *Second Language Learning Theories* (2nd edn), London: Arnold.

Nattinger, J. R. and DeCarrico, J. (1992) *Lexical Phrases and Language Teaching*, Oxford: Oxford University Press.

Nesselhauf, N. (2005) *Collocations in a Learner Corpus*, Amsterdam: John Benjamins.

Nevalainen, T. (2009) 'Number agreement in existential constructions: a sociolinguistic study of eighteenth-century English', in Filppula, M., Klemola, J. and Paulasto, H. (eds.) *Vernacular Universals and Language Contacts: Evidence from Varieties of English and Beyond*, London: Routledge, 80–102.

Nikula, T. (1996) *Pragmatic Force Modifiers: A Study in Interlanguage Pragmatics*, Jyväskylä: University of Jyväskylä.

Östman, J.-O. and Fried, M. (eds.) (2005) *Construction Grammars: Cognitive Grounding and Theoretical Extensions*, Amsterdam: John Benjamins.

Pagel, M., Atkinson, D. Q. and Meade, A. (2007) 'Frequency of word-use predicts rates of lexical evolution throughout Indo-European history', *Nature* 449 (11): 717–20.

Pawley, A. and Syder, F. H. (1983) 'Two puzzles for linguistic theory: nativelike selection and nativelike fluency', in Richards, J. C. and Schmidt, R. W. (eds.) *Language and Communication*, London: Longman, 191–225.

Promodrou, L. (2008) *English as a Lingua Franca: A Corpus-Based Analysis*, London: Continuum.

Ranta, E. (2006) 'The "attractive" progressive: why use the *-ing* form in English as a lingua franca?', *English as a Lingua Franca*. Special Issue of *The Nordic Journal of English Studies* (ed. A. Mauranen and M. Metsä-Ketelä) 5 (2): 95–116.

Ranta, E. (2009) 'Syntactic features in spoken ELF: learner language or spoken grammar?', in Mauranen, A. and Ranta, E. (eds.) *English as a Lingua Franca: Studies and Findings*, Newcastle upon Tyne: Cambridge Scholars Publishing, 84–106.

Ringbom, H. (1993) *Near-Native Proficiency in English*, Turku: English Department Publications, Abo Akademi University.

Ringbom, H. (1998) 'Vocabulary frequencies in advanced learner English: a cross-linguistic approach', in Granger, S. (ed.) *Learner English on Computer*, London: Longman, 41–52.

Römer, U. (2005) *Progressives, Patterns, Pedagogy*, Amsterdam: John Benjamins.

Sankoff, G. (2002) 'Linguistic outcomes of language contact', in Chambers, J. K., Trudgill, P. and Schilling-Estes, N. (eds.) *The Handbook of Language Variation and Change*, Oxford: Blackwell, 638–68.

Seidlhofer, B. (2004) 'Research perspectives on teaching English as a lingua franca', *Annual Review of Applied Linguistics* 24: 209–39.

Selinker, L. (1972) 'Interlanguage', *IRAL* 10 (3): 209–31.

Silva-Corvalan, C. (1998) 'On borrowing as a mechanism of syntactic change', in Schwegler, A., Tranel, B. and Uribe-Etcxebarria, M. (eds.) *Romance Linguistics: Theoretical Perspectives*, Amsterdam: John Benjamins, 225–46.

Sinclair, J. McH. (1991) *Corpus Concordance Collocation*, Oxford: Oxford University Press.

Sinclair, J. McH. (1992/2004) 'Trust the text', in Ravelli, L. and Davies, M. (eds.) *Advances in Systemic Linguistics: Recent Theory and Practice,*. London: Pinter, 1–19. Reprinted in Sinclair, *Trust the Text: Language, Corpus and Discourse*, London: Routledge, 9–23.

Sinclair, J. McH. (2004a) 'The search for units of meaning', in Sinclair, *Trust the Text: Language, Corpus and Discourse*, London: Routledge, 24–48.

Sinclair, J. McH. and Mauranen, A. (2006) *Linear Unit Grammar*, Amsterdam: John Benjamins.

Stubbs, M. (1996) *Text and Corpus Analysis*, Oxford: Blackwell.

Swales, J. M. and Burke, A. (2003) '"It's really fascinating work": differences in evaluative adjectives across academic registers', in Meyer, C. and Leistyna, P. (eds.) *Corpus Analysis: Language Structure and Use*, Amsterdam: Rodopi, 1–18.

Szmrecsanyi, B. and Kortmann, B. (2011) 'Typological profiling: learner English versus indigenized L2 varieties of English', in Mukherjee, J. and Hundt, M. (eds.) *Exploring Second-Language Varieties of English and Learner Englishes*, Amsterdam: John Benjamins, 167–87.

Tagliamonte, S. A. (2009). 'There *was* universals; then there *weren't*: a comparative sociolinguistic perspective on "default singulars"', in Filppula, M., Klemola, J. and Paulasto, H. (eds.), *Vernacular Universals and Language Contacts: Evidence from Varieties of English and Beyond*, London: Routledge, 103–29.

Thomason, S. G. (2001) *Language Contact*, Edinburgh: Edinburgh University Press.

Ventola, E. and Mauranen, A. (1991) 'Non-native writing and native revising of scientific articles', in Ventola, E. (ed.) *Functional and Systemic Linguistics: Approaches and Uses*, Berlin: Mouton de Gruyter, 457–92.

Wray, A. (2002) *Formulaic Language and the Lexicon*, Cambridge: Cambridge University Press.

6 *Discourse explicitness*

When people find themselves talking in a foreign language to others who are also using a foreign language, they adapt to the circumstances immediately. Speakers seem to be guided by a general awareness that there is much less certainty about shared ground, and that they need to take special care to make themselves understood and be prepared for unfamiliar features in their interlocutor's speech. Although much that passes is familiar and similar to what anyone says and does in their first languages, there is a strong element of uncertainty and unpredictability in conversations using a lingua franca. In the case of ELF in particular, a site of complex second-order language contact, speakers need to cope with diversity and unpredictability on many fronts simultaneously, as it were, to deal with 'superdiversity' (Vertovec 2006). This makes demands on speakers and calls for heightened sensitivity to interlocutors' communicative intentions and responses. Being attuned to the social environment helps cope with this task and attend to relevant cues from the interlocutor so as to adapt one's own behaviour appropriately.

A natural way of coping with unpredictability is enhancing clarity. People typically adjust their speech towards clearer and more explicit expression when faced with communicative uncertainties; for instance, speaking to people they meet for the first time, very young or very old people, people under visible stress or pain, and so on. Clarity and explicitness serve speakers' interests by increasing their chances of getting their contributions understood as intended. But more than that, clarifying and explicating strategies are cooperative: participants have common interests to achieve communication, and striving for clarity is a way of working towards this goal together. Speakers cooperate to keep things going, to share and develop understanding, arguments, and knowledge.

A tendency to enhance explicitness on crossing cultural and linguistic boundaries is known from other environments, too, notably from translation. One of the best established 'translation universals' (Baker 1993; Mauranen 2007a) is that translators add clarifying matter to the text as they translate, which in turn has the effect that translated texts are regularly longer than their originals (Johansson 1998). This translational feature has been termed 'explicitation' by Blum-Kulka (1986). Similar tendencies have been observed in lingua franca discourse (Cogo & Dewey 2006; Mauranen 2007b): speakers raise the level of explicitness to help hearers keep track, to secure uptake of their intended meanings, and to show cooperativeness. Conversely, in the listener's role, it has been noted that ELF speakers tend to support the current speaker by signalling listenership, i.e. indicating understanding with encouraging feedback in a similar manner to native speakers in L1–L2 interaction (Kurhila 2003). Explicitness seems to facilitate the conveying of message content, and thereby serve the content orientation reportedly characteristic of ELF speech (cf. Chapter 2). At the same time it is no less important in managing interaction. In this chapter both the content and the interactional aspects will be addressed. The chapter focuses on some principal means of making discourse explicit especially as it concerns discourse organising: metadiscourse, local organising, and topic negotiation are under the spotlight. The next chapter picks up a different angle on related themes, and looks at speakers' clarificatory strategies through their use of repetition and rephrasing. Unlike the last two, more corpus-based chapters, this chapter looks into topics best addressed with discourse analysis, and mostly draws on transcript samples from the ELFA corpus.

6.1 Metadiscourse

Human language has the fascinating capacity of being able to talk about itself. This reflexivity (Lyons 1977), or metalanguage, is apparently not shared by even the most sophisticated animal communication systems as far as we know. It is among the features that distinguishes humans from animals, along with a theory of mind, exceptional short-term memory capacity, and a high level of self-awareness. Thus, we can say things like *I was gonna say* ... or *I'm very glad you brought that up*, and we use such expressions regularly for navigating through conversations, managing meanings and interaction on the way. This self-referential capacity, which has surfaced in linguistic research since Roman Jakobson's work in the 1950s, is a fundamental aspect of language.

A very early study of metalanguage in discourse was Schiffrin (1980) on 'metatalk', which analysed language about language in speech, in a somewhat provisional way. It was nevertheless in written text analysis that metadiscourse research more widely took off around the late 1980s (Crismore 1989; Vande Kopple 1985; Mauranen 1993a, 1993b), with a special interest in academic text.

Metatext or metadiscourse research has retained a central position in text studies ever since (see e.g. Hyland 2005; Ädel 2006; papers in Ädel & Mauranen 2010), but even today there is little investigation of spoken metadiscourse in proportion to the field as a whole. Among the exceptions are Luukka (1992) and Ädel (2010), who have compared written and spoken data in academic contexts and Mauranen's (2001, 2002a, 2003a, 2004a) analyses of ENL academic speech. In ELF, there has understandably been much less work so far, but what there is has taken speaking, not writing, on board: Penz (2008, 2009) has investigated metadiscourse in professional groups speaking ELF and Mauranen (2005, 2007b, 2010) has studied it in academic ELF speech. Both have found that ELF speakers make ample use of metadiscourse. Other studies on ELF speech strategies have touched upon metadiscourse somewhat tangentially (Firth & Wagner 1997; Meierkord 1998), generally noting that ELF speakers do not engage in much negotiation of ambiguity, with metadiscourse casually subsumed under this general heading, but instead let things pass and 'make them normal' (Firth 1996). This early research was far less clear about the nature of ELF than the studies in this millennium and generally worked on very restricted data, so that it makes more sense to say that ELF research on metadiscourse is very recent.

As metadiscourse studies have proliferated in the last 20 years or so, they have also diversified. Less so in their continued focus on writing, especially in academia, but notably in their definition of the object of study. Besides the conceptualisation of language as a self-referential, reflexive system, broader notions of metadiscourse have been employed from fairly early days (Vande Kopple 1985; Crismore 1989). Widening the scope of metadiscourse beyond reflexivity probably reflected a growing awareness in linguistics of the interactive aspects of language. Since the 1980s linguists have become increasingly aware that interpersonal features are ubiquitous and that even the most objective-looking written text incorporates an interactive dimension. As it has been the objective kind of written text that has attracted the bulk of metadiscourse studies, this data type may also have affected conceptual preferences. The interactivity of text, in effect its speech-like characteristics, were a new revelation in text-linguistic studies and understandably became the centre of attention.

The all-encompassing notion of metadiscourse as comprising everything that is non-propositional in text, the Hallidayan 'non-ideational' text matter, or what lies outside Sinclair's 'autonomous plane' (1992/2004), has by now largely served its purpose of raising awareness about the nature of written text. Research into interactive aspects of language has expanded and diversified enormously since the early eighties. Studies of hedging, discourse particles, stance, evaluation, vagueness, etc. have undergone remarkable development and turned into burgeoning research fields in their own right.

It is not fruitful for the pursuit of insightful descriptions of language to subsume all interactional matter under metadiscourse. To take hedging as an example, a tendency can be observed of hedging to co-occur with metadiscourse in both ENL (e.g. Mauranen 2001, 2003a) and in ELF (Mauranen 2005, 2009). I have called this 'discourse collocation', because it is an attraction between two discourse phenomena, not between lexical items (as in collocation) or grammatical items (as in colligation). The likely explanation can be sought in the nature of social interaction: while metadiscourse imposes the speaker's perspective on the discourse, it not only clarifies things to hearers, but also reduces the negotiability of interpretations. One of the principal uses of hedging, on the other hand, is to open up for negotiation the meanings being made in ongoing discourse. The combination of hedging and metadiscourse thus serves to restore a balance between effectively putting forth a speaker perspective and keeping it negotiable. That this combination appears in ELF suggests it is not confined to Anglo-American cultural environments, or a manifestation of a native command of English, but is a more fundamental feature of discourse. Now, if we opt for a very broad conceptualisation of metadiscourse, subsuming hedging within it, we lose insights of this kind, because they all count as instances of metadiscourse – possibly of different types, but their co-occurrence and above all their individual contributions are easily lost in such accounts. Similar cases could be made for evaluation, stance, or presenting a persona, for example. Ädel (2006) is an example of a successful analysis of texts with a framework that has a clear theoretical foundation in a careful definition of a 'focused' view of metadiscourse, limiting it to text about the current text itself, and expressions of writer–reader interaction in it (Ädel 2006: 44, see also Ädel 2010).

To maintain a clear distinction from the integrative approach to metadiscourse, I have often preferred to use the term 'discourse reflexivity' for discourse about the ongoing discourse. Here I use the terms interchangeably when there is no danger of confusion, because 'metadiscourse' has become a widely known and established term, despite its many interpretations.

Metadiscourse makes discourse organisation explicit – hence its generally recognised role as 'guiding the reader' through the text. In speaking, metadiscourse serves similar functions: it helps organise discourse by signalling beginnings, changes of tack, and endings of sequences of interaction. It also helps to make predictions about what is to come, and review what has passed. It communicates speakers' intentions with respect to the functions of their own speech acts, and their understanding of their interlocutors' turns. There are other means of organising discourse and making it explicit, but talking about language is among the most flexible and sophisticated.

When spoken discourse replaces written text as the object of metadiscourse analysis, certain key parameters are immediately altered, with inevitable consequences for analytical models. Because speaking takes place with hearers present, relating to the immediate environment, it looks outward to the circumstances of talking. Speech is therefore necessarily situation-focused. In monologues, such as lectures and conference presentations (which were the exclusive data of Luukka's 1992 work), the difference between written and spoken text need not be dramatic; it is dialogic speech that brings forth alterations.

6.1.1 Metadiscourse in monologue

Let me just quickly go through these similarities between spoken and written metadiscourse with some examples before moving on to the major differences. In monologues, especially if they have been prepared in advance, such as lectures or presentations, speakers prospect ahead, make retrospective references, resume earlier topics, and make transitions, much like writers. Extended turns in discussions have similar features in a more limited way. Example (6.1) from a conference presentation illustrates these prospective and retrospective uses: it first reminds hearers of what ground has been covered so far (*we have been looking at*), where the speaker is going next (*we shall now see*), and finally resumes an earlier point on which the upcoming talk is going to build (*as mentioned previously*).

(6.1)

> ... *we have been looking at* (xx) ... symbolic content with which is it is adorned, *we shall now, see* how all this applies to the catalan case. *as mentioned, as mentioned previously* the foundation ...

These organising elements often label the function of the talk ahead (*by way of illustration let us now consider*) or just covered (*this was just a brief presentation I gave you*). Instead of making promises about what will follow, they can act as disclaimers, indicating what is *not* to be expected (*my lecture will not deal with Catalonia as a whole*).

Reflexive discourse points out which parts of the talk are the important ones, thus indicating priorities and emphases (*my point is*). Speakers also engage in what we might call 'reflexive commentary' when they talk about their terminological or conceptual choices metadiscursively (6.2):

(6.2)

> ... *we can indeed speak, in terms of* a symbolic nationalist landscape

In monologue, speakers even refer to their hearers much like writers refer to their readers as readers (*so here you clearly see that* ...). As in writing, we can identify such other-oriented discourse in instances like the following, where the speaker addresses hearers directly (6.3):

(6.3)

> ... in europe *if you may know* appreciation of hostile rough and rugged landscapes such as mountains or marshlands, is real real relatively recent ...

These can provide a platform for a passage to be launched, as if in preparation for a topic providing an explanation of why something is taken up, as in (6.4), which prompts a hearer to expect some sketch of Catalan geography to follow:

(6.4)

> ... *i don't know if you are familiar with* the catalan geography

The 'here-and-now' nature of spoken presentation means that situational deixis is used a fair amount of the time. As visuals normally accompany presentations, references to what hearers can see are intertwined with metadiscursive commentary (6.5):

(6.5)

> ... *here we have a statement er which i'm not going to read aloud* it's taken from the main page of this people first network website ...

Presenters also keep verbalising when something unexpected happens, such as a mistake with their visuals (*oh sorry*), and pepper their presentations with small verbal responses to minor problems as they go along (*oh what's that*):

(6.6)

> ... *we can see here the main reasons* for people sending e-mail from the rurals rural stations *i'd like to* ***oh what's that****, i'd like to point out that* er

er the profiles user profiles and the reasons for communicating are a little bit different

Deixis seems to replace the more elaborate references to what recipients can see for themselves in written metadiscourse (*as can be seen in Table 3*). The references nevertheless seem to serve similar functions. The monologic uses of metadiscourse are indeed not far from written discourse.

6.1.2 Metadiscourse in dialogue

Turning to dialogue, the departure from writing is more radical. Given the much greater demands that dialogue makes on interactional management, discourse reflexivity plays a larger and more multifarious part in fast-evolving social interaction. Language about language is an instrument for navigating the joint construction of messages in interaction. Speaker and hearer roles alternate constantly between participants, sometimes very quickly, and always in real time; participants must relate to each other actively all the time, making their contributions relevant to the changing states of the discourse. Discourse reflexivity helps operate the staging of the discourse and keep track of the mutual relevance of participants' turns.

While dialogic metadiscourse performs some relatively similar tasks to monologue, others arise only in relation to what other speakers say: speakers indicate how their speech relates to the current state of the discourse, how their contributions are to be taken, how they understand their interlocutors' speech, and what needs clarification. We can discern something of a continuum from pre-planned monologue to spontaneous dialogue, as suggested, for example, by Tanskanen (2000). Eggins and Slade have also observed in their analysis of casual conversation that longer turns, or 'extended turns', tend to have considerable internal organisation, as opposed to 'chat', where the characteristically rapid turn changes do not allow for much internal organisation (1997: 227). However, even in those functions where dialogue is comparatively similar to monologue, dialogue manifests a far more pronounced and explicit orientation to others. Participants must cooperate with each other to construct arguments, agreements and disagreements, judge the relevance of contributions to the points that are made, introduce and conclude topics. Participants have their own agendas, and competition is part of dialogic discourse.

Let us look at a straightforward example of a seminar discussion, which is not particularly argumentative, but working out a description and an interpretation. The talk is concerned primarily with reporting back on field observations and discussing their import. The discipline is occupational health, and S2 is a senior staff member chairing the session.

(6.7)

<S2> yeah but *if we take now the the paper mill first and then go after a while to the to the institute of occupational health then* </S2>
<S1> *and how* <S9> [yeah] </S9> *[about] the maintaining* because i i i think that the mo- most of them are working with er with maintaining situations and </S1>
<S8> yes </S8>
<BS7> yeah [80 85 are in the technical] </BS7>
<S1> [so so they are they are not just sitting] there </S1>
<BS7> technical but er 15 are administrators </BS7>
<S2> yeah so the education for for most of the people is something engi- engineering or technical </S2>
<S8> yes most of [them] </S8>
<BS7> [yeah] [(xx)] </BS7>
<S2> [most of them] </S2>
<S10> most of them are engineering </S10>
<S1> i i i think that </S1>
<S8> [well technical personnel (*they would be called*)] </S8>
<S1> [maybe not maybe] just technicals </S1>
<SU> technical </SU>
<S2> mhm yeah </S2>
<BS7> yeah technicals perhaps yeah </BS7>
<S9> [so this blue-col-] </S9>
<S5> [erm i'm you know] i'm getting @a bit@ confused </S5>
<S9> yeah [there's a] </S9>
<S5> [*are*] *we talking about the paper mill* </S5>
<S9> [*yeah paper mill*] </S9>
<SS> [*yes mhm-hm*] </SS>
<S2> [*pa-*] *paper mill we are talking about the paper mill now* [*first*] </S2>
<S9> [yeah] this blue-collar job er it involves people like the operators who operate it from the computer and see whether the machines operate in the way they suppose to be and there are also workers in the the paper the finishing part they were also the blue-collar <S2> yeah </S2> workers yeah </S9>

The extract illustrates the process of co-constructing discourse in a polylogic speech event. Several participants contribute to the emerging message, often speaking at the same time and vying for turns. They overlap and interrupt each other. Clearly, different participants have their own agendas as well as different interpretations of what was significant in the environment observed for reporting, and also of the terms that apply (I shall return to the negotiation of terms in Chapter 7). At the same time, cooperation features prominently: participants align their turns to those of others, repeat each other's wordings, use back-channelling (*mhm*), and employ numerous agreement markers (*yeah*, *yes*, *mhm-hm*). Thus, we can see competition and cooperation simultaneously at work, with cooperation underpinning the competition – without cooperation no communication would be achieved at all.

To turn to metadiscourse specifically, the chair (S2) in lines 1–2 makes an organising move. While it is a perfectly conventional move on the part of a chairperson, it immediately illuminates the distinction between monologic and dialogic discourse: the chair is not organising his own talk, but that of the entire speech event, with consequences for other speakers' freedom of movement. As can be seen, the distinction between managing language and managing the situation gets somewhat blurred – to a notable extent, the discourse constitutes the situation, it does not just take place within a situational frame. Although chairpersons do have duties and privileges, they do not hold dictatorial rights in academic genres. Immediately, in lines 3 to 5, one of the student participants (S1) chips in to suggest an addition to the agenda, which concerns maintenance work (*maintaining*, as her approximation goes). After some talking, another student (S5, line 23) makes a metadiscursive move: he interrupts a fellow student and shifts the discourse onto the interactive plane (cf. Sinclair 1992/2004) by first indicating that he is confused (line 23). This does not throw others off the track, as S9 apparently continues developing the topic. But again he gets interrupted by S5, who continues his metadiscursive intervention (line 25). S5 now makes it explicit that it is the discourse topic he is talking about, and this elicits a series of relevant responses, both from S9 and simultaneously from several students collectively (line 27), then from the chair, who confirms their responses. An immediate return to the 'autonomous plane' follows, that is, to the contents, or 'message', and S9 resumes his topic, successfully finishing a turn without further interruptions.

6.1.3 Other-oriented metadiscourse

As the last example in the previous section showed, one clear difference between monologic and dialogic metadiscourse is in interactional management. In addition to regulating turn-taking, management metadiscourse imposes structure and order on the situation as a whole. The next three examples illustrate these basic types, showing how metadiscourse helps to take the floor (6.8), to yield or offer the floor (6.9), and impose order on the situation (6.10):

(6.8)

> *erm i wanted to say that er generally ...*

(6.9)

> *... would you like to explain it for us ...*

(6.10)

> *... we shall we talk about gender difference that's the main focus*

At least equally important and perhaps less obvious, or at least less visible in metadiscourse research, is what we might call 'other-orientation' in dialogue. Dialogic exchanges are characterised by a far more prominent and explicit orientation to other people who are present than is discernible in monologue even when it is rich in interactive signalling. This comes out in sharp relief in the co-construction of arguments, which is particularly typical of academic genres. We can roughly distinguish three main roles in other-oriented reflexivity. Let us call these 'elucidation', 'interpretation', and 'springboard'.

1. **Elucidation.** The speaker wants the previous speaker to clarify, confirm, or expand on what he or she has said (6.11).

(6.11)

> <S1> i- is you are you *are you saying that* er, the imagery of which the mountains are part this imagery of landscape ...

2. **Interpretation.** The speaker offers an interpretation of what the previous speaker meant.

(6.12)

> ... using quantification over possible worlds *so you're saying* things ...

3. **Springboard.** The speaker paraphrases the previous speaker's meaning as a point of departure for a new direction in the discussion.

(6.13)

<S1>... er i found this really interesting that *the mention that you made* about er, common defence of the territory or ways m- modern (world) is becoming er an important platform for political mobilisation with new activism er and this somehow er, er instead of political parties er acting as as important points of reference for these movements i i think this is something that is going on (over all) er, there seem to be various ideologies ...

These kinds of metadiscourse affect interaction differently: while elucidation requires a response from the hearer addressed, interpretation leaves them such an option, but does not necessarily assign an obligation to respond. The third type, springboard, virtually precludes a hearer response, securing the floor to the current speaker. Springboard is an other-oriented way of constructing arguments, a fitting illustration of co-constructing argumentative discourse, where the speakers develop points that their interlocutors have made, take them to new directions, or take pains to refute them. It appears more common than the other kinds in the ELFA corpus (Mauranen 2009).

In the competitive and cooperative activity of 'doing dialogue', speakers also make self-references, for example to offer their interpretations of what is going on (6.14), to justify themselves (6.15), or to make evaluations (6.16).

(6.14)

but but er *what i'm gathering here is that* it's this is more about it is catalonia that is being protected and not not any environment

(6.15)

... it's one er of the reasons that *i explained why* er (xx) has emerged almost 25 years of the

(6.16)

<S4> ... and thinking of whether this is a environmental movement or something else *i think it's very interesting question* and er because one of the, one could say maybe paradoxes ...

In the dialogic construction of arguments, self-references also serve to emphasise the speaker's self-consistency, especially with *what I'm saying* and *I'm not saying*, much along the lines discovered earlier with ENL seminar discussions (Craig & Sanusi 2000; Mauranen 2004b), as can be seen in (6.17) and (6.18). For resuming earlier stages of the argument, self-references are a useful means of promoting the speaker's position and making it appear consistent (6.19).

(6.17)

<S2> ... *what i'm saying is* that er, this is less and less politically useful, erm because ...

(6.18)

<S2> ... but until now the situation is like that, so, *i don't say that this i'm not saying* that these mobilisations are ...

(6.19)

... provokes *as i said* the necessity of er finding er mhm elements, in the landscape

Speaker and hearer references are complex in polylogic interaction: the two discourse roles available, 'I' and 'you', alternate quickly between participants (cf. Sinclair & Mauranen 2006), in contradistinction to monologic discourse, where the references maintain comparative stability and consequently develop a particular speaker–audience relationship. In polyadic talk, the discourse roles in themselves are fairly abstract, but on the other hand the participants are more personally involved than in the relative safety of monologic one-to-many speaking. Participants' face needs must therefore be attended to; discourse reflexivity can play a part in this in its role of indicating how the speaker intends his or her meaning to be taken. These expressions range from relatively straightforward announcements of how the upcoming turn is to be understood (6.20 and 6.21) to clearer disclaimers indicating awareness that something might be taken negatively (6.22 and 6.23), and to forewarnings that what follows is going to be negative (6.24 to 6.26).

(6.20)

... because i think that well *let's put it as a question* can there be a quality as such independently from ...

(6.21)

... or i- *if i, put it more clearly* where can we see this culture ...

(6.22)

... then just some minor things *nothing to criticize you* ...

(6.23)

... *i'm also going to put it a bit more sharply* than you do yourself, on the relationship between ...

(6.24)

... *to put it blunt if you put it a bit bluntly* ... so that's what i find problematic

(6.25)

... *this is not criticism but* ...

(6.26)

... *now i'm going to be nasty* ...

The last two are similar to what Brown and Levinson (1987: 171–2) call 'hedges addressed to politeness strategies' as they directly notify the hearer of a face threat that follows (see also Riekkinen 2009 who discusses them as lexical hedges). As the examples show, ELF speakers are quite adept at performing such facework, and not much held back by the constraints of operating in a foreign language. Hedges overlap in part with modality and accomplish similar things in interaction. It is therefore interesting at this point to note that Mortensen's (2010) findings on modal expressions in ELF student group-work discussions were in essence like those in L1–L1 discussions, whether the L1 was English or Danish. It would seem that hedging and modality are used in both interactive and epistemic functions in much the same ways, at least in comparable genre contexts.

6.1.4 Ongoing discourse and beyond

A few speech-event types in university environments are sequential events, occurring in chain-like series, in which, after initial sessions, participants refer with increasing frequency to topics and discussions in earlier sessions. Seminars, lecture courses, and conferences would be typical examples. It is therefore possible to distinguish metadiscourse about the ongoing discourse from that concerning other sessions in the series (Ädel 2006 makes a similar distinction between 'metatextual' and 'intertextual reference' in writing). Although it is a distinction that one would not expect in any way to reflect differences between L1 and L2 speaking, I nevertheless found differences between ELF and ENL data in the way the verb DISCUSS was used (Mauranen 2005): both speaker groups used metadiscoursal DISCUSS for organising discourse, but in the ELFA corpus it was mostly (in two-thirds of the occurrences) used for talking about the current situation ('immediate discourse organising', Example 6.27), whereas in the MICASE corpus the prevalent use (again in two-thirds of the instances) was 'long-range organising', that is, talking about the serial event as a whole (6.28).

(6.27)

> ... the point is here that we are talking about northern europe and only *we are discussing about turkey* er that is @ ...

(6.28)

> ... uh that will although it's an interesting question, and maybe one *we could discuss within the framework of this class* it probably is not relevant, to ...

Clearly, this difference does not reflect language proficiency – it shows a different preference for functions that are recognised and in this sense normal in both discourse communities. It is a subtle shift, and does not impinge on any established rules of Standard English, even if we might speculate that it arises from a perception among ENL speakers that DISCUSS has a more 'distal' sense than, say, TALK. The clearly distinct preference patterns would seem to indicate that this is not simply a matter of broadening a functional meaning, or ignoring a functional distinction by ELF speakers, which might reflect simplification. It is a matter of use that most speakers are probably not aware of. But in this respect it resembles the most thoroughly studied domain in sociolinguistics, phonological variation, which has attracted great interest precisely because choices relating to accent are often not within speakers' conscious awareness. Discourse level, beyond-the-utterance and beyond-the-sentence phenomena also generally seem to fall outside people's conscious awareness of 'language', and therefore provide good material for discovering their spontaneous choices.

The distinction between the current speech event and those that are temporally distant is nevertheless less clear-cut in spoken than in written genres, which renders the borderline between intertextual and intratextual metadiscourse fuzzier in spoken text. The sharpness of boundaries varies from the clarity of meetings or casual encounters in the street, which have recognisable beginnings and endings, to conferences with interlinked talks and seminars with presentations, lectures, or pre-readings followed by discussion. It is always possible, and even common, to refer to earlier occasions and what was said on them, as illustrated in the next example from a conference (6.29), but a symposium or a longer seminar session as a whole could arguably be taken to be one event with several phases.

(6.29)

> ... it's always linked to the culture that produces symbols *as we have just seen* in a way *in claudio minca's lecture in the morning*

The multiple uses of discourse reflexivity that ELF speakers handle in both monologic and dialogic speaking reflects the position of metadiscourse in communication and, at the same time, the nature of using a lingua franca. As to metadiscourse, the capacity of language to talk about itself, and thereby add to the versatility, precision, and complexity of communication, seems to be a vital component for handling sophisticated communicative tasks. Its adoption in ELF supports the hypothesis that it is a discourse universal, in other words a fundamental aspect of human discourse. Metadiscourse is a way of making discourse more explicit, and in this sense it is 'hearer-friendly' in analogy to the 'reader-friendliness' that has been suggested as its central contribution to text. Making talk explicit to the hearer is a kind of 'recipient design', and it is easy to see it as an 'act of consideration to the listener', following McCarthy's characterisation of the use of headers (1998). As we have seen above, metadiscourse can also be put to good use as an instrument for manipulating the discourse to a speaker's own agenda; these are two sides of the same coin, as cooperation and competition generally are in spoken interaction. Cooperation underpins all successful spoken interaction, and clarity enhances cooperation.

In ELF speech, the chief implication of discourse reflexivity seems to be that interactional needs are attended to even when the primary focus of communication is on content, and even when the mastery of a particular linguistic code is not perfect. Metadiscourse enacts a 'plane-change' (Sinclair 1992/2004). It arrests the flow of message construction for a while, whether in advance or in retrospect, leaps from the textual world of 'content', shared experience, to the real world of interaction. This is something that ELF speakers manage well. ELF speech engages in facework as well as complex manoeuvring of discourse in interaction, and indicates sensitivity to situational demands. Small and more homogeneous communities use less metatext in their writing because more can be expected to be shared among its members (see Mauranen 1993a,b), and we can postulate a similar dimension for speaking.

As ELF speech is produced in circumstances of considerable heterogeneity, one would expect a heightened need for explicitness and clarity. Performing successfully in such interactional work is not hampered by infidelities of form with respect to Standard English, although they occur continually (*also other thing*; *to put it blunt*; *I will give you the introduction*). Many metadiscursive expressions are highly conventionalised in ENL, and as we saw in Chapter 4, ENL conventions can successfully be flouted in ELF as long as the intended function is recognised by interlocutors. Slightly unusual forms of metadiscourse likewise seem to serve their purposes (*if you may know*; *I go into conclusion and give a erm particular definition of democracy*). The interactional dimension of language is as natural to L2 as to L1 speaking, and equally crucial to communicative success. It is not something extra that can be added to mastery of form at high levels of proficiency only; quite the contrary, communicative means that enhance clarity are likely to be more serviceable than those concentrating on accuracy.

6.2 Indicating local organisation

We saw in the previous section how talking about talk was an integral part of ELF speech and how speakers may fruitfully draw upon this aspect of speech when designing their talk with listeners in mind. I would like to focus in this section on what speakers do to help their interlocutors keep track of the unfolding discourse. At the same time, I want to shift the angle a little and concentrate on a small group of anticipatory devices, because anticipation is crucial to comprehension. Anticipatory mechanisms feed material into our processing systems for making guesses about what is to come, and what we actually encounter then confirms or refutes our guesses. Moreover, these devices operate quite locally, and thus narrow down the focus from metadiscourse in general, where the scope can range from very local to a global organisation of the discourse at hand.

It seems on the basis of earlier research that ELF speakers are adept at organising the macro-structure of their talk (for example Mauranen 2009). Some speakers clearly have better rhetorical skills than others, but there seems to be no obvious connection to any particular mother tongue, or even whether one is speaking an L1 or an L2. Suviniitty (2010) has investigated lecturing in ELF at a technological university, and she shows how lecturers who received the highest scores for comprehensibility from students used interactive signalling far more than those who got low scores. Language proficiency in itself was not involved, and ENL speakers did not necessarily come up on top.

Lectures and conference presentations are normally well planned in advance, but not often read out loud from a written script. In certain disciplines and some cultures, reading is more common than in others, but in the ELFA corpus this was not practised except on rare exceptions – such as doctoral candidates' initial presentations in defences (the 'lectio praecursoria'), or the reading out of quotations presented in visuals. Presenters thus speak freely for the most part, adjusting their speech to their audience as they go along (cf., for example, Bamford 2004; Crawford Camiciottoli 2005, and specifically on ELF lectures, Suviniitty forthcoming).

Importantly, in free speech, the linearity of the delivery gains more prominence than in written text, even though both are monologues and in principle in full control of the presenter. Linearity in spoken language implies the primacy of local text organisation over a long-term focus, since working memory spans are limited and maintaining coherence demands that hearers can keep up with the line of thought as it unfolds in real time. In monologic presentations speakers can fall back upon visuals, which helps all participants keep track of the overall organisation, and they are consequently made much use of. In conference presentations an important purpose is of course to lead to a discussion section following the presentation, and here the situation is even more demanding: questions and comments need to be formulated quickly and be readily comprehensible to the presenter. The presenter, in turn, must respond immediately and make the responses relevant to the comments. All of these turns in academic conferences tend to be fairly extended, and require all parties to think on their feet and simultaneously weave internal organisation into their contributions.

If local discourse organising plays a fundamental role in successful management of meanings, people should be able to do it in foreign languages as well as their own. With less entrenched repertoires, speakers may be more inclined to resort to a variety of means that are aimed at clarifying their intended meanings than they would in their native languages. Whether such clarifying strategies are more pronounced in ELF than among ENL speakers is not simple to assess because phenomena of this kind tend to be hard to quantify. However, an interesting study on the MICASE corpus by Marx and Swales (2005) did quantify some expressions that are highly relevant to local discourse organisation. This provides a nice point of comparison to frequencies in ELF talk, even though it prioritises the ENL perspective. Marx and Swales's study started out by talking about 'self-repairs', noting that even though speakers commonly reformulate what they have just said as a matter of course, they can also use certain phrases to announce that they are going to try again, saying more or less what they said previously. Assuming a general tendency to enhanced explicitness among ELF speakers, we would expect them to use proportionally more announcements of rephrase intentions than comparable ENL speakers.

As Marx and Swales (2005) point out, new formulations of what was just said can elaborate or try to make clearer what was meant or how it is to be interpreted. In this respect the markers they investigated fall nicely in line with the topics explored in this chapter. But although 'self-repair' is a term that is in general use, it seems to imply that something went wrong with the initial formulation, which is not always the case (Chapter 7). I shall be using the more neutral term 'self-rephrasing', and talk about 'rephrase markers' to refer to the actual items used for announcing self-rephrases.

To carry out the comparison, I used the first half of ELFA (0.6 million words) and limited the range of expressions to Marx and Swales's (2005) selection without adding any new ones. Like them, I weeded out manually expressions that taken in their context do not announce reformulations (*what I mean to say is*), that is, did not function as rephrase markers. A sheer quantitative overview reveals striking differences (Table 6.1).

Table 6.1 shows two things: first, that ELF speech does indeed announce self-rephrasing far more often than ENL speech, and secondly, that the most favoured expressions in the speaker groups are not the same. Both are interesting findings, and both can be related to things that we have had hunches about. The greater frequency of announced rephrasing can point to a greater overall tendency for self-rephrasing in ELF, which seems to correspond very well to anecdotal evidence (I shall come back to this later). However, it can also point to the tendency towards explicitation in ELF, in line with other observations in this chapter, which have shown ELF speakers striving for greater explicitness in search of mutual understanding.

The other finding, that the favoured expression is specific to ELF, even though quite common in ENL speech too (here it is the second most frequent expression, the only other large class apart from the preferred ENL type), is also worth noting. It has been a common enough observation in SLA studies that L2 speakers tend to resort to a smaller variety of near-synonyms or functional equivalents than would be available in the target language. This is an economical strategy, and seen from that perspective also a rational one. That English is an additional language to ELF speakers is clearly in evidence here, and starting from the many gaps compared to the ENL data points in the same direction as the conspicuous frequency of *I mean*. However, we must keep in mind that there is an inbuilt and very common

Table 6.1 Self-rephrase markers

	MICASE	ELFA
in other words	224	9
(I) mean	50	438
trying to say	19	4
another way	18	-
that is to say	16	3
namely	15	17
i.e.	14	-
meant	11	1
what I'm saying is	7	-
clarify	4	-
rephrase	4	1
more specifically	2	-
misspoke	1	-
Total	385	473
Total /100,000w	**21.4**	**78.8**

Comparing announcements of self-rephrasing in MICASE and ELFA corpora. The numbers in the columns are absolute occurrences of rephrase markers; the final row gives normed figures as occurrences per 100,000 words.

bias in this comparison in that it starts from ENL speech, and easily renders ELF inadequate when viewed from that direction.

The original analysis by Marx and Swales (2005) starts from ENL intuitions, not bottom-up from observations in a corpus-driven fashion. Such practices are still seen in many corpus searches and they are particularly common in ENL speakers' well-intended practical help to second-language learners. While it provides a shortcut to corpus searches and does not of course affect frequencies, it implicitly retains native-speaker intuition as the core of language use, brushing aside the possibility that something other than what is open to introspection might be found in large corpus data. This has repeatedly been shown to be an incorrect assumption in corpus linguistics (see e.g. Sinclair 1991, 2004). In the case of functional categories, such as hedging, stance, or metadiscourse, or indeed announced self-rephrasing, alternatives to intuition for getting at the range of expressions available in the language all require painstaking qualitative analyses of data, and are thus far slower than intuition-driven studies. The criticism that can be levelled at the latter route is that the data that is analysed would always seem to be too small to cover all possibilities that might occur. Different combinations of the two approaches and alternation between their viewpoints would seem to yield better findings than either on its own.

The conspicuous preference of *I mean* in ELF speech certainly seems to invite a qualitative analysis, even though on a restricted sample, and the next section will tackle this.

6.3 *Close-up on* I mean

In the comparison of announced self-rephrasing in ENL and ELF speech, *I mean* came up as the preferred marker in ELF far more than any other. To see how it actually works in context, I switched to a qualitative method and selected five conference presentations and their discussion sections, looking at every instance of *I mean*. In all, 67 cases came into view. A clear majority were in discussion sections, but as some discussions went on far longer than others, numerical differences were large: discussions ranged from zero to 26 occurrences. The presentations were of roughly equal length, about 20 minutes, and although some presenters went over their allotted time, there was not so much variation (from two to seven instances). The uses of *I mean* across presentations and discussions were essentially of the same kinds. Such similarity is perhaps not entirely surprising in that none of the presenters was reading from script, but compared to the marked differences in metadiscourse it is interesting to note how the same distinctions of context or situation are not relevant to all expression types. Conference discussions typically involve long turns, which generally tend to have more internal structuring than the short turns of casual conversations.

What speakers used *I mean* for was overwhelmingly to change tack: *I mean* was used in longish turns and it marked the start of a new direction, for example to make a concession, a digression, add an explanatory or evaluative comment, or an exemplifying or elaborating sequence. Marx and Swales originally characterised their announced self-repairs as 'phrases that a speaker might use when he or she wanted to tell the interlocutors that an attempt to fix a speech mistake, clarify an idea, or rephrase an ambiguous utterance was coming up' (Marx & Swales 2005). The weight of the characterisation lies on the assumption that speakers use these expressions to flag their intention to repair a formulation they were not happy with; as spoken words cannot be erased, speakers can try to amend their blunders by making additions and elaborations. This repair work is presumably to make up for some potential ambiguity, lack of clarity, or risk of misunderstanding that they feel their first formulation

Table 6.2 I mean *in ELF conference talk*

Tack changes	67%	(45)
Self-repairs	18%	(12)
Fillers	12%	(8)
Other	3%	(2)
Total	**100%**	**(67)**

Five conference presentations and their ensuing discussion sections. 'Tack changes' stands for starting a new direction, like units with a new function or parenthetical remarks. 'Self-repairs' include reformulating expressions and false starts, 'fillers' are hesitation markers, and 'other' unclear cases.

might cause. As we expect much more uncertainty about the formulation of expressions when people are not speaking their first language, the greater number of rephrase markers in ELF seems unsurprising. However, I ran a comparison of rephrasing in an ENL and in an ELF seminar (Chapter 7), in view of which this assumption appears less self-evident: when repeats and hesitations were removed, actual rephrasing was not remarkably common in ELF.

Before looking at examples, it is useful to glance at the distribution of *I mean* in its categories of use (Table 6.2). The dominant category is, then, 'tack change', which accounts for roughly two-thirds of all occurrences, while repair announcements cover nearly a fifth, and fillers just over a tenth.

Rephrase marking is undoubtedly an important use of *I mean*, but the picture that emerges from this sample is that speakers use it more as a discourse marker signalling an upcoming change. As can be seen in the examples below, *I mean* typically precedes a new phase in a speaker's turn. This is the category I am calling 'tack change'.

Moving on to the contextual uses, then, the speaker in the first example (6.30) begins a new subtopic, 'the economic value of traditional knowledge'. After claiming that the issue is not discussed any longer, she proceeds to make preparations for a different point, namely that traditional knowledge is worth protecting. She begins this argument by making a strong evaluative statement (that it is economically valuable), in this way establishing the basis for the argument she then goes on to develop. *I mean* marks the transition from the claim about the missing discussion to the basis of the next point; it signals a change in the functions of the two consecutive utterances and, at the same time, stages of the argument. Thus, far from stating the same thing again in different words, it marks discourse movement.

(6.30)

> then you have the economic value of traditional knowledge erm well there's there's no more discussion about that *i mean* traditional knowledge definitely has an important economic value so the stakes of protecting it would be in relation of er well getting protection against misuse

It is also common for speakers to comment on what they just said. Along with metadiscourse, other expressions can be employed in signalling the beginning of such new commentary phases; clearly, *I mean* is one of those expressions, as we can see in (6.31). The speaker here is talking about the limitations of analysing self-representations and then shifts his course and makes an evaluative comment (*it's not particularly surprising*) on the phenomenon itself, the self-representation that analyses cannot entirely capture.

(6.31)

> this is this kind of self-representation erm, it goes on an analysis about that goes only just it only goes that far *i mean* it it's not particularly surprising that people tried to put their own city in a positive light

This interplay with metadiscoursal commentary and *I mean* acting as a discourse marker can be seen nicely in the next example (6.32), where the speaker inserts a comment on her own discourse between a forward-looking marker *I mean* and a resumptive *but* (cf. Mazeland & Huiskes 2001), which signals a return to the main line of the argument (which, incidentally, is interrupted by a new side sequence beginning with *and*).

(6.32)

> russian foreign policy to these companies i would say i would argue *i mean* this is very @sarcastically@ argued **but** and now we have to switch back under putin that he really tries to get control back

Here we first have a plane-change, where the speaker is temporarily shifting to the interactive plane by using metadiscourse that prospects an argument (*I would say I would argue*). Instead of going on to present her anticipated argument, she postpones it, and instead frames it further by making a comment on it (*this is very sarcastically argued*), which comment, together with her laughter, gives it a concessive, almost apologetic air. The comment is introduced by *I mean*, and the next plane-change is marked by *but*. A very similar sequence is seen in (6.33), where the speaker also inserts a metadiscourse comment between *I mean* and *but*:

(6.33)

> so there are scientists that er after getting a certain permission can run field trials er open-air and they grow genetically modified plants and er and this study *i mean* i will talk about it er later on **but** er basically what we have been collect- er what we have been doing is

Many other, mostly elaborative, functions can be fulfilled by an *I mean* marker in constructing arguments and carrying out discussions, the main point being that there is a shift in function which immediately follows the marker. The speaker in (6.34) evokes an example as supportive evidence of his claim:

(6.34)

> <S18> of course there is a lot of to do with it *i mean* think about education <S32> mhm </S32> like *i mean* when you told that er information doesn't count <S32> mhm </S32> but but we do have a schooling system in our countries and and er if we @@ are that @pessimistic@ then we can pretty much end the end the schooling like ivan illich was pointing out 30 years ago </S18>

The second instance of *I mean*, following *like*, could be seen as ambiguous between filler and tack-change marker, but it certainly starts a new development, returning to a fellow participant's (S32) earlier point as if to prepare the ground for a counterargument. The counterargument then follows after *but*.

On occasion, the elaborations that speakers launch with *I mean* take on a clarificatory role, which comes close to the kinds of uses that announcements of rephrases were expected to have. Example (6.35) illustrates this.

(6.35)

> <S34> but er then i i will also ask a question how many are there experiences

like this in uzbekistan *i mean* if we would have er all the success cases of ICT in uzbekistan er as presentations how many people would be here in this room </S34>

Here the speaker comes closest to reformulating if not the utterance, at least the idea he seems to be putting forth as a question to the presenter. His first formulation of the question could be seen as a kind of preview of the elaborated version that follows *I mean*. Even so, his elaborated version does not seem to relate to the linguistic means he chose the first time. Thus, relating this to a self-rephrasing perspective, it seems to reflect no uncertainty about linguistic form, nor any attempted corrections.

As noted above, these examples are drawn from presentations and discussions alike, with the same functions in both. An exception perhaps is the turn-initial *I mean*, which occurred a couple of times (once by an ENL speaker and once by an L2 speaker, in different conferences), both times as part of an overlap when speakers were competing for turns. Here is the ENL speaker:

(6.36)

<S7>...i haven't i wasn't able look to very many from the other side i i don't i i hope it would [continue] </S7>
<S4> [mhm] mhm-hm [but] </S4>
<NS13> [*i mean*] yeah but in areas where, australian networks and (xx) was established, this works a whole lot better ...

Three speakers get into overlaps here: two L2 speakers, S7 and S4, and NS13, an ENL speaker. They are talking about building research networks in an emerging field. S4's minimal response (*mhm*) first overlaps with S7, and when he stops, she makes a start (*but*). However, NS13 starts simultaneously (*I mean*), and when S4 stops speaking, continues with another discourse marker (*yeah but*) and goes on with his turn.

Self-rephrases did of course occur in conference contexts, just as they did in other situations; Examples (6.37) and (6.38) illustrate this. In both, the difference from tack change is clear: the speaker either corrects a blunder or a slip of the tongue (6.37), or searches for an expression and reformulates the first attempts at saying something (6.38).

(6.37)

was saying very explicitly about the pro- needed to protect interest of russian energy companies so that is a question er *i mean* that is er my answer

(6.38)

<S25> [i think this *i mean*] this goes with the idea of *i mean* this modern western notion of of progress where you think

False starts are typical rephrase occasions. One common place for a false start is at the beginning of a turn (6.39), when the speaker literally starts over again:

(6.39)

<S4> isn't *i mean* here really there were so many sessions that re- real it was impossible to follow all these new ideas and we ...

Sometimes *I mean* is used for filled pauses, but there were relatively few of these in the sample. No more than eight (12%) looked as if they were used as 'fillers', or to play for time (6.40) as the speaker is searching for a suitable expression.

(6.40)

tha- thank you for your presentation i er it seems like *i mean* in uzbekistan there are many benefits of IT but er i have just one simple question

In all, it looks as if the strongly preferred use of *I mean* in ELF talk is to organise discourse by marking transitions, changes of direction, and plane-changes explicitly. Other notable but distinctly less frequent uses are those that have been associated with repair behaviour, such as rephrasing and hesitation. The impression emerges from these observations that *I mean* is used more deliberately and with a clearer set of functions than merely being necessitated by lack of linguistic resources or the contingencies of online speaking. They seem to suggest that explanations of the high frequency of such markers might more readily be found in the enhanced explicitness tendency among ELF speakers than in their uncertainty about formulating expressions. Moreover, it might be the case that ENL speakers are equally motivated by factors other than the intuitively most obvious.

6.4 Negotiating topics

In addition to discourse elements, such as metadiscourse or discourse markers, syntactic means can also be brought to bear to enhance discourse clarity and explicitness: certain traits of syntax, particularly those that deal with topic or focus and manipulate word order to express them, for instance by 'fronting' or 'left dislocation', are typical features of spoken language that relate to the needs of dialogue. Fronting has different interpretations in syntactic theories, but basically means placing sentence elements other than subjects at the beginning of sentences or utterances, and has the effect of giving them prominence or the role of a sentence topic. In a broad interpretation, 'left dislocation' is a kind of fronting, where the element to be made focal or topical is placed outside the clause structure, but with a pronoun in the clause to stand for the full referent (*these differences **they** are important*). Such structures rarely make an appearance in foreign-language curricula, even though they are common in spoken language. ELF speakers nevertheless use them frequently. Part of the reason may be that left dislocation is a common feature in the spoken grammar of many languages, and when encountered in English will be familiar to L2 users without deliberate teaching. It may be at least latent in many ELF speakers' linguistic repertoires independently of their experience of English.

Topic and focus are important aspects of helping interlocutors keep up with each other's contributions as conversation unfolds; the cooperative development of discourse involves ensuring a shared understanding of the current topic. Therefore, any changes in topic referents a participant wants to make need to be sufficiently transparent for the interaction to proceed smoothly.

Sometimes speakers seem to forget to make the relevance of their topic clear, as in (6.41), where the speaker starts out with a referent he has in mind (*the strain*) but which is new at this point of the discourse. He then seems to have second thoughts about whether others are with him because he relegates the beginning to a false start and restarts without a pause (*as for the strain*), marking it more clearly as a topic change, and after S2's encouraging back-channelling he expands the original formulation a little (*the work strain is there*) and then goes on with his turn.

(6.41)

<S10> yeah so actually you know *the strain is there as for the strain* <S2> yeah </S2> *the work strain is there* because if in at any stage especially the finishing point ...

S10 above managed his topic introduction after some retracing, but there are other common means of introducing new referents to discourse. In monologues or extended turns, topic changes are often signalled by discourse markers or metadiscourse. In dialogue, introducing new topics can be done in a number of ways. Consider the following instances:

(a) *okay then the mental workload* it's sometimes difficult to assess that of course but er what ...
(b) *i have a question* about the procedural aspect of democracy ...
(c) th- *this is about multiculturalism* i i would like to know if ...
(d) *concerning* the chemical i asked a question about whether like er how do they manage the waste product ...
(e) er *about* the origin of NGOs er does NGOs from the source ...
(f) *what about* rejection er rejection <S7> yes </S7> it's er (it's not usual), on the liver, rejection </S5>
(g) <S7> because *the diagnosis of brain death it* always happens in the afternoon ...

These are all turn-initial topic introductions from seminar discussions. The first does the introduction with a discourse marker (*okay then*), as is usual in the middle of monologues and long turns, and then moves on to the topic referent (*the mental workload*). In (b) the speaker uses metadiscourse (*I have a question*), and so does the speaker in (c), although in a slightly less conventional way. In (d) and (e), the topic referent is introduced by prepositions, and in (f) an introductory phrase (*what about*). The last one uses 'left dislocation': she presents the topic referent (*the diagnosis of brain death*) as a noun phrase on its own, and then continues with a clause where a pronoun (*it*) stands for the topic. While all of the examples are common and conventional in ENL speech as well, it is the last type that we focus on.

'Left dislocation' is typical of spoken grammar, which may be the reason why it has been treated dismissively in formal grammars, as the term itself suggests. In spoken discourse analysis, it has been seen as a way of highlighting or foregrounding the topic. Carter and McCarthy (2006) talk about it as 'topic slot' or 'header'. They see it as the speaker's means of orientating the hearer, and accordingly characterise it as an 'act of consideration to the listener' (McCarthy 1998: 77). From a social interactionist perspective, Pekarek Doehler (2001) has shown the construction to be motivated by situational factors rather than syntax alone. Ford et al. (2003) call it 'negotiating referent'. In their analysis, the fundamental role of this structure is to ensure that interlocutors have the same topic in mind before going on. Adapting their term a little, I talk about 'negotiating topic' or 'topic negotiation' for syntactic devices like this, hoping to highlight their interactional nature and avoid the pejorative overtones of 'dislocation' suggesting a syntactic problem where something is out of joint. Likewise, it is better to keep clear of terms like 'left' and 'right' in describing speaking, to avoid undue written language bias. Obviously, speaking takes place in time, not in a spatial sequence. In brief, topic negotiation is a way of ensuring that hearers are clear about what speakers are talking about.

Topic negotiation is performed skilfully in ELF discussions towards the beginning of turns as in (6.42), but it is not limited to turn-initial positions (6.43).

(6.42)

<S9> [yeah] *this blue-collar job* er *it* involves people like the operators who operate it from the computer ...

(6.43)

<S3> ... so it's like the people you know *the people they* don't understand like what's happening but in the world bank report ...

In (6.43) the topic element at the beginning marks a new stage in a long turn where the speaker explains a complex situation; at this point he changes tack, moving on to the consequences of what he has been describing. As the two examples show, the topic referents can be singular or plural, animate or inanimate, abstract or concrete. Individual referents as in (6.44) and (6.45) are not very common compared to groups of people (6.46), abstract objects (6.47), institutional objects (6.48), and groups of objects (6.49). In consequence, *they* is a far more common pronoun referent in this construction than *he*, *she*, or *it* (Mauranen 2007b).

(6.44)

... you know in the swedish original version *pippi longstocking she*'s extremely strong and she's lifting er er her own horse ...

(6.45)

... *our other basic industry paper and pulp it* was successing as well so it's not totally the rise of information society ...

(6.46)

<S7> erm in the te- terminal phase of the wilson's disease *the patients they* also get the encephalopathy ...

(6.47)

... *these different layers of identity they* are by no means mutually exclusive so you can ...

(6.48)

... because er the *the estonian government they* made some kind of simplifying towards the citizenship law for the russians so ...

(6.49)

<S6>it was something that the *the fat drops they* they can be like very small vesicules or ...

With this construction, which highlights the topic, speakers manage the flow of the discourse so that the content development is secured, and at the same time attend to the interactional needs of the situation. It shows, again, how the two facets of discourse are closely intertwined, and how the same means can be used to achieve both content- and interaction-related purposes. Content orientation does not entail indifference to interaction.

A very similar discourse strategy to the topic negotiation in the previous examples, even though syntactically slightly different, is illustrated in (6.50) and (6.51). This structure also has the effect of separating the topic from the rest of the message by announcing it first and following it up with a pronominal reference in a full clause:

(6.50)

<S6> the the question is just if if *if the first loan if if it* came from the IMF or if the first debt actually came from somebody totally

(6.51)

<S2> is it possible that *an alcoholic,* that *he* doesn't get any of these diseases that he lives like hundred and twenty years </S2>

Both of these topicalise the key referent by starting but not continuing the embedded clause where it appears in subject position. Instead they interrupt the clause after the subject-topic, and then resume the clause with the conjunction (*if*, *that*) and make a pronoun reference to the subject noun phrase. This tactic resembles a false start in that the clause is begun anew after abandoning it, but it does not discard the first start. Quite the contrary, after the topic noun has already been expressed it is treated as a valid part of the discourse; otherwise the pronominal reference would not make sense. This is therefore a variant structure of topic negotiation, with an equivalent discourse effect: making the topic clear and prominent.

The mirror image of topic negotiation as a 'header' is what Aijmer (1989) termed 'tail', and is also known as 'right dislocation' or a 'noun phrase tag' (Biber et al. 1999: 139). A tail also works as a clarifying strategy. In this structure, the clause with a pronominal reference is followed by a full noun phrase as if an afterthought (… ***it** was quite acceptable for the scholars too **peace policy***). McCarthy (1998) notes its tendency to co-occur with evaluative contexts and the heavily interpersonal overlay it gives to the clause. The tail construction is not very frequent in academic discussions, which makes it difficult to assess whether there is an equivalent tendency to occur in evaluative contexts. But it may well be so, and evidence from ELFA is certainly supportive, as the following examples (6.52–6.57) indicate.

(6.52)

<SU> and *it* should be a boy *the child* </SU>

(6.53)

<S5> … and *it's difficult @@, this case* case but i think it's er good er reason to to have biopsy and er </S5>

(6.54)

… this becomes completely vacuous that that er there's no point in er, *it becomes completely uncontroversial this principle*, er …

(6.55)

<S7> … *they* are too weird tests *your colleague took*, I-G-A I-G-G I-G-N </S7>

(6.56)

<S7>… so if you get the new liver because of alcohol you must stop drinking absolutely <P:08> and they do it. and *they are in very tight control those alcoholics* …

(6.57)

<S2> *it* seems to be a very complex erm <S1> mhm </S1> phenomenon [*adaptation*, in in in] <S1> [yeah yeah mhm] </S1> erm a variety of aspects …

Each of these cases is embedded in an evaluative context. This is interesting because it shows how ELF speakers can be remarkably sensitive to interactional overtones. One possibility for explaining this might be in the direction of discourse universals. It could be hypothesised that similar interactional functions are necessary across languages, and this gives rise to comparable discourse structures, even if they are not an exact match in terms of clause syntax. If this is the case, discourse universals may turn out to play a role in what Chambers (2004) calls 'vernacular universals', although Chambers talks about lexicogrammatical, not discourse, features. The relatively common presence of such structures in ELF spoken by people from typologically very distant languages suggests that there are points of convergence in discourse phenomena that apparently play useful roles in situations of high complexity and unpredictability, and that they may favour syntactic structures that enhance explicitness.

There is also an observation to be made from the point of view of processing, which is perhaps clearest in (6.57) above. The strategy of externalising the topic noun phrase from the principal clause that conveys the rest of the message also has the effect of helping to dish out the message in processable portions – as usual, to the benefit of both the speaker and the hearer. In (6.57) the piecemeal presentation of the elements in this reflective talk allows for an interlocutor's back-channelling to keep up with the delivery. In this way the speaker gets feedback while thinking and speaking on his feet. Keeping track is assisted from the spreading out of the references, and interactional signalling maintains cooperation.

Speakers also resort to clarifications on the hoof, as if were, interposing nominal referents after pronoun references, apparently to ensure referential clarity. Just a few examples will suffice (6.58–6.60):

(6.58)

<S6> do do *they these immunoglobulin* show vasculitis or (what) </S6>

(6.59)

<S3> of course a couple of questions erm *this citizenship* how much does *it* influence the people are *they the russians* allowed officially to work and everything </S3>

(6.60)

<S7> ... so the donor is ready in the afternoon and *they, the transplantation group* goes *late afternoon* to the donor ... </S7>

In (6.59), the speaker makes use of topic negotiation (*this citizenship* how much does *it* influence) and clarification by interposed noun (*they the Russians*) within the same turn. Many tactics can thus combine to maintain coherence and clarity in delivery, helping along a smooth progression of contributions with all interactants on the same track. The structural devices discussed in this section show that speakers adapt to the demands of the ELF situation at many levels, including syntactic structuring. Negotiating topic is not only a means of increasing clarity in discourse, but also of orientation to the interlocutor. It can be seen as an accommodation strategy in the wider sense (cf. Chapter 2, Section 2.3.3), one that foregrounds cooperation.

Topic negotiation thus seems motivated by the needs of dialogue. The structures involved are most naturally seen as being shaped by face-to-face interaction, whereby they support conclusions drawn in discourse-based grammars. As Du Bois (2003) put it: 'Grammars do best what speakers do most.' Or, in more general terms, 'Discourse drives grammar, not the reverse' (McCarthy 1998: 78).

In the absence of quantitative comparative data from ENL speech, it is futile to speculate whether topic negotiation should be particularly characteristic of ELF – yet my field observations would suggest that this might be the case. Not only are examples easily found in the ELFA corpus, but fluent, highly educated non-natives in international meetings or interviews in the media appear to resort to these structures noticeably often. If this should be the case more generally, this strategy might also facilitate processing – and, as commonly is the case (cf. Chapter 5), for speakers and hearers alike.

That ELF speakers use topic-negotiation devices is interesting from the point of view of language teaching, where spoken grammar is not a central curricular item despite the emphasis on other aspects of speech. It is intriguing that they are used in ELF all the same; this rather tends to undermine explanations that ELF speech is essentially just learner language resulting from imperfect learning.

6.5 Summary

This chapter has focused on manifestations of explicitness in ELF talk. The point of departure lay in an earlier observation suggesting that explicitness might be characteristic of ELF talk, which takes place in heterogeneous environments, in contrast to the implicitness that appears to thrive in small, relatively homogeneous communities. This can be related to the tendency observed in other cross-cultural communication situations, such as translation, to enhance explicitness.

Three kinds of explicitness were taken up: metadiscourse, anticipatory markers of local organisation, and negotiating topics.

We also used ELF data analyses to question the adequacy of native-speaker intuition as a research method: an example in this chapter was the use of *I mean* as a discourse-structuring device whose functions went far beyond the intuitively posited hesitations and announced self-rephrases.

In the light of the analyses, the centrality of explicitness in ELF talk is hardly in doubt. Even though all features were not readily quantifiable, those comparisons that were carried out pointed to enhanced explicitness in ELF relative to ENL.

In terms of the co-construction of shared knowledge, or 'content', explicitation seems to have a facilitating effect by helping to keep track of topic development and to chunk up the important contributions to manageable portions. The principal means for achieving this are topic-negotiation strategies. Explicitation also assists processing in providing a number of clues for hearers to work on, which from the speaker's point of view increases the chance of getting through to hearers.

It looks clear from these analyses that interactional aspects of language are just as central to lingua franca speech as they are to any language use: interactional needs of communication are not overridden by an excessive content-orientation, as has been sometimes suggested (see Chapter 2). The notable cooperativeness, observed in many studies, was also manifest here. What clearly looks like being relegated to a secondary role is grammatical accuracy, as interaction does not seem to be much hampered by uncertainties and fluctuations in grammar. Yet certain discourse-based structures that feature strongly in facilitating smooth interaction are characteristic of ELF speech. This raises questions with regard to SLA, since the structures taken up here are not parts of the typical ELT syllabus.

Extensive use of explicitation strategies may also have macro-level sociolinguistic consequences, which are probably slow to take shape but which are either a consequence of an orientation to enhanced explicitness or enabled by it. A direct consequence would be an increase in transparent structures, analyticity instead of syntheticity, and some indications of this can perhaps be already seen in ELF favouring periphrastic structures, such as the *-ing* form instead of the simple present. A less direct consequence would be a generally heightened readiness to accept and freedom to create innovations. Clearly, ELF speakers show a good deal of linguistic creativity in producing novel expressions that solve the communicative problem at hand, even if they result in ungrammatical forms or non-existent lexis from a Standard English viewpoint. While much of this passes unnoticed, some patterns begin to stick and multiply, as we saw in Chapter 5. Extensive explicitness prepares a good breeding ground for such processes, as it provides enhanced contextual support for anomalous forms to thrive in.

References

Ädel, A. (2006) *Metadiscourse in L1 and L2 English*, Amsterdam: John Benjamins.

Ädel, A. (2010) '"*Just to give you kind of a map of where we are going*": a taxonomy of metadiscourse in spoken and written academic English', *The Nordic Journal of English Studies* 9 (2): 69–97.

Ädel, A. and Mauranen, A. (eds.) (2010) *Metadiscourse*. Special issue of *The Nordic Journal of English Studies* 9 (2).

Aijmer, K. (1989) 'Themes and tails: the discourse functions of dislocated elements', *Nordic Journal of Linguistics* 12: 137–54.

Baker, M. (1993) 'Corpus linguistics and translation studies: implications and applications', in Baker, M., Francis, G. and Tognini-Bonelli, E. (eds.) *Text and Technology: In Honour of John Sinclair*, Amsterdam: John Benjamins, 233–50.

Bamford, J. (2004) 'Gestural and symbolic uses of the deictic here in academic lectures', in Aijmer, K. and Stenström, U.-B. (eds.) *Discourse Patterns in Spoken and Written Corpora*, Amsterdam: John Benjamins, 113–38.

Biber, D., Johansson, S., Leech, G., Conrad, S. and Finegan E. (1999) *The Longman Grammar of Spoken and Written English*, London: Pearson Education.

Blum-Kulka, S. (1986) 'Shifts of cohesion and coherence in translation', in House, J. and Blum-Kulka, S. (eds.) *Interlingual and Intercultural Communication: Discourse and Cognition in Translation and Second Language Acquisition Studies*, Tübingen: Gunter Narr, 17–35.

Brown, P. and Levinson, S. (1987) *Politeness: Some Universals in Language Usage*, Cambridge: Cambridge University Press.

Carter, R. and McCarthy, M. (2006) *Cambridge Grammar of English*, Cambridge: Cambridge University Press.

Chambers, J. K. (2004) 'Dynamic typology and vernacular universals', in Kortmann, B. (ed.) *Dalectology Meets Typology*, Berlin: Mouton de Gruyter, 127–46.

Cogo, A. and Dewey, M. (2006) 'Efficiency in ELF communication: from pragmatic motives to lexico-grammatical innovation', *Nordic Journal of English Studies* 5 (2): 59–93 (https://guoa.ub.gu.se/dspace/ bitstream/2077/3148/1/5-2-Cogo-Dewey.pdf).

Craig, R. T. and Sanusi, A. L. (2000) '"I'm just saying ..." Discourse markers of standpoint continuity', *Argumentation* 14: 425–45.

Crawford Camiciottoli, B. (2005) 'Adjusting a business lecture for an international audience: a case study', *English for Specific Purposes* 24 (2): 183–99.

Crismore, A. (1989) *Talking with Readers: Metadiscourse as Rhetorical Act*, American University Studies, Ser. XIV, vol. 17, New York: Peter Lang.

Du Bois, J. W. (2003) 'Discourse and grammar', in Tomasello, M. (ed.) *The New Psychology of Language*, vol. II, Mahwah, NJ: Lawrence Erlbaum, 47–87.

Eggins, S. and Slade, D. (1997) *Analysing Casual Conversation*, London: Cassell.

Firth, A. (1996) 'The discursive accomplishment of normality: on "lingua franca" English and conversation analysis', *Journal of Pragmatics* 26: 237–59.

Firth, A. and Wagner, J. (1997) 'On discourse, communication, and (some) fundamental concepts in SLA research', *The Modern Language Journal* 81: 285–300.

Ford, C. E., Fox, B. A. and Thompson, S. A. (2003) 'Social interaction and grammar', in Tomasello, M. (ed.) *The New Psychology of Language*, vol. II, Mahwah, NJ: Lawrence Erlbaum, 119–43.

Hyland, K. (2005) *Metadiscourse*, London: Continuum.

Johansson, S. (1998) 'On the role of corpora in cross-linguistic research', in Johansson, S. and Oksefjell, S. (eds.) *Corpora and Cross-Linguistic Research: Theory, Method, and Case Studies*, Amsterdam: Rodopi, 3–24.

Kurhila, S. (2003) *Co-constructing Understanding in Second Language Conversation*, Helsinki: University of Helsinki.

Luukka, M.-R. (1992) *Akateemista metadiskurssia*, Reports from the Language Centre for Finnish Universities no. 46, Jyväskylä: University of Jyväskylä.

Lyons, J. (1977) *Semantics*, Cambridge: Cambridge University Press.

Marx, S. and Swales, J. M. (2005) 'Announcements of self-repair: "all I'm trying to say is, you're under an illusion"' (www.lsa.umich.edu/eli/micase/kibbitzer.htm).

Mauranen, A. (1993a) *Cultural Differences in Academic Rhetoric. A Textlinguistic Study*, Frankfurt: Peter Lang.

Mauranen, A. (1993b) 'Contrastive ESP rhetoric: metatext in Finnish – English economics texts', *English for Specific Purposes* 12 (1): 3–22.

Mauranen, A. (2001) Reflexive academic talk: observations from MICASE', in Simpson, R. and Swales, J. M. (eds.) *Corpus Linguistics in North America*, Ann Arbor: University of Michigan Press, 165–78.

Mauranen, A. (2002a) '"A good question": expressing evaluation in academic speech', in Cortese, G. and Riley, P. (eds.) *Domain-Specific English: Textual Practices Across Communities and Classrooms*, Frankfurt: Peter Lang, 115–40.

Mauranen, A. (2003a) '"But here's a flawed argument": socialisation into and through metadiscourse', in Leistyna, P. and Meyer, C. F. (eds.) *Corpus Analysis. Language Structure and Language Use*, Amsterdam: Rodopi, 19–34.

Mauranen, A. (2004a) 'Spoken corpus for an ordinary learner', in Sinclair, J. McH. (ed.) *How to Use Corpora in Language Teaching*, Amsterdam: John Benjamins, 89–105.

Mauranen, A. (2004b) 'Talking academic: a corpus approach to academic speech', in Aijmer, K. (ed.) *Dialogue Analysis VIII: Understanding and Misunderstanding in Dialogue*, Tübingen: Max Niemeyer, 201–17.

Mauranen, A. (2005) 'English as a lingua franca – an unknown language?', in Cortese, G. and Duszak A. (eds.) *Identity, Community, Discourse: English in Intercultural Settings*, Frankfurt: Peter Lang, 269–93.

Mauranen, A. (2007a) 'Universal tendencies in translation', in Anderman, G. and Rogers, M. (eds) *Incorporating Corpora: The Linguist and the Translator*, Clevedon: Multilingual Matters, 32–48.

Mauranen, A. (2007b) 'Hybrid voices: English as the lingua franca of academics', in Fløttum, K., Dahl, T. and Kinn, T. (eds.) *Language and Discipline: Perspectives on Academic Discourse*, Newcastle: Cambridge Scholars Press, 244–59.

Mauranen, A. (2009) 'Spoken rhetoric: how do natives and non-natives fare?', in Suomela-Salmi, E. and Dervin, F. (eds.) *Cross-Linguistic and Cross-Cultural Perspectives on Academic Discourse*, Amsterdam: John Benjamins, 199–218.

Mauranen, A. (2010) 'Discourse reflexivity: a discourse universal? The case of ELF', *Nordic Journal of English Studies* 9 (2): 13–40.

Mazeland, H. and Huiskes, M. (2001) 'Dutch "but" as a sequential conjunction', in Couper-Kuhlen, E. and Seltin. M. (eds.) *Studies in Interactional Linguistics*, Amsterdam: John Benjamins, 141–69.

McCarthy, M. (1998) *Spoken Language and Applied Linguistics*, Cambridge: Cambridge University Press.

Meierkord, C. (1998) 'Lingua franca English: characteristics of successful non-native – non-native speaker discourse', *Erfurt Electronic Studies in English* (http://webdoc.sub.gwdg.de/edoc/ia/eese/eese.html).

Mortensen, J. (2010) 'Epistemic stance marking in the use of English as a lingua franca: a comparative study of the pragmatic functions of epistemic stance', PhD thesis, University of Roskilde.

Pekarek Doehler, S. (2001) 'Dislocation à gauche et organisation interactionnelle. *Marges Linguistiques*' 2: 177–94 (www.marges-linguistiques.com).

Penz, H. (2008) 'What do we mean by that? ELF in intercultural project work', paper presented in ESSE 9, the Ninth International Conference of the European Society for the Study of English, Aarhus, Denmark, 22–26 August 2008.

Penz, H. (2009) 'Metadiscourse in ELF project discussions', paper presented at the Second International Conference of English as a Lingua Franca, 6–8 April 2009, University of Southampton.

Riekkinen, N. (2009) '"This is not criticism, but…": softening criticism – the use of lexical hedges in academic spoken interaction', unpublished MA thesis, University of Helsinki (www.helsinki.fi/elfa).

Schiffrin, D. (1980) 'Meta-talk: organizational and evaluative brackets in discourse', *Sociological Inquiry* 50 (3/4): 199–236.

Sinclair, J. McH. (1991) *Corpus Concordance Collocation*, Oxford: Oxford University Press.

Sinclair, J. McH. (1992/2004) 'Trust the text', in Ravelli, L. and Davies, M. (eds.) *Advances in Systemic Linguistics: Recent Theory and Practice*, London: Pinter, 1–19. Reprinted in Sinclair, J. McH., *Trust the Text: Language, Corpus and Discourse*, London: Routledge, 9–23.

Sinclair, J. McH. (ed.) (2004) *How to Use Corpora in Language Teaching*, Amsterdam: John Benjamins.

Sinclair, J. McH. and Mauranen, A. (2006) *Linear Unit Grammar*, Amsterdam: John Benjamins.

Suviniitty J. (2010) 'Lecturers' questions and student perception of lecture comprehension', *English as a Lingua Franca*. Special issue of *Helsinki English Studies* (ed. A. Mauranen and N. Hynninen) 6: 44–57.

Suviniitty, J. (forthcoming) 'It ain't how you say it, it's what you say: a student perspective on Lectures in English as a Lingua Franca', PhD thesis, University of Helsinki.

Tanskanen, S.-K. (2000) *Collaborating Towards Coherence: Lexical Cohesion Across Spoken and Written Discourse in English*, Turku: University of Turku, Department of English.

Vande Kopple, W. J. (1985) 'Some exploratory discourse on metadiscourse', *College Composition and Communication* 36: 63–94.

Vertovec, S. (2006) 'The emergence of super-diversity in Britain', Working Paper No. 25, Centre on Migration, Policy and Society, University of Oxford (www.compas.ox.ac.uk/fileadmin/files/pdfs/Steven%20Vertovec%20WP0625.pdf).

7 *Repetition and rephrasing*

When I was working with a group of graduate students with a variety of second-language data, one expressed great surprise at having received results contrary to her firm expectations based on research literature: she had expected to see a much higher rate of self-repairs in EFL than ENL, but this was not what the data showed. L2 learners did not use self-repairs at an exceptionally high rate (Lonkila 2010). What she found was a self-repair rate very similar to what she had gleaned from the literature on L1, and more importantly, its frequency did not differentiate more advanced learners from less advanced ones, nor more highly rated students from lower-rated ones in a team-evaluated foreign-language speaking test (see 'HY-talk': http://blogs.helsinki.fi/hy-talk/suullisen-kielitaidon-arviointitutkimus/in-english/). The other students in the group were equally astonished, but as soon as they had recovered from their initial surprise, they came up with possible explanations. One was that maybe L2 speakers plan their utterances more carefully in advance than L1 speakers, and therefore have less need for repair. Perhaps. However, you cannot have it both ways: self-repairs cannot be a sign of dysfluency (as is normally seen to be the case in L2 speech) and fluency (as is usual when we talk about L1) at the same time. Yet we seem to entertain these discourses side by side, just as we do with repetition. Ever since Tannen's seminal book (1989) on the many uses of repetition in speaking, we have begun to see it as a normal and useful characteristic of speech (albeit slowly; see e.g. Biber et al. 1999:1053–55, where it is a sign of dysfluency). Repetition, repairs, and rephrasing are closely interrelated. They are all 'saying the same thing again', whether in the same or in a modified wording. There is thus a good case for seeing self-rephrasing or self-repairs as a type of repetition.

What about ELF? If there turns out to be little difference between learners and native speakers in the number of self-repairs, we would expect ELF to be no different, and the same might be extended to repetition. However, what learners do in test conditions need not be a very accurate indicator of what speakers do in real life, and quantitative comparisons are rendered questionable by such circumstantial differences. While it is therefore useful to keep in mind findings about learners and ENL speakers, it is necessary to investigate ELF, again, as language use of its own kind and in its own right. In this chapter we probe ELF for manifestations of repetition and rephrasing. As ubiquitous phenomena in spoken interaction, they relate to all the other traits that we have been exploring in the previous chapters, and throw light on talk from primarily two of the three viewpoints outlined in Chapter 2: the cognitive perspective of language processing and the microsocial perspective of interaction – with some suggestion of possible ways of usage diffusion as well.

7.1 Repetition in speech

Speaking which proceeds with a lot of self-repetition, especially in public arenas, tends to annoy hearers and impart an air of insecurity on the speaker's side. Although all conversations regurgitate the same things a few times, a person who does it too often is generally considered a bore. Yet repetition is everywhere; it is a basic building block of discourse.

Repetition in conversation has been studied fairly thoroughly. It is easy to notice, and it crops up in the smallest databases. Tannen (1989) was perhaps the first to bring to general awareness the many roles that repetition plays in discourse. Despite its roles in interactive discourse and its inevitability in speech, repetition has typically been construed as problematic; along with hesitations and pauses, it has been taken to signal processing difficulties, and in language learners especially, dysfluency and lack of competence. To some extent this negative view of repetition must be put down to what Linell (1982/2005) calls 'the written language bias', that is, assessing speaking in reference to the written standard. In this light, spoken language is typically described in negative terms, such as limitations, contingencies, and uncertainties: working-memory capacity, for example, is characteristically seen as a constraint on fluency rather than as a resource of processing; although working memory is limited, presumably natural languages have developed to fit within its limits. Both SLA and psycholinguistic traditions view language essentially from the perspective of an individual speaker (see e.g. Levelt 1989; Field 2003). In contrast, the textlinguistic study of written text has given a firm status to repetition in rhetorical analysis (e.g. Winter 1977; Hoey 1983), where its pivotal role in cohesion (Halliday & Hasan 1976) and effectiveness have been analysed from a reader's viewpoint. Very similar rhetorical structures are discernible in spoken monologic presentations (Mauranen 2009).

Repetition is often partial, and in some cases virtually indistinguishable from false starts, where a speaker begins an utterance, then changes tack before finishing it. Many false starts are restarts with exactly the same wording (*open s- open source software*), even though others are not and seem to result from second thoughts (*for examp- because it's*). Further down this cline we find rephrasing, where the speaker changes his or her wording to improve on the first formulation, to correct it, to make it clearer, or for emphasis or effect. Repetition and rephrasing are thus multifunctional. As Marx and Swales (2005) put it in their study, announced self-repairs (discussed as markers of rephrasing in Chapter 6) are 'phrases that a speaker might use when he or she wanted to tell the interlocutors that an attempt to fix a speech mistake, clarify an idea, or rephrase an ambiguous utterance was coming up'.

A number of studies on ELF have shown that repetition is common and comes in different manifestations ranging from self-repetition and rephrasing to other-repetition and discourse organising, which are crucial in helping prevent communication breakdowns, as well as in co-constructing comprehensibility and interactional cooperation (e.g. Mauranen 2006a, 2007b; Cogo 2009; Kaur 2009). In this, ELF speech is much like first language use; it uses repetition for gaining processing time, ascertaining comprehensibility, marking discourse boundaries, showing interactive alignment and affiliation, and structuring monologue.

Although the term 'self-repair' is well established in the field, it seems to imply that something went wrong with the initial formulation, which does not tally with the facts. Speakers can rephrase quite normal and unobjectionable expressions, and at least in the case of ELF, the first formulation can be more 'correct' than the new (*an unequal unequals amount of*). Rephrasing can also have pragmatic motives other than making expressions clearer or easier to understand, for example with second thoughts about having expressed something perhaps too abruptly (cf. 'concessive repairs' in Couper-Kuhlen & Thompson 2005). I shall therefore prefer the more neutral term 'self-rephrasing' and use it here.

7.2 Repeats as repetition

At the outset, repetition seems a more than obvious phenomenon, since it simply means saying the same thing twice. Yet what gets repeated is not quite straightforward to delimit. Biber et al. (1999) make a useful distinction between repetitions of a single word in speech (*the,*

the, the), which they refer to as 'repeats', and 'repetition' as a general term, covering also what they call 'deliberate repetition'. I shall adopt their term and talk about single-word repetitions as 'repeats'.

A harder task is to make a precise distinction between verbatim repetition and rephrasing. As basic ways of saying the same thing more than once, we might separate them by limiting repetition to verbatim cases. It would nevertheless still remain a simplification especially in speech: do pitch or loudness count, for example, or small morphological modifications? At the other end, how far can rephrasing and paraphrasing go and still be regarded as variations of the 'same', in terms of meaning or effect? The speaker can make it explicit (by using expressions such as *in other words*, *what I mean is …*) that he or she intends the meaning to stay the same despite new phrasing, but hearers may still interpret it to mean something different. But as we saw in Chapter 6, for instance, the expression *I mean* has other very different functions from just indicating that a reformulation is coming up. The problems of classification are considerable, if precise objective categorisation is required. But it may not be so relevant in categorising natural language; the important matter is to discern the basic types, and accept that borders tend to remain fuzzy.

It seems that strictly verbatim repetition is less common than modified repetition: repetitions of longer phrases, especially, tend to involve some alterations to the first utterance. Thus, repetitions can be 'fuzzy matches' involving similar if not identical stretches of speech, which listeners nevertheless recognise as repetitions. Such 'matching' (see Sinclair & Mauranen 2006) is based on close formal similarity (*Japanese mushrooms… sort of Japanese mushrooms*). On the basis of sheer formal properties, then, we can talk about repetitions of two kinds: exact repetitions of individual words (repeats), and more or less precise repetitions of longer units (matches). A certain fuzziness in the classification remains, but this reflects the general nature of linguistic categorisation and indeed observation.

A further complication arises from the ordinary practice of saying what unmistakably seems to be the same thing twice, but in clearly altered terms (*the poor nutrition level*, *this poor diet*). Rephrasing is a common enough habit among teachers, who want to make sure that their students understand and hopefully also remember what they have been told, but it occurs time and again in ordinary conversation, and is not infrequent in academic discussions. If matching is a somewhat fuzzy category, rephrasing on the basis of semantic similarity is even fuzzier. Nevertheless, for a simple similarity of sense it is always possible to apply a replacement test: does the meaning of the utterance remain the same if one expression of the pair is replaced by the other?

Even though it is clear that the repetition of a meaning is as significant as repeating a form, and in itself adds something to the unfolding discourse (e.g. emphasis, focus, or stance), the semantic replacement test can act as a rough guide for a semantic match, which I refer to as a rephrase. I avoid the term 'self-repair', unless it is clear from the context that a correction was intended (and achieved), because it is unnecessarily negative and implies that a perfectly ordinary spoken tactic is somehow problematic, drawn upon when speakers have got themselves into trouble. It is also one of those terms that subtly hint that speech is a corrupt version of language proper.

7.2.1 Repeats in monologue

The shortest and most mechanical kind of repetition is the 'repeat' type, the simple repetition of a single item or a very short sequence (*of, of, of* ...), and based on large ENL reference corpora, this is the most common type of repetition (Biber et al. 1999). The general motive for using them is the speaker's need to buy time – while he or she keeps talking – but what makes repeats interesting is that they tend to occur non-randomly at certain points in discourse. Biber et al. emphasise the planning logjams caused by the start of a major syntactic boundary: 'The evidence of repeats confirms that speakers have to plan hardest when embarking on major syntactic units, including finite clauses and full noun phrases' (Biber et al. 1999: 1059). Boundaries are importantly involved also in Levelt's (1989) classic work on speaking, which nevertheless stresses the occurrence of repairs towards the end of a unit, rather than the one that is to begin.

> a speaker's selective attention to his own output increases toward the ends of phrases. During speech a speaker's attentional resources are mainly used for message planning, but by the ends of phrases attention can momentarily shift in order to evaluate the current speech output. (Levelt 1989: 467)

Unit boundaries are in both interpretations the crucial point of occurrence for hesitation phenomena. As Field explains it with regard to pausing:

> At the end of a clause, we need to remove what is in our speech buffer (i.e. the group of words we have just produced) and to replace it with a new chunk of speech for the next stage of the utterance. Pausing seems to be vital to this process. (Field 2003: 36)

The other reason that most sources tend to agree on for repeats, pauses, and hesitations, including the three cited here, is lexical search. This ENL example from MICASE illustrates both (7.1):

(7.1)

> .so you know *they they they they* cre- created large luxury cars which you know at least sold among people um *of of of* higher incomes.

The extract from a lecture is flanked by two short pauses (marked [.]). The first repeats (*they*) occur at the beginning of a major unit, in this case a clause. Immediately preceding the repeat sequence are a discourse marker (*so*) and a cajoler (*you know*), which together with the pause further serve to mark a boundary in the monologue. The false start that follows (*cre- created*) strengthens the impression that the speaker is playing for time between meaningful content units. The second repeat sequence (*of*) occurs in the middle of a noun phrase, again preceded by a hesitation marker (*um*), and seems to be occasioned by the speaker's searching for a suitable descriptor of the people who might buy the kinds of cars he is talking about. This is not, however, a major but a minor boundary.

In ELF we find similar examples: in a lecture monologue, boundaries where clauses or new topics begin are likely places for repeats to occur (7.2), and so are minor boundaries (7.3).

(7.2)

> there was a heroic story of course *that er that that* finns originally came from the east and then they moved ...

(7.3)

> all the people on the globe are *of of* the same origin ...

None of the last three examples can be attributed to the speakers' efforts to keep the floor, because they come from lecture monologues where the lecturer need not worry about that. Rather, they seem to comply with one of the more abstract principles for online production articulated in Biber et al. (1999: 1067): 'keep talking'.

Some repeats seem to coincide with lexical search. In the following case (7.4), the ensuing search result is immediately repaired, which seems to indicate that the speaker is somewhat uncertain about the precise form of *distinctive*. The first outcome looks like an approximation of the target item, but once the speaker has retrieved the target at the second go, he seems happy with the result, as evidenced by his continued use of this form for the rest of the lecture.

(7.4)

> most people still in finland believe that because we have *a a a distinct distinctive* language ...

7.2.2 Repeats in dialogue

Interactional demands in dialogic exchanges differ from those of lectures, and even though academic discussions tend to have comparatively long turns, turn-taking is a major interactional task. When turn-changes occur, participants shift into primarily interactional mode, until the return to the 'contents' of the discussion has been made. The beginning of a turn is likely to cause the heaviest increase in the new speaker's processing load, as he or she has to cope with the simultaneous tasks of getting the floor and planning the utterance. The expectation is therefore for repeats to accumulate turn-initially, and there seems to be plenty of evidence for this. In this example (7.5) from a seminar discussion, the speaker's repeats fade out once he has cleared the initial stage of his turn:

(7.5)

> <S6> *the the* question is just *if if if* the first loan *if if* it came from the IMF or if the first debt actually came from somebody totally different and the IMF is supporting to reduce this debt

Personal subject pronouns tend to occur at the beginnings of clauses and are thus likely to be repeated also at the beginnings of turns. This is nicely illustrated by instances from a seminar where four ENL speakers participated along with nine non-native speakers. Turn-initial first-person pronouns were repeated by both (7.6, 7.7).

(7.6)

> <NS4> i i think the first question is to be wealth where erm is it wealth in a [in a]

(7.7)

> <S1> yeah i i think you're right </S1>

It would seem intuitively natural that ELF speakers use more repeats than ENL speakers, because processing a second language taps more of a speaker's resources than processing a first language. Although comparisons are not straightforward to make, I ran a simple quantitative comparison based on trigrams, that is sequences of three consecutive words, in MICASE and ELFA. The comparison[1] showed that among the most frequent 100 items differentiating ELFA from MICASE were four repeat sequences (*in in in, to to to*, *the the the*, and *of of of*, in this order), but none differentiating in the reverse direction (i.e. MICASE from ELFA). This supports the hunch that repeats are more common in ELF speech on the whole, although some common repeat types, such as *if* or personal pronouns did not distinguish the corpora. The comparison also showed, again along the lines of everyday experience, that there are more hesitations in ELF. Hesitations are unreliable to compare across corpora on account of different transcription conventions, but there were over twice as many trigrams with hesitations in ELFA than in MICASE. It is interesting to note, however, that repeats seem to act differently from rephrases.

The repeat sequences that differentiate the two corpora also appear to lend some support to the interpretation that major boundaries trigger repeats. Repeats of *and*[2] are of course likely to occur at syntactic junctures, while the definite article is likely to precede subject nouns, and thus be expected in clause-initial positions like pronouns. The prepositions, on the other hand, would seem to indicate that prepositional phrases (and in the case of *to*-infinitives) constitute boundaries relevant to planning and retrospective evaluation, as Levelt (1989) already proposed. This would imply that chunks in processing are shorter than a sentence or clause, as has been suggested in the literature and as was discussed above in Chapter 2. The studies suggesting this, Cheng et al. (2008), like Sinclair and Mauranen (2006), used both native and non-native speech as their data. In this respect, then, in the length and boundary marking of chunks, there does not seem to be much difference between ELF and ENL, despite the already noted greater frequency of repeats.

In addition to short grammatical items, individual content words were also repeated. These are not likely to show up high in corpus searches, because the tokens are 'local', that is, all different (*legislate, legislate*; *finally finally*; *westwards westwards*), even though the repeat type itself is not unusual. Even so, going through several randomly chosen transcribed hours of speech, it looks as though repeats cluster on grammatical items: prepositions, pronouns, and articles. It is thus mainly at various junctures expressing relations between units that playing for time takes place, whereas the focal elements that carry the most important meanings appear not to be subject to repetition of the repeat type. Planning thus seems to prepare for expressing the main points, not take place during their articulation.

It looks as if the same tendency to avoid repeats of the focal meaning-bearing elements goes for slightly longer repeated sequences as well (Example 7.8). In this way they allow for lighter processing passages between items that are heavier content-wise.

(7.8)

> those jobs are better paid *and they are and they are* better paid because they are more productive

When explanations for repeats, pauses, and hesitations have been sought, the perspective has virtually exclusively been that of the speaker's limited processing capacity. Clearly, however, short-term memory capacity, which is at stake here, is equally small (or large) in hearers, as was already discussed in Chapter 2. A refreshing remark is therefore that made by Field (2003: 36), who speculates that speakers who hesitate and insert a lot of pauses assist the non-native listener because they mark proportionately more word beginnings and endings. His observation is made in respect of ENL speakers, but it should equally apply to ELF. While assisting L2 speakers can hardly count as a plausible motive or explanation for an omnipresent feature of language, the suggestion is nevertheless a step towards a dialogic view of the phenomenon. Repeats, which like other minor 'dysfluencies' are part of normal speaking, probably help both speakers and hearers keep track. Fluent stretches tend to alternate with less fluent stretches in speech production (as we saw in Chapter 2, Section 2.2.2), and this is probably a welcome rhythmic alternation to both speakers and hearers, who collaborate closely to achieve communication and need less intense phases in addition to more intense ones. Field may well be right in surmising that L2 hearers could benefit from this in particular, and since it is a common feature in L2 speaking, the high frequency of repeats may well be conducive to successful ELF communication in allowing more processing time and marking boundaries.

7.3 Self-rephrasing

As we move on from repeats to larger and freer units, false starts are a category only observable in speech. They can be very similar to repetitions, as (7.9) shows, and occur in the same kinds of places.

(7.9)

> ... and *er dif- diverse- diversity in the other sec- sectors such such as* mining industry and trade ...

Like repeats, false starts are a normal part of speaking. They tend to gather at turn-initial points, as below (7.10), where repeats and repeated sequences also occur (*there are there are there are places where*; *if they they, if they do do the erm the work of states*), turn-internal junctures, and generally between what seem to be the central points of meaning that the speaker is trying to get across.

(7.10)

<S11> [okay] erm *wh- wh- wh- what* i'm just curious (of) names or or examples you use er <S10> mhm </S10> and you said er one time that er *there are there are there are* places where NGOs execute their government's programme er like (xx) for children on the streets but are they still NGOs and *if they they, if they do do* the erm the work of states are they still NGOs or if they if they act (xx) for the state are they still NGOs </S11>

Although false starts are commonly regarded as particularly characteristic of non-native speakers, and thereby seen as problems that interfere with speaking and should be eradicated if possible (e.g. Skehan 2005), it is not clear why they should present any difficulties to listeners. Quite the contrary, they seem to fulfil a useful function, just like repeats, in giving respite from high-attention processing, and giving time at the beginnings of turns for orientation to the next stage of the discourse for all participants.

7.3.1 *Self-repairs*

False starts can be recognised by a new start that follows them. They may not result from any error in the original start, nor result in a correction, and are therefore best seen as particular kinds of 'rephrases' rather than 'repairs', unless a clear error-and-correction sequence is noticeable. However, self-repairs do occur, as illustrated by the next two examples. In (7.11), the speaker appears to have second thoughts about the appropriate form for the desired level of generalisation – although no article-repair is made for *liver*.

(7.11)

<S7> *all the bil- all bilirubin* come from liver </S7>

(7.12)

<S6> in the textbook they said it said that nowadays they give livers even *from for* alcoholics <S7> yes </S7> what do you think about it is it ethically right </S6>

In (7.12), self-repair is also an appropriate term, because the speaker appears to have realised that he has produced an unintended meaning and hastens to put it right. Sometimes self-rephrasing shows clear signs of searching for an appropriate syntactic form (7.13).

(7.13)

<S2> ... and er after the independence *they have they had* a a new president er socialist leader... er i think he did a good job but *er he has been he was er criticised* by western countries ... </S2>

In other cases it is not obvious that the form is the primary target for rephrasing even though it is affected. The tense shifts in (7.13) affect meaning, but the tense distinctions that English makes between the present, the perfect, and the simple past tenses does not match tense distinctions in many other languages, so it is unclear to what extent this shift actually alters the sense intended, or interpreted. In example (7.14) the speaker engages in some repetition, but the replacement of *might be* for *may be* seems more related to the meaning, the level of confidence the speaker wishes to convey. This phenomenon has been analysed as 'concessive repair' by Couper-Kuhlen and Thompson (2005). By this they mean speakers' self-rephrases that tone down their first formulation of a view or statement. Couper-Kuhlen and Thompson have observed concessive repairs with strong or polarised views, which the speaker immediately goes on to soften up. In this example, the view is not strongly expressed to begin with, but the rephrase can be interpreted as a mitigation also in the light of the later *at least I think* in the same turn.

(7.14)

<S2> yeah, i mean one underlying tendency for this this big dilemma *may be might be* the this kind of obsession in progress that the modern west at least i think has ...

Sometimes self-rephrasing appears to be motivated by lexical choice. In the next example, the speaker seems to realise the first choice (*investigating*) was not quite what he wanted to say (*evaluating*), so he goes on to replace it. At the same time he changes the form of the object noun phrase into the plural as well. The context does not indicate whether he had been evaluating one university or many, so it remains unclear whether the latter rephrase led to greater or lesser accuracy of meaning.

(7.15)

<S1> [in in es-] in tallinn <S4> yeah in tartu </S4> i've been *investigating* this university so *evaluating* this universities last spring </S1>

An important aspect of self-rephrasing is clarification on the speaker's part. Whether it leads to an improvement on the first expression or not is not necessarily relevant; we can assume an 'emic' perspective, in which case the participants' viewpoint is the relevant one, not that of the researcher or outside expert, who looks at the discourse from an 'etic' angle. The example below is from a monologue, and the lecturer himself appears satisfied with the latter formulation (*it's not even idea*) because he continues without modifying it further, even though to an outside analyst it looks more problematic than the first (*there was no idea*).

(7.16)

there was no idea it's not even idea of democracy in those days

As we have seen, self-rephrasing sometimes verges on self-repair. While its clarificatory role may not always appear evident in these cases, when we move on the cline towards paraphrasing, it becomes unmistakable. As we proceed in Example (7.17) below from (a) to (e), rephrasing goes from what looks like incidental, even perhaps half-conscious in (a), slightly more intentional in (b), because it is marked by *or*, to more deliberate rephrasing in (c), which brings to mind familiar pedagogic practices. The next one (d) is clearly marked as saying the same thing using different wording, and finally (e) seems to be seeking purposeful rhetorical effect.

(7.17a)

because here, is the er *the point the place* in which they regulate the market,

(7.17b)

that kind of stuff and or beliefs belong to the 19th century

(7.17c)

the poor nutrition level this poor diet

(7.17d)

there was minimum social and career mobility which meant, or we could say that poor people had no chance for career mobility

(7.17e)

> unless we have an effective global framework erm which are the effective challenge ethical challenge of of in promoting sustainable development we will never reach a sustainable development *in the coming future in the time to come.*

The last examples show self-rephrasing moving closer to paraphrasing and, along the way, a growing focus on meaning. While some rephrasing is clearly oriented to amending form (like 7.16), in other instances paraphrases of the same sense may appear to the speaker to be more accurate or more appropriate (like 7.17a, b), and in yet others, the speaker may want to make specifications or alterations to meaning (7.14). Adding or removing hedges would be typical alterations in meaning, and so are additions of a detail or specification, as in (7.18), where we see the speaker interrupting his noun phrase to insert a specification.

(7.18)

> already had a very developed *communica- elec- electronic communication systems* compared to bigger countries

Many researchers have noted that ELF communication tends to be noticeably content-oriented, as discussed in the previous chapter. While they may well mean different things with it, one interpretation is that as hearers are focused on following the meaning, or the contribution to the 'message' that the current speaker is making, they pay as little attention as possible to form, unless it gets in the way of making sense of the intended meaning. Purely form-based rephrases do not necessarily assist the hearer, as illustrated in the following turn and the minimal response token (7.19):

(7.19)

> <S5> and then there are the serum albumin and protein (xx) to to see to see the capacity of the liver to to <SIC> synthetise </SIC> proteins and so you you see how it *work* <S6> [yes] </S6> [it] *worked* </S5>

Speaker 5 corrects himself (*worked*), but S6 has already responded to the content of what he said by the time he utters the repaired form. Such hearer behaviour is in line with Kurhila's (2003) findings on native/non-native exchanges: non-native speakers made many reformulations, but native speakers did not correct them, or provide the correct form as confirmation of a successful repair. Instead, they oriented to the contents and responded accordingly. Form-based rephrases are nevertheless very frequent in ELF, as I shall show presently. This lays open to question the traditional explanation in SLA studies, which Kurhila also makes, that L2 speakers make reformulations in the hope that their L1 interlocutors provide the correct model as a response to their signalled uncertainty about the form. In ELF, speakers cannot rely on each other for language authority – and indeed, other-corrections are rare.

Minor self-repairs of form, such as those adjusting a morphological detail, do not add much to clarity, unlike rephrases which affect meaning. Such small amendments do not seem to be of much interactional consequence (as seen in 7.19). A more plausible explanation that I would like to propose is that they indicate particular aspects of language processing, related to entrenchment. Many of these are likely to accompany the processing of a language whose items and forms are less entrenched than is usually the case in speakers' first languages. It is possible that searches for items that are not firmly connected through many neural pathways take slightly longer, and the retrieval of a new alternative follows after a delay, even though one item has already been uttered. If speakers monitor and evaluate their production more actively towards the ends of units, as Levelt (1989) suggested, the second alternatives, if judged to be better than those first accessed, might then be likely to turn up at that point. This is just one of the many indications of shaky entrenchment, such as approximations, discussed in Chapter 4 in more detail.

7.3.2 Rephrasing in ELF and ENL

Well aware of the problems involved in using very small samples, I ventured a glimpse into randomly picked parallel extracts of just 1,000 words of polylogic seminar discussion drawn from ELFA and MICASE to check if the received view (even though not supported by Lonkila's (2010) results on learners reported at the outset of this chapter) that L2 speakers engage in more rephrasing than ENL speakers is supported by ELF data. I want to stress the highly tentative nature of the comparison, whose principal value perhaps lies in the hypotheses that arise from it for further testing. It nevertheless suggests certain clear differences between ENL and ELF speech, which makes it interesting.

To get at self-rephrasing proper, I ignored repeats (*they they they*) and hesitations (*erm*, *uh*, *i-its*, *le-let's*), which is also more compatible with the rephrasing markers discussed in Chapter 6. Repeats may well play a role in accounting for the commonly held belief that ELF speakers rephrase themselves more; as we saw above, among the best trigram differentiators of ELFA from MICASE were indeed a few repeats. Moreover, there is evidence that if repeats are counted in, L2 speech has remarkably high frequencies of repetition (e.g. Kurhila 2003). In contrast to this general picture, the simple count from the seminar samples yielded a result with ENL speakers actually rephrasing more: MICASE showed 15 rephrases in 1,000 words and ELFA 10. Thus, ELF speakers appeared to rephrase *less*, not more than ENL speakers. Although this quantitative difference is proportionally large, it is not entirely reliable given the small size of the sample. What is more interesting is the qualitative difference that emerged from these discussion extracts.

I compared two more things: first, restarts and minor adjustments, that is, how proper restarts after false starts compared to minor adjustments without restarts. Secondly, how rephrases affecting form compared to those affecting meaning. What I call 'adjustments' occurred when some rephrasing was made on the fly as it were, without abandoning the message but continuing the main clause structure already begun (7.21). While there are always borderline cases, the distinction is in principle clear. In the first example (7.20) the structure starts again from a reporting clause when the speaker seems to have lost track of what she wanted to say in the reported clause (and the reporting clause *I don't think that* is also replaced by a new one *I don't have this feeling that*). The second example (7.21) shows how a speaker just replaces a prepositional phrase begun with an article by one without an article, but the syntactic structure, or the narrative line around the adjustment, is not affected.

(7.20)

i don't think that it's in not for a *i don't have this feeling that* ... (ELFA)

(7.21)

and just hear it and *go to the to home* and er require ... (ELFA)

Adjustments were roughly equally common in both (ELFA 8, MICASE 7), whereas restarts following false starts were clearly more common in ENL (ELFA 2, MICASE 7). If the result is repeated elsewhere, minor adjustments might contribute to explaining the common intuitive perception that people have of L2 speakers correcting themselves more.

A more dramatic difference emerged when rephrases were divided according to whether they involved a change of just form (as in 7.22) or of meaning (7.23).

(7.22)

> i agreed with uh, Justin's contention *about that, that about the fact that,* you know um, i- it's very hard to prove (MICASE)

(7.23)

> there are only so many people off the str- i mean, by your theory will get all the people off the streets (MICASE)

The outcome of this comparison that I found surprising was that no rephrasing affected meaning in this extract of ELF, while half of the ENL rephrasing (7/15) did. Even though the sample is too small for wide-reaching conclusions, it suggests that it is structures (at levels from morphology to syntax) that ELF speakers seem to be adjusting and modifying most. In itself the finding that form is often adjusted in ELF is not surprising, quite the contrary, as it is well in line with observations on processing (Chapter 4) – the surprise was that no meaning adjustments were in evidence in the ELF sample, although they did appear in ENL in an equally small sample. That ELF speakers would not rephrase meanings at all is not borne out by other analyses; as we already saw above (e.g. in 7.12), ELF speakers' reformulated expressions can involve new lexical choices, sometimes with more specific meanings than the first time around, and we also saw ELF speakers engaging in concessive repairs (e.g. in 7.14). But even if there is only a proportional quantitative difference, that is, less meaning rephrasing in ELF than ENL, this is interesting and worth further checking.

So far we have discussed repetition as self-repetition, starting from involuntary repeats and ending up with rephrasing for clarity or effect. The vital role of repetition and rephrasing for achieving comprehensibility in ELF discourse was discussed in Chapter 5 (see also Kaur 2009; Mauranen 2006a). In these contexts, the focus has been mainly on the speaker's self-repetition. But alongside a speaker's playing for time, clarifying and organising his or her own discourse, repetition of an interlocutor's speech plays important roles in co-constructing dialogue, as will be discussed in the next section.

7.4 Repetition and interaction

We can observe more than processing through repetition. Interaction and facework draw on repetition in a quite noteworthy manner. Making one's talk clear and explicit is in itself a way of adapting to interlocutors, a form of recipient design, and can be seen as accommodating to interlocutors in a wide sense of accommodation (Cf. Chapter 2, Section 2.3.3). Speakers tend to adapt especially if they do not know each other well or cannot assume much in terms of shared knowledge or linguistic habits. ELF speakers seem to be well aware of this, and utilise repetition and rephrasing for explicitation. Much self-repetition and paraphrasing is occasioned by normal contingencies of spoken interaction, in which ELF is no different from any other kind of speaking. So, for example, after overlapping or simultaneous speech, repetitions and paraphrases are common (Kaur 2009). But in addition to making themselves clear and their points comprehensible to their interlocutors, speakers also actively engage with each other and use repetition as a resource for achieving this. Importantly, other-repetition ('allo-repetition'), repeating the interlocutor's expressions, is brought to play.

Other-repetition, or 'echoing', as I like to call it, is a strategic resource that can show alignment with the speaker of the original utterance (e.g. Kangasharju 2002; Lichtkoppler 2007). Cogo (2009) recently analysed other-repetition in ELF conversations and noted that it serves a number of functions, two of which were particularly prominent in her study: maintaining rhythmic synchrony and showing alignment with the speaker of the original utterance. Cogo's conversational data was generically rather distant from the academic discussions that are the focus here, but provides a good backdrop against which to view other-repetition in ELF talk in this more institutional environment. Which features are ELF, which might be generic, and what is likely to be shared by all people communicating in face-to-face situations? For the analysis at hand, I looked particularly closely at echoing in three graduate seminar sessions (over six hours altogether) in different disciplines (sociology, medicine, and cultural studies), but drew on other available seminar data for more examples as well.

Speakers' orientation to content is plain in these discussions; conceptual issues are raised and talked about, and even though participants build and maintain social relationships at the same time, there is no doubt about the primacy of content, or the 'message'. The interactants engage in conceptual work, negotiating notions relevant to the topics at hand and discussing the most appropriate terms and labels for the concepts. A prominent aspect of the discussions is a search for consensus on terms and definitions. In this consensual orientation, university discussion strongly (and perhaps surprisingly) resembles casual conversation (Eggins & Slade 1997); we are reminded again of one of the questions the MICASE corpus project sought answers to from the start: is academic speech more like academic writing or like other kinds of speaking? The answer, which was not at all obvious at the outset, much as it may seem so in hindsight, was that it is more like talk than like academic writing, as already discussed in Chapter 4. The drive towards consensus seems to cohere with the tendency to keep criticism more muffed or muted than positive evaluation, even though criticism is an inherent element of academic genres. Agreement, praise, and positive evaluation are more directly and openly brought forth than criticism and disagreement (see e.g. Mauranen 2002a,b).

7.4.1 Echoing in search of content

We thus find that much of the discussion in seminars revolves around conceptual issues: what is meant by a concept labelled with a given term, how participants define their understanding of concepts and their interrelations, and what distinctions apply. Questions of these kinds are taken up and negotiated, and common understanding is actively sought. Repetition is drawn on as a useful way of keeping track of topics and the progress that is being made. Example (7.24) illustrates this process. It is a little long, but S10's first turn in the extract sets the scene at this stage of the discussion so that the conceptual and terminological negotiation is perhaps easier to see in context.

(7.24)

<S10> yeah er the pressure groups are are only er one part of the erm er the general non-government organisation it is not part of the erm advocacy non-government organisation liberation (while ma- er) some erm (xx) project and the erm there there are the operation groups because they er their activity is based on the fields and they operate er for example er in the school in the field of (xx) human rights not in direct er er relation with the erm most important institutions er international institutions so er they don't signify the er politics of these institution but they erm in like like *pressure groups* but er erm by means the direct acts actions </S10>
<S11> okay erm </S11>
<S1> trade union <SU> mhm </SU> is a [*pressure group*] </S1>
<S10> [*a pressure group*] </S10>
<S1> not a NGO <S10> yeah </S10> which [one] </S1>
<S11> [(i'd say)], *pressure groups* [erm] </S11>
<S10> [press-] er it's *the pressure group* </S10>
<S1> it's *a pressure group* </S1>
<S10> mhm in my opinion yes </S10>
<S1> yeah i i think you're right </S1>

<S11> and i think the main difference is that er *pressure groups* er represent an interest whereas er NGOs er both represent and try to to improve the situation of the interest </S11>

Three speakers negotiate the meaning of 'pressure group', and particularly its relationship to 'NGO'. S10 in her lengthy first turn is using both terms as given, after which S1, who is the seminar chair, queries the extension of the concept 'pressure group' as employed by S10 – does it include trade unions? S10 replies by repeating the term, in effect saying 'yes'. S1 pursues the notion further, asking whether trade unions also qualify as NGOs. S11 chips in and puts forward the 'pressure group' interpretation. S10 now hastens to express her support for the same interpretation by repeating *pressure group* again, and S1 reproduces this understanding once more by another repetition. S10 confirms it as her view (*in my opinion*), and S1 indicates agreement (*I think you're right*). Finally S11 goes on to make the distinction quite explicit, giving reasons for his interpretation, by now accepted as the shared view.

Three speakers thus participated in co-constructing this conceptual clarification, where repeating the label for the focal concept worked to maintain cohesion and conceptual clarity by keeping references and agreements highly explicit. Repeating *pressure group* after S11 had taken the view that trade unions are pressure groups not NGOs seems pivotal here in establishing the agreed interpretation. It is reaffirmed by two indications of agreement (*in my opinion yes*; *I think you're right*), which is quite typical of these discussions: positive evaluations get repeated by participants, just as agreement tends to be – the consensus that has been reached is, as it were, sealed in this way before the point is relinquished and the discussion moves on to new topics.

Repeating a word or phrase gives prominence on the item agreed on and, I would like to argue, maintains clarity about which concept, idea, or item is the focal one, and in this way is a very useful means for negotiations concerning concepts. It also puts more emphasis on the agreement than a mere *yes* or *yeah*, both of which are used not only as general markers of agreement but also as minimal responses, back-channelling, turn organisers, and comprehension checks among other things; they have so many uses that they cannot carry much prominence or emphasis. Example (7.25) illustrates the added value of repetition over merely indicating agreement:

(7.25)

<S6> ... and the ASAT is all in the cytoplasm and in mitochondria so [that's why] <S5> [yeah] </S5> the ALAT rises more easily </S6>

<S3> and is *more specific* </S3>
<S6> yeah *more specific* that's right, <COUGH> </S6>
<S5> and then there are the serum ...

S3 adds a detail on what S6 has just been saying about ALAT, and S6 endorses the contribution by echoing her words (*more specific*). This is a seminar on internal medicine, where one of the students (S6) is the chair. In the last two examples, then, echoing works in a confirmatory move when speakers join forces to construct messages.

There are many ways in which ELF negotiations can be complex, not least in the kinds of environments we are concerned with: apart from being linguistically and culturally complex, these situations also have several participants who speak, that is, they are polylogic. The extract that follows (7.26) is illuminating on this score, with the main point jointly constructed by seven participants (out of the altogether ten that were present). This is a seminar on occupational health with the seminar leader a senior staff member who chairs the session. The extract was already partly discussed above in connection with metadiscourse (Example 6.7; Chapter 6).

(7.26)

<S2> yeah but if we take now the the paper mill first and then go after a while to the to the institute of occupational health then </S2>
<S1> and how <S9> [yeah] </S9> [about] the maintaining *because i i i think that the mo- most of them are working with er with maintaining situations* and </S1>
<S8> yes </S8>
<BS7> *yeah [80 85 are in the technical]* </BS7>
<S1> [so so they are they are not just sitting] there </S1>
<BS7> *technical* but er 15 are administrators </BS7>
<S2> yeah so the education for *for most of the people is something engi- engineering or technical* </S2>
<S8> yes *most of [them]* </S8>
<BS7> [yeah] [(xx)] </BS7>
<S2> *[most of them]* </S2>
<S10> *most of them are engineering* </S10>
<S1> i i i think that </S1>
<S8> [well *technical personnel* (they would be called)] </S8>
<S1> *[maybe not maybe] just technicals* </S1>
<SU> *technical* </SU>
<S2> mhm yeah </S2>
<BS7> yeah *technicals perhaps* yeah </BS7>

After the chair (S2) has established the order of dealing with the topics, S1 suggests that maintenance staff in the paper mill be talked about. S8 and BS7 agree; then BS7 and S1 compete for the floor for one turn, and BS7 manages to get it. The chair gives a paraphrase interpretation of what he makes of the reports of S1, S8, and BS7 so far, repeating BS7's *technical*. S8 accepts the interpretation, by repeating *most of them* from S2's formulation. BS7 makes a supportive response, then S2 starts another turn with *most of them* again, but S10 interrupts, repeating both *most of them* and *engineering*. In this way, general acceptance has been signalled to the point made jointly by S1, S8, and BS7 that a large majority of the paper mill employees are technical workers involved in maintenance and have a technical or engineering education. Coming to this has taken several rounds of expressing agreement, not only by a number of *yeah*s and *yes*'s, but by noticeably repeating central noun phrases (*most of them*, *engineering*, and *technical*).

The talk then moves on to a suitable occupational label for these employees. S8 makes the first suggestion (*technical personnel*), S1 prefers plain *technicals*, an unknown student *technical*, with S2 and BS7 coming in support of the second one. Again reaching this consensus has involved fuzzy matching and repetitions of *technical* four times by as many speakers. It illustrates the way topics can be closed with positive evaluation, as has earlier been observed in written genres (e.g. Hoey 1983), and additionally that indicating agreement is an important part of closing topics. The agreement is thus collectively ratified as it were, and at the same time the collective and repeated confirmations signal group affiliation and build it up. Speakers show their involvement and interest by participating and indicating agreement. Silent acceptance can do the job of signalling group consensus, but it rests on shakier ground than when agreement is voiced.

7.4.2 *Echoing in search of form*

Interactional echoing can also serve the purposes of linguistic support, which one might expect to be more prominent in lingua franca communication than in L1 talk. On occasion, a participant is clearly at a loss to know what the target word or term might be and asks for help:

(7.27)

<S6> mhm, erm i don't know it's wa- it was only the that my position becau- about these position of these two women they're,

focus- focusing on gender they're *i don't know what's in english* it's er maybe female activist or something like that <SS> [@@] </SS> [@*i don't know what's it@] is it emancinet* but </S6>
<S1> [@uh-huh *emancipated@* women they're normally] </S1>
<SS> [@@] </SS>
<S5> yeah what have we really *emancipated* </S5>
<S1> well what what mean what does it mean that you're really *emancipated* </S1>
<SS> [@@] </SS>
<S6> [*emancipated*] </S6>
<S4> i think it's a kind of er radical feminists </S4>

In this example (7.27), S6 first uses a paraphrase (*these two women they're, focus- focusing on gender*), then announces that she is looking for an English expression that would convey her intended meaning (*I don't know what's in English*), and continues with another paraphrase (*female activist*), making it clear that this is an attempt to get closer to the target, but not the term she had in mind (*maybe ... or something like that*). Other participants laugh in sympathy, but are apparently not clear about what her target is. Then, while joining in the laughter, S6 repeats the help appeal (*I don't know what's it*), and finally suggests an approximation of her target term: (*is it emancinet*). This time it is close enough for others to recognise it and be able to help, and S1 provides the usual form of the term. Although S1 gives the correct form, she does so in passing, as it were, continuing with the discussion at the same time, before she is interrupted by general laughter. S5 then continues to develop the topic by picking up the term now established and asking a question related to it (*what have we really emancipated*). S1 chips in to rephrase S5's question in a more grammatical form (*you're really emancipated*). During the general laughter that follows again, S6 echoes the term once more, perhaps to rehearse or reaffirm the form she had just been looking for. A fourth speaker, S4, then carries on the discussion by suggesting an answer to the question posed by S5.

The example illustrates the simultaneous achievement of several things – content-oriented development of topics and negotiation of concepts, cooperative solving of language problems, and doing face-work. All these aspects of the discussion clearly constitute a joint achievement. We can see here how problems of language are adeptly dealt with on the side, as the co-construction of shared knowledge takes place. Echoing each other's phrases is done by somewhat fuzzy matching, as if imperceptibly doing corrective or clarificatory language work, but above all it maintains topical focus and indicates the relevance of the new points to the earlier ones, in this way aligning the turns to previous speakers' turns. By contributing to the emerging shared knowledge, the participants thus show affiliation to each other at the same time and with largely the same linguistic means.

7.4.3 *Echoing as relational practice*

The speakers engage in a good deal of facework also beyond affiliative repetition: the general laughter is friendly, and relieves the stressful experience of not finding the right words. In a similar way, allusions to notoriously difficult issues raised in earlier discussions, such as the meaning of 'really emancipated', trigger general laughter, which relieves tension and renders the difficulty a shared experience. This is part of the 'relational practice' that Holmes and Marra (2004) talk about. As Pullin Stark (2009) notes, humour and laughter constitute relational work, and thereby contribute to good workplace relationships. Clearly a very similar role can be attributed to these strategies more generally in academic groups. Thus, although the orientation to content was clearly observable here, as in the earlier extracts in this section, it does not preclude a simultaneous orientation to interaction and facework.

In the next two examples, repetition and laughter are both used in the exchange where they seem to help create a friendly, unthreatening atmosphere. Moreover, in these brief snippets from one seminar, the maintenance of good social relations appears to take priority over content orientation (7.28, 7.29).

(7.28)

<S2> yeah </S2> of course and this kind of [socialisation] <S2> [yeah] </S2> and to take a child as a social-cultural phenomenon not only from didactic point of view but pedagogy as you mentioned <S2> yes </S2> yeah <NAME> but also <NAME> mhm-hm <S2> mhm-hm </S2> <COUGH>, you were talking also (about genres) [maybe (that)] </S1>

<S2> [yes well there are] *different* ways of </S2>

<S1> very [*different* @@] </S1>

<S2> [presenting literature but] you know i have i have this sociological interest in [literature] <S1> [uh-huh] </S1> because that is my er main interest ...

(7.29)

<S3> the author a- also well organised some some happenings @in schools@ er so it was er comparable to [this] <S2> [mhm-hm] </S2>

what you mentioned so i think sex and shopping is may- @ or may be really@ </S3>
<SS> [@@] </SS>
<S2> [yeah these are *the the the hot- the hottest issues* @@] </S2>
<S1> [*hot hot issues provocations hottest @hottest issues@* probably yeah] </S1>
<S2> <COUGH> <S1> mhm </S1> yeah </S2>

Joking and laughter are effective means of managing relations, and as Pullin Stark (2009) observes, they manifest resourcefulness and achievement in lingua franca use. Repetition of each other's wordings is much involved in achieving humour in interaction, and it simultaneously shows affiliation, as S1 is clearly doing in the last two examples. In (7.28), she echoes S2's words and then laughs, making her turn both friendly and jokey. In (7.29) there is general laughter already, following S3's reference to a lightly taboo topic and laughing about it. S2 then tops up the laughter episode by labelling them *the hottest issues* and laughing herself, at which point S1 follows suit, repeating her wording a couple of times, laughing. After this they return to the main topic in a more serious tone.

When speakers start using each other's phrases or linguistic mannerisms, we can also see this as a kind of echoing, although it might perhaps strike the observer as more trivial. Yet, although such repetitions may well be less conscious than the negotiation of terms and concepts, or indicating agreement or generating humour, they nevertheless carry subtle but intriguing hints about real-time diffusion of expressions. The speaker (S4) in the next extract (7.30) uses a phrase, innocent-looking in itself (*in a sense*), which is used by one of the others (S2) very frequently, and in whose speech it has become a kind of mannerism (... *but in a sense i've er it's hard to explain these things*). The extracts come from a long seminar discussion where S2 talks a good deal, defending her own paper, and uses *in a sense* almost to the point of monotony. S4 speaks less but is also active; she expresses a strong attraction to topics relevant to S2's field of interest but voices somewhat opposing views to S2. At a fairly late stage of the discussion, S4 uses S2's favourite phrase (7.30):

(7.30)

<S4> yeah but that also has to do with the er method of of [filming] <S1> [mhm- hm] </S1> and making the film <S2> yeah but it's </S2> it's *in a sense* it's dogmatic even this film al- although it's not a dogma </S4>

The phrase has become quite noticeable in the discussion, with S2 playing a rather dominant role, and perhaps particularly salient to S4 who tends to take an opposing stance. The emotional load that S2's mannerism thus has for S4 may be apt to induce her to use it too, perhaps involuntarily or even against her will, much as people start humming melodies that have subliminally caught their attention even though they may not like them.

A more interesting detail in this case is that S2 also uses the phrase in a non-standard way, producing *in a sense that* several times (... *it this film isn't anti-religious in a sense that she bess just has her own way of believing in god* ...). This non-standard form is also picked up by S4 (7.31):

(7.31)

> <S4> but i just it's hard for me to understand that you can be at the same time you can be very sure of yourself *in a sense that* you know what's your mission and you you know what you have to do <S2> [mhm] </S2> [but still] you can be you're so unstable i find it difficult to [understand yeah] </S4>

The last two examples give rise to a couple of other interesting observations: first, to whatever extent ELF speakers turn to each other as models of language use, standard and non-standard forms do not get noticeably differentiated. If this is how expressions spread, they do not pass through any 'standardisation filter', but other factors, such as salience, memorability, and interactional meaningfulness are more likely to play decisive roles. The other observation relates to repetition: echoing other speakers' wordings need not show affiliation (although it does align turns). Speaker 4 did not agree with S2's approach or interpretations most of the time, and on both of the occasions shown here she was calling them in to question. Of course, unlike the examples of interactive negotiation above, in this case other-repetition did not follow the first utterance immediately. Neither did it focus on a lexically central item; *in a sense* is a hedge, or in the non-standard use attested here part of a multi-word conjunction. It is relatively peripheral to the discourse, and therefore its role may be regarded as minor. Nevertheless, by latching on to an opponent's wording, S4 indicates cooperativeness in placing herself in the same discourse, but she does not indicate affiliation by doing this.

Echoing serves multiple functions in these polylogic discussions that are strongly oriented to the business at hand. Repeating other speakers' expressions, these speakers take up and continue topics that they deem to be important to the matter on the agenda. Other-repetitions thus make it clear what topics are being developed, and compared to, say, pronominal references they take fewer risks of misunderstanding. At the same time, importance and centrality judgements come to the fore by prioritising some topics over others. In this way, evaluative facets of discourse are attended to. Showing agreement by echoing is a matter of simultaneously being clear, placing emphasis, and doing facework. In brief, echoing is instrumental in making contributions to the shared knowledge that is being developed as well as the interactional concerns in these discussions.

Shared knowledge is constructed by talking about issues of content; echoing helps negotiate interpretations of central concepts and facts – we could talk about 'matching speaker perspectives'. Multiple indications of agreement seem to be an appropriate way of closing topics, and showing alignment and affiliation at the same time. Compared to Cogo's (2009) findings, these content-oriented polylogic discussions did not seem to show much that could be interpreted as rhythmic synchrony, but much that showed alignment. Again, a strong orientation to content does not override interactional concerns, and language resources are put to both uses without apparent difficulty.

7.5 Summary

This chapter has focused on the many roles of repetition in ELF talk. Repetition was observed above all in dialogic interaction, and its fairly well-known rhetorical power in organising monologue was not touched upon here. Repetition in dialogue brought up on the one hand aspects of individuals' processing in the alternating capacities of speaker and hearer, and on the other hand in interactional cooperation.

ELF speech seemed to show proportionally more form-based rephrasing than ENL speech. The comparisons were not based on large data samples, but the direction seemed clear, and the result seems relatively easy to relate to other findings. Minor adjustments of form, for example adjusting morphological details, came up from different analyses. One thing that they suggest is that these are less well entrenched linguistic structures, as second-language structures presumably are, and that certain minor fluctuations in form are common and not communicatively disturbing.

The more striking finding came from the analysis that suggested there might be less meaning-based adjustment in ELF than in ENL. If true on a larger scale, this might open new questions on any kind of second language use. It merits further investigation.

In terms of processing, it looks as if repetitions of different kinds serve similar purposes in making processing a more palatable task to both speakers and hearers. Repeats that seem to indicate that the speaker is playing for time appear at various kinds of junctures in discourse – between chunk boundaries and clause boundaries, for instance. Thus they occur between elements that are principal message-bearing units and the most crucial contributors to the evolving shared understanding of content. In this way, the repeats, together with hesitations and filled pauses, facilitate processing for both speakers and hearers by dishing out the message in shortish chunks. At the same time, this helps separate the main elements from the more peripheral ones and provides brief breaks, breathing spaces as it were, between fluent stretches which are likely to require more planning as well as more receptive processing capacity. In these respects, there would not seem to be any principled distinction between ENL and ELF processing, although ELF may manifest and need more of these breathing spaces. This also has repercussions on facilitating comprehensibility and interaction, and would perhaps be something for ELT to consider.

Self-rephrasing and repairs reflect the complexity of processing and invoke a multi-layered view of language: the different linguistic levels of processing may not progress in perfectly aligned chunks (Chapter 2). Instead, a certain staggering has been noticed in the processing of units at different levels. Traditionally distinguished levels of language may not be central units in processing, and may proceed at different speeds. Forward planning may simply get interference from delayed hits from earlier searches. This may then show itself in form-related self-rephrases, as the speaker's online problem-solving results in new items after a time lag.

False starts can also serve useful functions, instead of just indicating planning or processing difficulty. They tend to concentrate in turn-initial positions, where planning and processing loads naturally intensify, not least because turn-taking involves complex simultaneous attention to both interactional and content-related concerns. This concerns all participants, and the initial repetitions and rephrases give everyone a chance for reorientation before the important points by the new speaker come up.

Repetition in dialogue supported the findings in previous chapters that while there is a distinct content-orientation in ELF talk, this does not rule out interactional concerns. In the light of the present analyses, ELF speaking is interaction-oriented like any face-to-face communication. Repetition served the simultaneous achievement of several interactional things – content-oriented development of topics and negotiation of concepts, cooperative solving of language problems, and doing facework.

A clear connection to the explicitation tendency discussed in Chapter 6 can be seen in other-repetitions, or echoing (see also Chapter 4).

Echoing helps keep track of topics being developed less ambiguously than, say, pronominal references. This is in line with Warren's finding (2006) that other-repetition was more common among L2 speakers in Hong Kong than among ENL speakers; the more general explicitness tendency may go a long way in explaining the Hong Kong results as well. Moreover, echoing seems to facilitate negotiating interpretations – or 'matching speaker perspectives', which is an important facet of achieving communication.

While echoing can serve to show agreement, and thus simultaneously facilitate clarity, placing emphasis, and doing facework, it does not always need to show affiliation. This was suggested by one analysis in particular. The value of this finding is that it draws a clear distinction between cooperativeness in a 'weak', or neutral sense, underpinning all communicative interaction, and in a 'strong' or positive sense, showing affiliation and agreement. Thus, cooperativeness by itself can be signalled by echoing, which places the speaker in the same discourse as the addressee, but it can serve as a springboard for disagreement just as well as agreement. In this sense, it can be related to the chief functions of metadiscourse in Chapter 6: it is cooperative to the extent that it establishes a shared perspective or point of departure between participants, but it does not follow that agreement is reached. This again indicates the close connection between interactional and message-related facets in constructing successful discussions.

Finally, this chapter also suggested that ELF speakers' echoing each other's turns of phrase may have more lasting consequences. This is a similar case to *registrate* in Chapter 2, where we also saw adoption of another speaker's form in progress. In neither case is there any telling whether the speakers continue using the forms, and whether they will spread. However, we also saw in Chapter 4 instances of fairly widespread non-standard forms in ELF speech. An important point here is that as forms diffuse in ELF interaction, standard and non-standard forms do not get noticeably differentiated. Expressions do not pass through a 'standardisation filter' to spread. Other factors are more likely to come into play, such as salience, memorability, and interactional meaningfulness. What we are seeing here are mechanisms conducive to change, even if change itself may take a long time to establish itself and be detected.

Notes

1. Using the Keywords function in Wordsmith Tools. The comparison produces a rank-ordered list of the most frequent trigrams and shows which ones best differentiate one corpus from the other.
2. Not among the 100 best differentiators, but still high as the 125th.

References

Biber, D., Johansson, S., Leech, G., Conrad, S. and Finegan E. (1999) *The Longman Grammar of Spoken and Written English*, London: Pearson Education.

Cheng, W., Greaves, C. and Warren, M. (2008) *A Corpus-driven Study of Discourse Intonation*, Amsterdam: John Benjamins.

Cogo, A. (2009) 'Accommodating difference in ELF conversations: a study of pragmatic strategies', in Mauranen, A. and Ranta, E. (eds.) *English as a Lingua Franca: Studies and Findings*, Newcastle-upon-Tyne: Cambridge Scholars Publishing, 254–73.

Couper-Kuhlen, E. and Thompson, S. A. (2005) 'A linguistic practice for retracting overstatements: "concessive repairs"', in Hakulinen, A. and Selting, M. (eds.) *Syntax and Lexis in Conversation*, Amsterdam: John Benjamins, 257–88.

Eggins, S. and Slade, D. (1997) *Analysing Casual Conversation*, London: Cassell.

Field, J. (2003) *Psycholinguistics*, London: Routledge.

Halliday, M. A. K. and Hasan, R. (1976) *Cohesion in English*, London: Longman.

Hoey, M. (1983) *On the Surface of Discourse*, London: George Allen and Unwin.

Holmes, J. and Marra, M. (2004) 'Relational practice in the workplace: women's talk or gendered discourse?', *Language in Society* 33 (3): 377–98.

Kangasharju, H. (2002) 'Alignment in disagreement: forming oppositional alliances in committee meetings', *Journal of Pragmatics* 34 (10): 1447–71.

Kaur, J. (2009) 'Pre-empting problems of understanding in English as a lingua franca', in Mauranen, A. and Ranta, E. (eds.) *English as a Lingua Franca: Studies and Findings*, Newcastle upon Tyne: Cambridge Scholars Publishing, 107–25.

Kurhila, S. (2003). *Co-constructing Understanding in Second Language Conversation*, Helsinki: University of Helsinki.

Levelt, W. (1989) *Speaking*, Cambridge, MA: MIT.

Lichtkoppler, J. (2007) '"Male. Male." – "Male?"' – "The sex is male." The role of repetition in English as a lingua franca conversations', *Vienna English Working Papers* 16 (1): 39–65 (www.univie.ac.at /Anglistik/views_0701.PDF).

Linell, P. (1982/2005) *The Written Language Bias in Linguistics: Its Nature, Origins, and Transformations*, London: Routledge.

Lonkila, A. (2010) 'Self-repairs in learner English', unpublished MA thesis, Department of English, University of Helsinki.

Marx, S. and Swales, J. M. (2005) 'Announcements of self-repair: "all I'm trying to say is, you're under an illusion"' (www.lsa.umich.edu/eli/micase/kibbitzer.htm).

Mauranen, A. (2002a) '"A good question": expressing evaluation in academic speech', in Cortese, G. and Riley, P. (eds.) *Domain-Specific English: Textual Practices Across Communities and Classrooms*, Frankfurt: Peter Lang, 115–40.

Mauranen, A. (2002b) '"One thing I'd like to clarify ..." Observations of academic speaking', in Nurmi, A. (ed.) *Helsinki English Studies*, vol. II: *Corpora in Today's English Studies* (www.eng.helsinki.fi/hes/).

Mauranen, A. (2006a) ‘Signalling and preventing misunderstanding in English as a lingua franca communication’, *International Journal of the Sociology of Language* 177: 123–50.

Mauranen, A. (2007b) ‘Hybrid voices: English as the lingua franca of academics’, in Fløttum, K., Dahl, T. and Kinn, T. (eds.) *Language and Discipline: Perspectives on Academic Discourse*, Newcastle upon Tyne: Cambridge Scholars Press, 244–59.

Mauranen, A. (2009) ‘Spoken rhetoric: how do natives and non-natives fare?’, in Suomela-Salmi, E. and Dervin, F. (eds.) *Cross-Linguistic and Cross-Cultural Perspectives on Academic Discourse*, Amsterdam: John Benjamins, 199–218.

Pullin Stark, P. (2009) ‘No joke – this is serious! Power, solidarity and humour in Business English as a Lingua Franca (BELF)’, in Mauranen, A. and Ranta, E. (eds.) *English as a Lingua Franca: Studies and Findings*, Newcastle upon Tyne: Cambridge Scholars Publishing, 152–77.

Sinclair, J. and Mauranen, A. (2006) *Linear Unit Grammar*, Amsterdam: John Benjamins.

Skehan, P. (2005) ‘Understanding fluency in second language performance’, paper presented at the IATEFL Conference, 5–9 April 2005, Cardiff.

Tannen, D. (1989) *Talking Voices: Repetition, Dialogue, and Imagery in Conversational Discourse*, Cambridge: Cambridge University Press.

Warren, M. (2006) *Features of Naturalness in Conversation*, Amsterdam: John Benjamins.

Winter, E. (1977) ‘A clause-relational approach to English texts’, *Instructional Science* (Special issue), 6 (1): 1–92.

8 *Applications, implications, and the way ahead*

In this concluding chapter, we look at ELF in relation to the implications of the empirical explorations of the chapters above. To begin with, I shall address questions often asked concerning the practical relevance of investigating ELF, and more generally, the practical consequences of ELF to communication. Secondly, the findings of the preceding chapters are briefly reviewed in view of the theoretical postulates outlined at the outset. And finally, some directions for further research are sketched out in Section 8.4.

What are the practical consequences to the language professions of the better understanding of ELF yielded by its descriptive and theoretical explorations? A telling example of the situations that ordinary English users find themselves in comes from a Finnish IT expert whose company had merged with an Indian IT company a couple of years earlier. The Finnish representative was interviewed in the leading Finnish daily newspaper, and on the whole he was very happy with how the merger had turned out. As regards language, he made the following comment (my translation):

> We had a bit of a problem when they'd call us and we didn't always understand what they said in their Indian accent. We would rather have used email. But that was not working out, because speaking is so important to them. (*Helsingin Sanomat* 20.6.2010)

This is the kind of difficulty many language users report: it is not using English in itself that is the problem, it is the discrepancy between what many foreign-language learners have learned to expect on the basis of their educational experience and the kind of English they encounter in the real world. Clearly, school and university had not prepared the speaker's company for intercultural communication that goes beyond non-natives communicating with members of the 'target culture', which for English mostly means British and American cultures (e.g. Hynninen 2007; Vettorel 2008; Kopperoinen 2011). The same bias can be seen in the Common European Framework of Reference for Languages (CEFR) scales (e.g. Hynninen 2007), which are attuned to success with native speakers in the target culture. Sometimes the consequences of this well-intended but narrow orientation to Standard English can lead to more serious and ethically problematic consequences, as is described by Guido (2008) who investigated asymmetries and miscommunication arising between Nigerian immigrants and Italian welfare officers: the latter's expectations of reasonable ELF was based on their linguistic backgrounds, where second-language varieties from 'outer circle' English did not feature.

Many language professionals need to take ELF use into account in their daily work: language teachers, translators, and interpreters, and all those working with texts for international consumption, such as language editors and drafters of international laws. The teaching profession has been most concerned about ELF, presumably because it is their task to set objectives, guide their students towards the goals, and assess the achievements. Many excellent suggestions for taking ELF into account in teaching have been proposed, some of them based on extensive empirical research into ELF (e.g. Llurda 2004; Seidlhofer 2004; Dewey 2006; Jenkins 2006; Cogo 2007; Ranta 2009). In the present context, potential applications are discussed with academic ELF in mind, in line with the rest of the book.

8.1 Language teaching and testing

From the start, research into English for specific purposes (ESP) and for academic purposes (EAP) has been largely application-oriented, even though it has also branched out into basic research. Descriptive work of the language used in professional communities has underpinned both applications and theoretical interests. Spoken EAP corpora appeared late in the field (see Chapter 3), and the idea was, in line with the study and teaching of written skills, that observing closely what ENL speakers do would yield the best basis for teaching and assessing students with other first languages. In an environment where English is the main language of the university and the community at large, this is an understandable position. From a more global angle it is not. The wide variety of purposes that English is put to in the academic world, for instance in international student and staff mobility, research groups, and research centres, is in effect ELF.

A much-debated issue in the recent wave of internationalisation in the university world is the effectiveness of studying in a foreign language. Despite the mediaeval beginning of universities in Europe, entirely based on Latin which nobody spoke as their first language, or the long tradition of sending students abroad for programmes that were not available in a country that nevertheless needed professionals in the field (e.g. veterinary medicine in some European countries), let alone individuals in search of education to suit their especial interests, the very possibility of successful learning has been questioned. These doubts do not take into account the extensive literature on immersion programmes or CLIL. They have been voiced quite loudly in the Nordic countries (Jansson 2008; Davidsen-Nielsen 2009), where many academics fear for domain loss in their comparatively small national languages (Phillipson 1992, 2003; Zegers & Wilkinson 2005; Haberland et al. 2008; Mortensen & Haberland 2009; Preisler 2009). The two questions of effectiveness of learning in ELF and the threat English poses to small national languages often get mixed up in the debates, but they are really separate issues. It is beyond the scope of this book to go into questions of national language policy, but it is important to keep in mind that the infiltration of English into many domains of life in many non-English-speaking countries is a separate issue from the effectiveness of learning in a foreign language.

The debates aside, available empirical studies show that students do learn from ELF-medium instruction. Among recent studies on English-medium programmes outside English-speaking countries, Suviniitty (2008) found that Master's students of technology achieved the same success rates in their exams after the programme had switched to English as earlier when the programme had been run in their mother tongue. Airey (2009) compared undergraduates in English-taught and Swedish-taught courses in Sweden when their education included both. He found that while many students reported little difficulty in comprehending the contents of what they were taught, fewer questions were asked in English than in Swedish classes. Some first-year students, in particular, appeared to have difficulties in talking about topics related to their studies, and many encountered problems taking notes. However, as students went on with their studies and acquired discipline-specific knowledge and discourse skills, the differences in the language that was the medium of instruction disappeared. Smit (2010) found successful learning of the content matter on the professional programme she investigated in Austria, and noted that students passed their final exams. On the other hand, language and content learning were not so smoothly integrated, and participants assessed the development of their own language proficiency differently depending on what level they had started off with. Similar self-evaluations were found in Shaw et al. (2009) in Denmark and Sweden. In European universities the strongest early fears (Maiworm & Wächter 2002) about the detrimental effects of ELF-medium study programmes on learning have abated in the course of the last few years (Wächter 2008), possibly with increasing experience of such programmes. On the whole, while the debates continue in many places, the use of English as a lingua franca has become accepted as a fact of life in European higher education (e.g. Jakobsen 2009). To quote Wächter (2008): 'While the problem has not changed, Europe's higher education institutions have become accustomed to the communication situation in the international classroom. What once created frustrations is today viewed as a normal condition.'

It is nevertheless not self-evident that learning in English-medium instruction is equally successful in all circumstances and for all students – there may be considerable differences in cross-linguistic communication skills among teachers and students. For instance in Arnbjörnsdóttir and Ingvarsdóttir's (forthcoming) study, a third of Icelandic students reported extra effort in coping with English academic texts. Language teachers have an obvious role to play in support programmes, which have been set up in many universities. The crucial questions revolve around our understanding of the role of language in the process: what features and what aspects of language are most important, where do the thresholds lie, and what in the teaching process could we improve to facilitate learning? The ELF situation is not identical to other kinds of bilingual education, and therefore calls for its own research.

Many relevant studies have already been carried out, starting from Jenkins's (2000) study of the phonology of ELF, which helpfully distinguished those features of English phonology that are vital prerequisites for understanding from those that are less important. A vast territory in pronunciation and accent is still unexplored: suprasegmental features may be more important than segmental phenomena (Derwing 2003), and although essential accent intelligibility may be achieved fairly rapidly (Smit 2010), little is known of long-term accommodation. In the receptive role, speakers need to be exposed to a variety of accents, so as to avoid the kinds of difficulties illustrated in the example at the beginning of this chapter.

Studies over the last decade have found a few recurrent features of successful ELF communication that can be used as a basis on which to build meaningful pedagogical approaches. Among them, the preceding chapters have brought to the fore certain processes that have a bearing on developing pedagogy. The first thing to keep in mind is that the small number of misunderstandings that happen in ELF talk means that speakers by and large are able to take steps towards overcoming them spontaneously. The pronounced orientation towards cooperation that many researchers have noticed (see also Chapters 6 and 7) probably plays a role in bringing this about, and cooperative strategies may be worth emphasising in teaching English for international communication. Some speakers seem particularly adroit at accommodating to their interlocutors' speech – how much this varies between individuals is not clear, and even though accommodation theory (Gallois et al. 2005) tends to see this in terms of choices that reflect participants' relations to each other, individual variation may be more fundamental than that (see Chapter 2). To what extent accommodation is a teachable skill is uncertain.

A number of successful communication strategies relate to recipient design. Many of them are tactics that can most likely be taught, and at the very least awareness of them can be raised; where awareness-raising is enough and where actual practice should be provided needs careful analysis and empirical study. As was seen in Chapters 6 and 7, clarity and transparency are enhanced by explicitation, which takes many forms. Using discourse devices like metadiscourse, topic negotiation, tails, repetition, and rephrasing facilitate mutual intelligibility and can be taught as important communication skills. Moreover, clarity is not merely an end in itself, but as the use of these linguistic means shows, it is an important component in supporting interpersonal cooperation. The same means that boost intelligibility are considerate towards interlocutors, and some are quite flexible in serving a number of purposes in the management of interaction, like metadiscourse or rephrasing. Some pragmatic devices like hedging or back-channelling and minimal token responses serve primarily interactional needs, and all of the linguistic means can serve rhetorical purposes. Virtually all of these should be teachable. In a university context, they should be incorporated in language support for both teachers and students in English-medium courses. To support teachers, particular emphasis should be laid on cooperative and interactional methods in teaching. If the focus is on correcting lecturers' lexis, grammar, and pronunciation towards Standard English, the danger is that this leads to preparing lectures to be read aloud. This in turn minimises interaction and in effect reduces the chances that mutual intelligibility is achieved.

Testing and evaluation of proficiency is one of the key areas where ELF gives rise to a need to re-think objectives and practices. Assessment of language skills is carried out increasingly for environments where English is an international language in non-English-speaking matrix cultures. Such circumstances pose new demands for assessment because the highest levels of proficiency cannot be defined by simply pointing to an 'educated native speaker' or a 'near-native' level, as is traditional (even in the CEFR): the highest achievement level needs to be defined explicitly, and this is much harder. The field needs not only to embrace a new ideal, such as the 'educated speaker of English' without strings to nativeness, but also to spell out what this accomplished speaker should be able to do. The highest achievement in English cannot possibly be 'native-likeness' outside Anglo-American environments, but those features that make a 'good communicator' in today's world. It is no longer the monolingual native speaker, but more likely to be someone who can leap from one language or one mode to another, who can take advantage of a wide repertoire of linguistic and non-linguistic means, make quick shifts, and adjust his or her tactics according to the demands of a novel situation. Intercultural sensitivity and adaptation skills are crucial in successful communication in a globalised world, and more often than not they bear no reference to Anglo-American cultural presuppositions.

A second requirement is that assessment should not be left to the hands of ENL evaluators. They may not need to be excluded completely, but they cannot play the role hitherto assigned to them as the sole or ultimate judges of correctness and appropriateness. Appropriateness is particularly unsuitable for ENL assessment, because they are often monolingual and thereby bound to their linguistic and cultural backgrounds. What works best for an international context can be a very different matter from what is appropriate in an ENL perspective.

A corollary of moving towards international proficiency is that language testing should take place in interaction: the speakers to be evaluated for spoken proficiency should be observed as full participants with other international speakers. Interviews with native speakers (or even non-native ones) are not able to reveal speakers' communicative capacity in roles they will have to take in the reality of complex international communication. Assessing individual performance in isolation is becoming dated in any case, but it is particularly ill-fitting in ELF contexts and in academia: academic life is one of cooperation and interaction, and for successful participation in education or research, individually measured speaking ability does not serve the purpose.

8.2 Other language professions: interpreting, translation, and text editing

Interpreters are an important group of language professionals whose work conditions are greatly affected by ubiquitous ELF. Since international conferences are increasingly carried out in ELF, the need for conference interpreting is reduced. The same tendency to use ELF where interpreting might be an option is observable in the business world (see e.g. Kankaanranta & Louhiala-Salminen 2010) and among people working for the EU in Brussels (Kriszan & Erkkilä 2010). Another trend that shapes the profession in Europe is increasing relay interpreting, occasioned by the expansion of the EU. This relates to interpreters' use of their different working languages. Interpreters normally have a main working language, 'B language' (AIIC 2010) in addition to their mother tongue ('A language'), and one or more minor working languages ('C languages'). A recent development is that interpreters work bi-actively (Melchers & Shaw 2003) into their B language as well as into their A language. This goes against the traditional tenet, which held that interpreters and translators should only translate into their mother tongue. In smaller languages, such as the Scandinavian languages, Dutch, or Finnish, this has always been the reality, in contrast to German or French. The new demands on interpreters in larger languages are experienced as causing extra difficulty by interpreters themselves: they need to cope with a greater variety of accents and other non-native features, as they interpret a colleague's B language output. This came out in Albl-Mikasa's (forthcoming) study, which also found out that interpreters feel a need to accommodate to their non-native audiences in many ways. Both receptive and productive conditions are therefore altered. The interpreter's traditional professional expertise relies heavily on a native-like proficiency in his or her B languages, and the new demands requiring a broader repertoire of skills have a less clear impact on the future of the profession: will interpreters of the traditional kind become a 'luxury item', as many of them seem to fear? Or, alternatively, will there be demand for interpreters as language professionals who fit the description of the good communicator of the future, a plurilingual, adaptive, effective speaker?

Insofar as interpreters will be needed in the future, and clearly they will be in demand for a number of different purposes given the present-day rates of mobility and immigration in a heavily globalised world, their education must respond to the altered conditions. Community interpreting, including forensic interpreting, is likely to gain ground, and increasingly complex combinations of languages and cultures will require relay interpreting. It is crucial that interpreters develop proficiency in dealing with 'unusual' accents and expressions, which they currently report to be causing extra stress for them (Albl-Mikasa forthcoming). They will also need to learn good strategies of simplifying their own speech, which they, like most speakers, do spontaneously, but probably not everyone has equal natural talent in simplifying in a relevant way; therefore including such skills in professionals' education should pay off in increased effectiveness. It seems clear that interpreters also need to widen their cultural repertoires considerably as a consequence of ELF: the idea of a 'target culture' of native speakers is losing its relevance just as it is in teaching.

Large-scale use of ELF has altered the work of translators and text editors. Translations made for international consumption, such as user's manuals, software, and institutional documents usually go through two stages: an internationalisation process where they are translated or originally written for an international forum, and a localisation process which involves translation and adaptation for users in a particular region. The internationalisation process lays the foundation for the next step, and must cater for a wide range of users anywhere in the world. The same is true of technical communication (e.g. Suojanen 2002). In these domains successful professional work depends on an understanding of what makes texts comprehensible and clear for a wide international audience. Recent findings by Biber and Gray (2010) challenge many of our received assumptions on complexity in speech and writing, with implications for communicating in ELF yet to be explored. Whatever these turn out to be, it is clear that research in ELF needs to inform the development of translator and technical communicator education.

Text professionals who actually work in the academic domain, such as language revisers and science editors, try to help authors in making texts clear and effective. The tradition in this field has been very strongly based on the idea that 'good writing' equals 'good English', and ENL speakers have been seen as the natural resource to be called in to revise texts of academics from other language backgrounds (Ventola & Mauranen 1991; Mauranen 1997). Ventola and Mauranen discovered that language revisers mainly corrected lexicogrammatical errors, but did not touch textual organisation or pragmatic aspects, even if these showed culture-specific influences that deviated from Anglo-American preferences. Revisers justified this on the basis that they did not wish to interfere with the writer's preferred way of presenting themselves, and because they believed the writers knew what they were doing rhetorically (Mauranen 1997). This would in itself seem to be a fairly good strategy for an ELF-using world, since it seems that on several culture-specific textual features, it is Anglo-Americans who are the exception, and many other cultures have different preferences (for an overview see Swales & Feak 2000). Very similar things have been found among science editors, a profession that, like that of language revisers, is very much oriented to ENL speakers (see e.g. Burrough-Boenisch 2004, 2006).

Work in contrastive rhetoric (for an overview see Connor 1996) has convincingly shown that our textual practices and preferences develop in our socialisation into a particular culture of writing. Since writing cultures vary, there is no universal standard of 'good writing'. Least of all can we say that Anglo-American rhetorical preferences would be better suited to academic writing than other cultural text norms, as already discussed in Chapter 3. Clearly, science as an inherently and traditionally international enterprise has no natural link to any national culture; its centres have moved from place to place over the centuries. Thus, although educated native speakers undoubtedly have an excellent command of Standard English grammar and lexis, it does not follow that their stylistic or rhetorical preferences are superior to those of scientists who use a second language in their professional lives. When English is written for a worldwide audience, criteria for good rhetoric or effective text organisation may be quite different from those required in writing for a British or American audience. Anglo-American rhetoric is not necessarily the most effective, comprehensible, or 'natural' choice for structuring academic texts even if we use English. It goes without saying that it is not more 'scientific'.

Even though written text tends to be more conservative and resistant to change than speech, striving for clarity and effectiveness in a global community of academics means having to adapt to the real readership, not an ideal native-speaker reader. As things stand, non-native speakers of English often feel disadvantaged in academic publishing (Flowerdew 2001; Hewings 2006; Ammon & Carli 2007).[1] It is necessary to set this straight and acknowledge the hybridity of the discourses in academia (Mauranen et al. 2010b), the mix of Anglo-American and local discursive norms and preferences. It is in the interests of progress in research that the vast majority of researchers do not get sidelined by the minority who use their native language in publication. Academic authors need to raise their awareness of the kind of English that serves them best when they look for international recognition. Similarly, language editors and revisers, as an influential group in dealing with textual preferences, need to make informed choices about the advice they give their clients – which is not that they should sound as Anglo-American as possible. The new modes of online publishing are undoubtedly working faster for ELF than would any educational programme; digital media is changing writing (see e.g. Myers 2010), and academic communities adapt to that.

There are, of course, many other people who use ELF at work and need solid evidence on what works best in international communication, such as pilots, customs officers, medical practitioners, legislators, and people in many kinds of service work, from taxi drivers to hairdressers. We have been concerned with university discourses in this book, therefore the expanding ELF needs in the labour market touch our present orientation mainly indirectly, via language education. To ensure relevant teaching for these increasingly international groups implies that the education of language teachers at universities needs to take ELF on board. ELF for professional and vocational purposes is a field worth developing in teacher education; teaching English for communication with ENL speakers is not a primary goal for large parts of the world.

As ELF gains ground in international communication, the intercultural perspective comes increasingly to the fore – cultures and languages in contact influence each other, in immediate contact situations as well as in the longer term, as manifest in linguistic and cultural change. The future belongs to the good communicator, the flexible plurilingual individual who can adapt to ELF circumstances: accommodate and converge, and adapt to variability, to live with a more varied selection of English lects than has been customary for second-language users. This turns the tables on many native speakers – they may end up as not having the upper hand, and in fact find themselves at a disadvantage. Many ELF speakers, on the other hand, have considerable experience of communicating with others who do not share their linguistic background, and this gives them an edge over those who have been treading on familiar ground.

8.3 Key points on ELF

This book has been looking into ELF, describing it as second-order language contact between similects arising from first-order contacts between English and a good proportion of the world's other languages. As discussed throughout, ELF thrives in complex, multilingual communities and networks, which generate linguistically intriguing features in lexis, structure, phraseology, and discourse. A central thread in this fabric has been the influence that ELF might have on English as a whole, and how English might change as a consequence. It is almost axiomatic in studies of language change that we cannot predict it, but it is also true, as Milroy (2003: 146) observes, that 'we have a great deal of evidence that suggests that some types of change are more likely and more frequent than others'. ELF adds extra uncertainty to the usual difficulty, because we do not know in which respects the processes observed in earlier research on language change are valid. We could nevertheless venture some suggestions on the basis of what the empirical chapters give rise to.

Starting from the very general assumption that the speed of change is different in different layers or systems of language, the impact of earlier findings on ELF is indeterminate. Mostly, a hierarchy of influence has been suggested where lexis is affected to a greater degree and at a faster rate than structures, but in the case of second-language learners, the major and first-occurring cross-linguistic influence is structural (Thomason 2001: 64). In this view, structural influence in ELF is just as likely as lexical.

The hypotheses posited specifically for ELF at the outset of this book (Chapter 2) started from the three perspectives that were chosen as the point of departure intended to cross-illuminate the language of lingua franca communication: the macrosocial, the cognitive, and the microsocial. It was assumed that frequent similect encounters would lead to enhanced transparency: grammatical simplicity, lexical complexity, and explicitness in discourse. It turned out that all the features were more multifarious and more intricately intertwined than background assumptions would have led us to believe, but that at a general level some support was found for all the hypotheses. Still, it is the variegated nature of each that is of more interest than confirmation of what could be expected.

To begin with grammar, structural simplification was found, most clearly in regularised morphology. Yet simplicity was not straightforward: wider, but not random, variability was found in comparison to ENL. Moreover, non-standard structures were not necessarily simple. They could be quite complex, or simplicity was not a relevant basis of comparison. The most noticeable difference from ENL was far greater structural fluctuation, even in one speaker's use, suggesting weaker structural entrenchment. Many structural features also show affinities with non-standard dialect features and with World Englishes of the postcolonial varieties (see also Ranta 2006, 2009, forthcoming). The forms that grammatical complexity takes in ELF should become easier to investigate on a larger scale with tagged ELF corpora; the findings on academic ELF will be very interesting to compare to Biber's findings on structural differences between spoken and written ENL academic discourse (Biber & Gray 2010). For similar comparisons in ELF, we will need written corpora to be compiled.

The second hypothesis concerned lexical complexity. Some support for this came in the proliferation of forms by morphological productivity, which resulted in neologisms as well as approximations. However, the main trend went right against this hypothesis: lexis seemed to concentrate on the most common words. A very similar phenomenon was discernible as has been noted in translations, namely the tendency of the most frequent words to be proportionally even more frequent. Taken together, these findings suggest that language contact strengthens 'core' vocabulary at the expense of rarer words. Comparing this with the historical 'megatrend' of the most frequent word groups being the most stable (Pagel et al. 2007; Pagel 2009) further solidifies the interpretation that frequent words are extremely robust and central to communication. As a small number of the most frequent words also accounts for most running text, the general picture of communication by lexis is sharpened by these ELF findings: communication is secured by recycling the same central vocabulary over and over again, both in unfolding discourse and in language as an abstract, collectively stored system. The most common vocabulary contains few lexical words, and any conclusions that might be drawn on the more distinct clustering of the most frequent items at the top of the distribution curves needs to take this into account: such 'simplification' need not imply general lexical impoverishment, but it may retain equal or greater variability among rare lexical words.

The central word types in the stable evolutionary groups were represented in ELFA, as expected. In ENL, spoken data was far more clustered on the most frequent words than a written text corpus used for comparison.

The other major process observed in the use of lexis was approximation, which produced items that are close enough to the target to be recognisable but not quite standard. In addition, a number of individual findings made it very clear that internal differentiation within lexis is considerable and shows a variety of tendencies in ELF; distinctions that obtain, for example, between grammatical, closed-class words, and lexical open-class words are vital, so are words in their interactional vs. referential functions, and there is still a vast territory to be covered in examining the behaviours of frequent and infrequent words. Overall comparisons of lexis have their uses, but ELF research must continue to address lexis differentially, to arrive at a better understanding of lexical processes from several angles.

The third general prediction for ELF concerned enhanced explicitness. The hypothesis was based on earlier research in contrastive rhetoric and translation studies as well as on ELF itself. It is a prominent characteristic of ELF, and was supported in many different ways: metadiscourse, anticipatory markers of local organisation, negotiating topics, rephrasing, and echoing were the main phenomena taken up and observed in their role of making discourse more explicit. Explicitness has many beneficial effects on communication between speakers with different backgrounds. For co-constructing shared knowledge, or 'content', it helps keep track of topics and gives clues to hearers to work on. Echoing whole phrases, for instance, is less ambiguous than pronominal references. From an interactional angle, forms of explicitation also serve the negotiation of concepts, cooperative solving of language problems, and doing facework. Echoing can indicate affiliation, and together with other signals of listenership such as backchannelling it contributes to the common ground that speakers need to construct. In brief, explicitation facilitates negotiation of interpretations – or 'matching speaker perspectives' – which may be a more arduous task in lingua francas than in conversations where speakers share more social and cultural assumptions.

In terms of processing, it looks as if explicitation such as repetition serves similar purposes in making processing a more palatable task to both speakers and hearers. For example, false starts tend to concentrate in turn-initial positions, where planning and processing loads intensify for both interactional and content-related concerns. The initial repetitions and rephrases give everyone a chance to prepare for what is going to be said next – while in interactional terms, hesitations in themselves serve important purposes. ENL and ELF should not differ in this, but there may be a need for more breathing spaces in ELF. Therefore the greater incidence of hesitations and repeats, very clear in ELFA, helps communication along. It may not be a good idea to dismiss it as 'dysfluency' or a problem; in the bigger picture, communication may become more fluent because the micro-level placeholders, hesitations, and false starts serve a useful purpose.

The final general hypothesis postulated in Chapter 2 was that speakers adapt to ELF circumstances by means of such interactional processes as accommodating and converging. These are basic building blocks in conversation that are also observed in language and dialect contact. Ample evidence was found to support both. It was nevertheless also hypothesised that an important ELF process would be adapting to variability. This is not directly testable with either corpus linguistic or discourse analytic means, but it remains a good hypothesis, which in principle would go a long way towards explaining the generally observable achievement of adequate mutual understanding in ELF. Evidence for or against this can best be gleaned from long-term investigation, and observations in Smit's (2010) study already seem to suggest that this might be the case. Hakala (forthcoming) takes this on board in his longitudinal study on ELF accents. There are various grounds for assuming that variability is normal in language, as any big picture of a natural language is able to show. Among other things it is quite common for new forms to establish themselves in language while old ones linger on as alternatives, sometimes for centuries (e.g. Hopper & Traugott 2003). A language also fosters different means of expressing similar meanings, making use of grammatical means, closed-class items, and open-class lexis, as Winter's (1977) 'Vocabularies 1, 2, and 3' show in contemporary Standard English.

Some more specific hypotheses were also put forward. ELF speakers were expected to approximate Standard English forms in their speech; this approximation should facilitate processing economy and improve chances of achieving comprehension in a rough-and-ready manner. Approximation turned out to be a ubiquitous phenomenon, as mentioned in connection with lexis; it was observable in every transcript and in different subsystems of the language.

Processing shortcuts for facilitating economy and fluency, such as multi-word sequences, were assumed to be similar to those that people use in their first languages. This was borne out in the large numbers of phraseological sequences that were discovered, many of them approximations, but the most common ones were very similar indeed to ENL. It is plausible that conventionalised phraseological sequences arise from processing motives and that they loosen up in SLU, largely on account of approximation processes and lesser entrenchment. They seem to work successfully in interaction despite their approximate nature. With such positive feedback to users, their non-standard forms are likely to survive, be strengthened, and possibly diffused via processes like accommodation. Their cognitive origin thus passes through interaction to macrosocial reality. In this respect we can expect speakers using ELF to engage in essentially similar processing to anyone in their first languages; for instance, what we saw happening in echoing (Chapter 4) other conversationalists' lexical items or multi-word units relates directly to the (ostensibly ENL-related) dispute concerning the roles of syntactic priming (Pickering & Garrod 2004; Gries 2005) vs. repetition of lexical forms (Howes et al. 2010) as a means of alignment in conversation. It would seem that investigating lexis and in particular phraseology in ELF would be a good way forward in taking this further.

An intriguing observation concerning multi-word sequences was that entirely or virtually identical expressions were found in environments where different speakers with different language backgrounds were using them independently of each other. These parallel developments of patterns indicate that ELF is a source of innovation with potential to influence the future of English. Phraseological sequences are a key element in language change, and ELF offers an excellent opportunity of tracking their progression. Phraseology straddles lexis and grammar; in this phraseological sequences are closely akin to calquing, which has been implicated as a conduit for structural influence of one language on another. 'Lexico-syntactic calquing' (Silva-Corvalan 1998) is an important means by which indirect structural diffusion takes place, as a consequence of lexical or pragmatic borrowing (Winford 2003). As lexical phrases are borrowed, their structural baggage comes along.

Altogether, academic ELF is very much like Standard English: the overwhelming majority of lexis, phraseology, and structures are indistinguishable from those found in a comparable corpus of educated ENL, including their frequency distributions. This comes out very clearly in corpus comparisons. Yet our everyday experience of ELF speech is that it is immediately recognisable and easily distinguishable from ENL speech. One explanation could of course be the exclusion of phonology from the present investigations, but even the transcripts, normalised for deviant pronunciation, are unmistakably not ENL. Why is this? The most obvious reasons are relatively minor infidelities of form, which manifest themselves in approximations, rephrasings, and non-standard syntax, together with apparent dysfluencies in execution, such as frequent repeats, hesitations, and pauses. The less obvious reasons relate to syntagmatic relationships: the standard forms in both n-gram sequences and lexical frequencies are most common, but the larger patterns and structures they enter into are far rarer, and new, emerging regularities do not show up among the top frequency items. Thus it is above all preference patterns that are changing in ELF use, and this is a slower process. Three generations were postulated as the likely timescale on which changes would be clearly in evidence. The systematicity in new forms is partly reflected in the structural similarities with non-standard dialect features, post-colonial World Englishes, and other second-language varieties, and learner language. Communication across Englishes is possible on the strength of the shared linguistic resources together with skilful communication practices. The shared language resources pass largely unnoticed because they are taken for granted, but they are there.

8.4 The way ahead

We have discussed English as a lingua franca in terms of 'second-order language contact', which takes place between similects, i.e. the lects that arise from speakers with a shared first-language background. This is unusually complex language contact, and on a scale that is unprecedented. The linguistic consequences are not easy to predict, but they open up intriguing questions. Does exceptionally complex contact lead to complex language? Or on the contrary to unforeseen simplicity? Complexity and simplicity are important issues in future ELF research. It is likely that different systems are differently affected – and it looks as though some key areas, lexis in particular, would benefit from more differentiated research approaches.

A fundamental question is what aspects of processing are involved in lingua franca speech that distinguish it from 'ordinary' speaking between same-language speakers. No doubt many factors contribute to this, many of them culture-bound in one way or another, but a point of interest to linguists is that language probably assumes a more central role in lingua franca encounters than in environments of same-language communication. In the absence of much shared cultural and other world knowledge, communication depends to a greater degree on the successful handling of shared linguistic resources.

A key linguistic element on the basis of the present investigation lies in the way phraseological sequences take shape and instigate change in English. They combine lexical and structural elements, and straddle the three perspectives that constitute the backbone of our exploration of ELF.

From an interactional point of view, 'matching speaker perspectives' is the central concept that helps understand, and perhaps explain, the nature of lingua franca communication and how that shapes linguistic structures. Lingua franca speakers probably need to put in extra effort to achieve a sufficient level of successful communication, and securing this moulds the language. It is also a point where educational systems need to revise their approaches most: to impart useful communication skills, an understanding of the multifarious perspectives embodied in a global language is a vital challenge.

One of the clearest phenomena that have come up repeatedly in the analyses is that processing and interaction are intimately connected: things that appear to confer processing advantages seem to benefit both speakers and hearers. In other words, as participants alternate in speaker and hearer roles they draw on similar interactional processes. Most, possibly all, of the observed features served speakers and hearers equally well. It may seem unexpected, given that the separateness of the two perspectives has been emphasised in psycholinguistic and cognitive studies, but it is certainly worth exploring further.

For example, not only is the strong explicitation tendency in ELF an interactional success strategy facilitating cooperation; it probably also helps non-standard forms to survive and diffuse. Explicit discourse strategies support top-down processing: they facilitate prospection, which helps listeners make efficient guesses and reduces the pressure placed on speakers to be accurate in their execution. It is easier for the speaker to take risks with exact pronunciation or the forms of individual items. The more use that interlocutors can make of top-down processing, the less chance there is that individual slightly misshaped items will hamper communication.

A phenomenon that cut across the three perspectives is frequency. It has recently been shown to play a crucial role in the evolution of vocabulary, to account for differences in language-internal patterning, and to be implicated in speakers' processing speed and accuracy. Frequent encounters with the same items have been evoked in explaining the maintenance of complex forms in close-knit communities and in long-term accommodation, leading to new dialect acquisition. Unlike many ELF phenomena, frequency is not observable directly in interaction, although interaction is where frequencies get reproduced and thereby established. Observing frequent items requires large quantities of data. There is very much more that we can find out by taking frequency on board. Corpus data is crucial in this, and fortunately becoming more and more widely available. Written ELF corpora would be particularly welcome at this stage. They could help address some basic issues concerning ELF. In the comparison here, the differences in most frequent lexis were far greater between ENL speech and writing than between ENL speech and ELF speech. To understand the import of lingua franca use, it would be vital to include the written mode; the chance to plan carefully and to revise taps the user's resources quite differently, and to assess the potential impact of lingua franca use on English and its future will need data from written text to complement the speech data we already have.

ELF research is a multi-faceted domain. A number of threads lead to related fields of inquiry. The first is collaboration with the study of global Englishes of all kinds – what common trends are to be discerned, and what changes under way? How much can we see of 'vernacular universals', and are there important points at which communities of native speakers and those of non-native speakers part company with respect to them? Such research collaboration would help gain the big picture of the different strains of change that are going on in English in today's globalised world.

The second collaborative promise no doubt relates to learner language: findings from learner corpora, in particular, give valuable insights into commonalities between learner English and English in authentic second language use, and the comparing of notes should continue. Cross-linguistic influence is relevant to both, connecting, as it does, learners and users at the cognitive level.

A third thread leads to the study of other lingua francas. In addition to the ubiquity of English, a major linguistic consequence of globalisation is the enormous increase in language contact: with so much mobility and immigration, virtually any language, however local or small, can serve as a lingua franca between groups of immigrants or foreign workers. The implications to theoretical modelling of lingua francas are considerable: how general are our observations, and how much dependent on specifics of language typology or social determinants of the communicative situation?

Finally, and above all, there is the study of ELF in its own right: in this expanding field new questions present themselves constantly. The work that has been completed so far has been very much attuned to ELF in social interaction. This is undoubtedly the centre of interest in a field seeking to capture change in the making, and looking into human communication in one of its most central forms: talking to 'the other' – speakers who may have widely different experiences of life and cultural expectations, but who share enough linguistic resources to be able to achieve communication. Language as the shared resource gains particular weight – and consequently has a heavier burden to carry – under these circumstances.

Many other things that deserve investigation in ELF could be raised. It would nevertheless be a very long list, and still probably leave many important questions not only unanswered but unasked. The field is changing fast, and in a few years it is going to look very different from the way it does today. Research into ELF has only just begun.

Note

1. However, see Swales and Leeder (2012) for evidence that L2 speakers of English can get published and cited to a notable extent in international journals.

References

AIIC (2010) *Directory*, Geneva: International Association of Conference Interpreters.

Airey, J. (2009) *Science, Language and Literacy: Case Studies of Learning in Swedish University Physics*, Uppsala: Acta Universitatis Upsaliensis.

Albl-Mikasa, M. (forthcoming) 'Interpreting quality in times of English as a lingua franca (ELF): new variables and requirements', in Zybatow, L., Petrova, A. and Ustaszewski, M. (eds.) *Translationswissenschaft trifft Theorie*, Frankfurt am Main: Peter Lang.

Ammon, U. and Carli, A. (eds.) (2007) *Linguistic Inequality in Scientific Communication Today.* Special issue of the *AILA Review* 20.

Arnbjörnsdóttir, B. and Ingvarsdóttir, H. (forthcoming) 'ELF in academia: the effects of simultaneous parallel code use on students' learning'.

Biber, D. and Gray, B. (2010) 'Challenging stereotypes about academic writing: complexity, elaboration, explicitness', *Journal of English for Academic Purposes* 1 (19): 2–20.

Burrough-Boenisch, J. (2004) *Righting English that Has Gone Dutch*, Voorburg: Kemper Conseil.

Burrough-Boenisch, J. (2006) 'Negotiable acceptability: reflections on the interactions between language professionals in Europe and NNS scientists wishing to publish in English', *Current Issues in Language Planning* 7 (1): 31–44.

Cogo, A. (2007) 'Intercultural communication in English as a lingua franca: a case study', unpublished PhD thesis, King's College London.

Connor, U. (1996) *Contrastive Rhetoric*, Cambridge: Cambridge University Press.

Davidsen-Nielsen, N. (2009) 'Danish under pressure: use it or lose it', in Harder, P. (ed.) *English in Denmark: Language Policy, Internationalization and University Teaching*, Copenhagen: Museum Tusculanum Press, University of Copenhagen, 138–40.

Derwing, T. (2003) 'What do ESL students say about their accents?' *The Canadian Modern Language Review* 59 (4): 547–66.

Dewey, M. (2006) 'English as a lingua franca: an empirical study of innovation in lexis and grammar', unpublished PhD thesis: King's College London.

Flowerdew, J. (2001) 'Attitudes of journal editors to non-native-speaker contributions: an interview study', *TESOL Quarterly* 35: 121–50.

Gallois, C., Ogay, T. and Giles, H. (2005) 'Communication accommodation theory: a look back and a look ahead', in Gudykunst, W. B. (ed.) *Theorizing About Intercultural Communication*, London: SAGE, 121–48.

Gries, S. (2005) 'Syntactic priming: a corpus-based approach', *Psycholinguistic Research* 34 (4): 365–99.

Guido, M. G. (2008) *English as a Lingua Franca in Cross-Cultural Immigration Domains*, Frankfurt: Peter Lang.

Haberland, H., Mortensen, J., Fabricius, A., Preisler, B., Risager K. and Kjaerbeck, S. (eds.) (2008) *Higher Education in the Global Village,* Department of Culture and Identity, Roskilde University.

Hakala, H. (forthcoming) 'Accent accommodation in ELF speech: how and why?', PhD thesis, University of Helsinki.

Hewings, M. (2006) 'English language standards in academic articles: attitudes of peer reviewers', *Revista Canaria de Estudios Ingleses* 53: 47–62.

Hopper, P. and Traugott, E. (2003) *Grammaticalization* (2nd edn), Cambridge: Cambridge University Press.

Howes, C. Healey, P. G. T. and Purver, M. (2010) 'Tracking lexical and syntactic alignment in conversation', paper presented at the annual meeting of the Cognitive Science Society, *CogSci 2010*, Portland, OR, August 2010 (www.eecs.qmul.ac.uk~mpurver/papers/howes-et-al10cogsci.pdf).

Hynninen, N. (2007) 'Cultural discourses in CEF: how do they relate to ELF?', unpublished MA thesis, University of Helsinki (www.helsinki.fi/elfa).

Jakobsen, A. S. (2009) '"Ellers er det bare lige ud af landevejen": en interviewundersøgelse af ti underviseres holdninger til og erfaringer med engelsksproget undervisning ved det Biovidenskabelige Fakultet (LIFE)', unpublished MA thesis, University of Copenhagen.

Jansson, E. (2008) 'Vetenskapsengelska – med många frågetecken', in Jansson, E. (ed.) *Vetenskapsengelska – med svensk kvalitet?*, Stockholm: Språkrådet, 5–13.

Jenkins, J. (2000) *The Phonology of English as an International Language*, Oxford: Oxford University Press.

Jenkins, J. (2006) 'Current perspectives on teaching World Englishes and English as a lingua franca', *TESOL Quarterly* 40 (1): 157–81.

Kankaanranta, A. and Louhiala-Salminen, L. (2010) '"English? – Oh, it's just work!": a study of BELF users' perceptions', *English for Specific Purposes* 29 (3): 204–9.

Kopperoinen, A. (2011) 'Accents of English as a lingua franca: a study of Finnish textbooks', *International Journal of Applied Linguistics* 21 (1): 71–93.

Kriszan, A. and Erkkilä, T. (2010) 'Multilingualism among Brussels based civil servants and lobbyists: perceptions, practices and power positions', unpublished project report, Network of European Studies, University of Helsinki.

Llurda, E. (2004) 'Non-native-speaker teachers and English as an International Language', *International Journal of Applied Linguistics* 14 (3): 314–23.

Maiworm, F. and Wächter, B. (2002) *English Language Taught Degree Programmes in European Higher Education*, ACA Papers on International Cooperation in Education, Bonn: Lemmens Verlagsund Mediengesellschaft.

Mauranen, A. (1997) 'Hedging and modality in revisers' hands', in Markkanen, R. and Schröder, H. (eds.) *Hedging and Discourse: Approaches to the Analysis of a Pragmatic Phenomenon*, Berlin: de Gruyter, 115–33.

Mauranen, A., Perez-Llantada C. and Swales, J. (2010b) 'Academic Englishes: a standardized knowledge?', in Kirkpatrick, A. (ed.) *The Routledge Handbook of World Englishes*, London: Routledge, 634–52.

Melchers, G. and Shaw, P. (2003) *World Englishes*, London: Arnold.

Milroy, J. (2003) 'On the role of the speaker in language change', in Hickey, R. (ed.) *Motives for Language Change*, Cambridge: Cambridge University Press, 143–57.

Mortensen, J. and Haberland, H. (2009) 'Sprogvalg På danske universiteter i historisk perspektiv', *Sprogforum* 46: 8–13.

Myers, G. (2010) *The Discourse of Blogs and Wikis*, London: Continuum.

Pagel, M. (2009) 'Human language as a culturally transmitted replicator', *Nature Reviews Genetics* 10: 405–15 (June 2009) (doi:10.1038/nrg2560).

Pagel, M., Atkinson, D. Q. and Meade, A. (2007) 'Frequency of word-use predicts rates of lexical evolution throughout Indo-European history', *Nature* 449 (11): 717–20.

Phillipson, R. (1992) *Linguistic Imperialism*, Oxford: Oxford University Press.

Phillipson, R. (2003) *English-Only Europe? Challenging Language Policy*, London: Routledge.

Pickering, M. and Garrod, S. (2004) 'Toward a mechanistic psychology of dialogue', *Behavioral and Brain Sciences* 27: 169–226.

Preisler, B. (2009) 'Complementary languages: the national language and English as working languages in European universities', in Harder, P. (ed.) *English in Denmark: Language Policy, Internationalization and University Teaching*. Special issue of *ANGLES on the English-Speaking World* 9: 10–28.

Ranta, E. (2006) 'The "attractive" progressive: why use the *-ing* form in English as a lingua franca?', *English as a Lingua Franca*. Special issue of *The Nordic Journal of English Studies* (ed. A. Mauranen and M. Metsä-Ketelä) 5 (2): 95–116.

Ranta, E. (2009) 'Syntactic features in spoken ELF: learner language or spoken grammar?', in Mauranen, A. and Ranta, E. (eds.) *English as a Lingua Franca: Studies and Findings*, Newcastle upon Tyne: Cambridge Scholars Publishing, 84–106.

Ranta, E. (forthcoming) 'Universals in a universal language? Study into the verb-syntactic features of English as a lingua franca', PhD thesis, University of Tampere.

Seidlhofer, B. (2004) 'Research perspectives on teaching English as a lingua franca', *Annual Review of Applied Linguistics* 24: 209–39.

Shaw, P., Caudery, T. and Petersen, M. (2009) 'Students on exchange in Scandinavia: motivation, interaction, ELF development', in Mauranen, A. and Ranta, E. (eds.) *English as a Lingua Franca: Studies and Findings*, Newcastle upon Tyne: Cambridge Scholars Publishing, 178–99.

Silva-Corvalan, C. (1998) 'On borrowing as a mechanism of syntactic change', in Schwegler, A., Tranel, B. and Uribe-Etcxebarria, M. (eds.) *Romance Linguistics: Theoretical Perspectives*, Amsterdam: John Benjamins, 225–46.

Smit, U. (2010) *English as a Lingua Franca in Higher Education*, Berlin: De Gruyter Mouton.

Suojanen, T. (2002) 'Research utilization in Finnish technical communication', in Lewandowska-Tomaszczyk, B. and Thelen, M. (eds.) *Translation and Meaning*, Part 6, Proceedings of the Lodz Session of the Third International Maastricht-Lodz Duo Colloquium on 'Translation and Meaning', 21–24 September 2000, Lodz, Poland, 379–85.

Suviniitty, J. (2008) 'Good, poor, or excellent: students' perception of lecturers' English and comprehension of lectures', in Welsch, F., Malpica, F., Tremante., A., Carrasquero, J. V. and Oropeza, A. (eds.) *The Second International Multi-Conference on Society, Cybernetics and Informatics: Proceedings Volume IV*, Winter Garden, Florida: International Institute of Informatics and Systemics, 187–90.

Swales, J. M. and Feak, C. (2000) *English in Today's Research World: A Writing Guide*, Ann Arbor, MI: The University of Michigan Press.

Swales, J. M. and Leeder, C. (2012) 'A reception study of the articles published in English for Specific Purposes from 1990–1999', *English for Specific Purposes* 31: 137–46.

Thomason, S. G. (2001) *Language Contact*, Edinburgh: Edinburgh University Press.

Ventola, E. and Mauranen, A. (1991) 'Non-native writing and native revising of scientific articles', in Ventola, E. (ed.) *Functional and Systemic Linguistics: Approaches and Uses*, Berlin: Mouton de Gruyter, 457–92.

Vettorel, P. (2008) 'ELF: a possible mediating factor for teaching culture in the language classroom?', paper presented at Esse 9: the Ninth International Conference of the European Society for the Study of English, Aarhus, Denmark, 22–26 August 2008.

Wächter, B. (2008) 'Teaching in English on the rise in European higher education', *International Higher Education* 52: 3–4 (www.bc.edu/bc_org/avp/soe/cihe/newsletter/ihe_pdf/ihe52.pdf).

Winford, D. (2003) *An Introduction to Contact Linguistics*, Oxford: Blackwell.

Winter, E. (1977) 'A clause-relational approach to English texts', *Instructional Science* (Special issue) 6 (1): 1–92.

Zegers, V. and Wilkinson, R. (2005) 'Squaring the pyramid: internationalization, plurilingualism, and the university' (www.palmenia.helsinki.fi/congress/bilingual2005/presentations/zegers.pdf).

Appendix 1: Transcription key

This page contains the basic transcription conventions used in the ELFA corpus for facilitating reading. For more detail, consult ELFA Transcription Guide:
www.helsinki.fi/englanti/elfa/ELFA%20transcription%20guide.pdf

Utterance begins: <S1>
Utterance ends: </S1>

Unidentified speaker: <SU>
Several simultaneous speakers (usually laughter or sth): <SS>

Uncertain transcription: (text)
Unintelligible speech: (xx)

Laughter: @@
Spoken laughing: @text@

Brief pause while speaking 2-3 sec.: ,
Pause 3-4 sec.: .
Pause 5 sec. or longer, rounded up to the nearest sec.: <P: 05>

Overlapping speech (approximate, shown to the nearest word, words not split by overlap tags): [text]
Back-channelling: <S1> mhm </S1>
<S2> okay </S2>

Hesitations
/öö/ er
/(ö)m/ erm
/aa/ ah

Names of participants: <NAME>
Nonsense words: <SIC> text </SIC>
Reading aloud: <READING> text </READING>
Switching into a foreign language: <FOREIGN> text </FOREIGN>

Other events that affect the interpretation or comprehension of what is being said:

<PREPARING OVERHEAD 1:23>
<WRITING ON BLACKBOARD>
<APPLAUSE>
<WHISPERING>
<DISC / TRACK / FILE / CD CHANGE>
<COUGH>
<GASP>

Appendix 2: 200 most frequent words in ELFA and MICASE

This is raw data; neither list has been cleaned up in any way. This solution was adopted even though it creates some problems, mostly on account of different transcription conventions. However, any modification would have run the risk of treating the databases differently and each solution for modifying the lists had its downsides.

The asterisk (*) marks the cut-off point for the items (word types) which cover 50% of the whole data (word tokens) on each list.

ELFA			MICASE		
N	Word	Freq.	N	Word	Freq.
1	THE	51,835	1	THE	77,672
2	ER	42,390	2	AND	47,110
3	AND	31,533	3	YOU	39,959
4	OF	26,884	4	OF	39,764
5	TO	23,023	5	THAT	39,075
6	IN	21,767	6	TO	37,476
7	THAT	18,995	7	A	37,390
8	I	18,342	8	I	36,852
9	IS	17,933	9	IN	26,772
10	YOU	17,553	10	IS	26,601
11	A	17,300	11	IT	25,429
12	THIS	12,446	12	SO	20,258
13	IT	12,281	13	THIS	19,536
14	SO	11,681	14	UM	17,819
15	HAVE	9,305	15	UH	16,675
16	WE	8,971	16	LIKE	14,159
17	BUT	8,802	17	HAVE	13,301
18	ARE	8,680	18	IT'S	13,241
19	FOR	7,966	19	WE	12,944
20	YEAH	7,791	20	WHAT	12,902
21	THEY	7,398	21	BUT	11,950
22	IT'S	7,359	22	KNOW	11,552
23	ERM	6,954	23	OKAY	10,825
24	MHM	6,890	24	FOR	10,523

25	OR	6,494	25	ONE	10,485
26	THERE	5,885	26	THEY	10,260
27	BE	5,750	27	BE	10,217
28	NOT	5,553	28	YEAH	10,100
29	WAS	5,552	29	ON	9,939
30	ON	5,499	30	ARE	9,671
31	WHAT	5,307	31	IF	9,643
32	AS	4,887	32	WAS	9,642
33	IF	4,876	33	JUST	9,404
34	XX	4,853	34	DO	8,893
35	#	4,826	35	OR	8,723
36	CAN	4,822	36	NOT	8,717
37	WITH	4,735	37	THAT'S	8,276
38	THINK	4,524	38	ABOUT	8,144
39	LIKE	4,469	39	RIGHT	8,009
40	THEN	4,388	40	WITH	7,834
41	VERY	4,272	41	CAN	7,387
42	ABOUT	4,219	42	AT	7,308
43	BECAUSE	4,093	43	AS	6,956
*44	ONE	4,043	44	THINK	6,782
45	ALSO	3,994	45	THERE	6,725
46	WHICH	3,941	46	DON'T	6,723
47	SOME	3,906	47	THEN	6,299
48	FROM	3,826	48	ALL	6,033
49	THESE	3,353	49	TWO	5,567
50	AT	3,224	50	XX	5,335
51	KNOW	3,039	51	HERE	5,328
52	WELL	2,997	52	WELL	5,180
53	DO	2,954	53	WOULD	5,056
54	JUST	2,932	54	HOW	4,940
55	YES	2,918	55	NO	4,846
56	MORE	2,889	56	AN	4,792
57	WOULD	2,832	57	GET	4,765
58	ALL	2,715	*58	I'M	4,747
59	HOW	2,591	59	FROM	4,745
60	OKAY	2,574	60	HE	4,730
61	DON'T	2,573	61	THESE	4,663
62	HAS	2,554	62	BECAUSE	4,579
63	THAT'S	2,431	63	MEAN	4,523
64	BY	2,396	64	REALLY	4,438
65	SAY	2,379	65	YOUR	4,331
66	HM	2,294	66	SOME	4,316
67	AN	2,227	67	OUT	4,250

68	KIND	2,173	68	NOW	4,201
69	WILL	2,159	69	GONNA	4,185
70	HERE	2,158	70	SEE	4,172
71	OTHER	2,158	71	OH	4,157
72	NO	2,096	72	YOU'RE	4,152
73	WHEN	2,032	73	WHEN	4,078
74	NOW	1,992	74	UP	4,055
75	PEOPLE	1,965	75	WHICH	4,040
76	REALLY	1,924	76	MORE	3,995
77	SEE	1,907	77	MHM	3,890
78	YOUR	1,894	78	THERE'S	3,785
79	WERE	1,823	79	VERY	3,765
80	DIFFERENT	1,810	80	SAY	3,678
81	MY	1,765	81	PEOPLE	3,570
82	SOMETHING	1,697	82	WERE	3,547
83	MAYBE	1,661	83	OTHER	3,499
84	I'M	1,660	84	BY	3,422
85	TWO	1,631	85	GO	3,395
86	WAY	1,586	86	MY	3,282
87	BEEN	1,567	87	TIME	3,210
88	COULD	1,560	88	SOMETHING	3,175
89	MEAN	1,536	89	ME	3,150
90	ACTUALLY	1,522	90	WHERE	2,998
91	TIME	1,510	91	WAY	2,943
92	MUCH	1,491	92	HAD	2,892
93	ONLY	1,487	93	COULD	2,882
94	HE	1,459	94	HAS	2,880
95	THEIR	1,447	95	THEY'RE	2,880
96	FIRST	1,438	96	THEM	2,860
97	EXAMPLE	1,433	97	THINGS	2,739
98	COURSE	1,419	98	THING	2,645
99	THEM	1,418	99	THOSE	2,643
100	GOOD	1,416	100	KIND	2,613
101	WHERE	1,370	101	S	2,602
102	GET	1,333	102	DID	2,486
103	QUITE	1,315	103	THREE	2,479
104	WHO	1,310	104	WHO	2,473
105	SHOULD	1,291	105	ACTUALLY	2,467
106	USE	1,256	106	WILL	2,444
107	SAME	1,250	107	THEIR	2,423
108	ANY	1,213	108	DIFFERENT	2,394
109	GO	1,210	109	ALSO	2,375
110	HAD	1,205	110	LOOK	2,375

111	IMPORTANT	1,189	111	GOING	2,368
112	THERE'S	1,180	112	GOOD	2,344
113	MANY	1,173	113	WE'RE	2,310
114	EVEN	1,135	114	SHE	2,281
115	THAN	1,134	115	LITTLE	2,258
116	QUESTION	1,071	116	INTO	2,225
117	WHY	1,028	117	MAKE	2,219
118	SYSTEM	1,016	118	CUZ	2,192
119	THINGS	1,015	119	DOES	2,187
120	THOSE	995	120	FIRST	2,178
121	BETWEEN	994	121	WHY	2,162
122	WANT	988	122	GOT	2,142
123	SORT	982	123	OVER	2,126
124	POINT	962	124	POINT	2,093
125	MAKE	959	125	ANY	2,086
126	OUR	954	126	WANT	2,068
127	OUT	931	127	SORT	2,052
128	STILL	927	128	NEED	1,994
129	INTO	906	129	SAME	1,991
130	ME	903	130	WANNA	1,986
131	GOING	902	131	THAN	1,959
132	WORK	895	132	MUCH	1,943
133	SAID	887	133	LOT	1,905
134	THING	882	134	TAKE	1,879
135	PART	849	135	ONLY	1,860
136	MIGHT	845	136	BEEN	1,819
137	COUNTRIES	836	137	OUR	1,797
138	LOOK	832	138	BACK	1,742
139	UP	831	139	DIDN'T	1,698
140	S	830	140	FIVE	1,698
141	CASE	817	141	EVEN	1,674
142	WORLD	814	142	FOUR	1,672
143	FINLAND	808	143	DOESN'T	1,651
144	LOT	806	144	USE	1,646
145	NEW	795	145	SHOULD	1,610
146	FIND	792	146	HIS	1,595
147	DID	789	147	SAID	1,593
148	BIT	788	148	WORK	1,569
149	TAKE	788	149	PART	1,550
150	MOST	787	150	MAYBE	1,537
151	INTERESTING	785	151	PUT	1,525
152	PROBLEM	769	152	N	1,518
153	RIGHT	766	153	C	1,516

154	PER	758	154	THROUGH	1,515
155	RESEARCH	754	155	DOWN	1,496
156	NEED	746	156	WHAT'S	1,476
157	STATE	746	157	CAN'T	1,465
158	SOCIAL	742	158	MIGHT	1,457
159	DEVELOPMENT	713	159	LET'S	1,456
160	LET'S	702	160	D	1,420
161	AFTER	699	161	TALK	1,418
162	LITTLE	674	162	COME	1,417
163	COUNTRY	669	163	DOING	1,403
164	THREE	659	164	YES	1,385
165	SUCH	656	165	ALRIGHT	1,373
166	LEVEL	651	166	HER	1,347
167	SHE	643	167	ANOTHER	1,342
168	ANOTHER	640	168	TOO	1,296
169	INFORMATION	635	169	I'LL	1,264
170	YEARS	635	170	T	1,254
171	USED	634	171	MANY	1,251
172	US	631	172	US	1,250
173	DIDN'T	630	173	STILL	1,246
174	IDEA	614	174	BETWEEN	1,240
175	STUDY	614	175	AGAIN	1,235
176	COME	606	176	BEING	1,231
177	GOVERNMENT	603	177	HE'S	1,220
178	AGAIN	602	178	NUMBER	1,204
179	EDUCATION	600	179	SAYING	1,199
180	MAY	592	180	QUESTION	1,191
181	FINNISH	586	181	GIVE	1,166
182	LEAST	586	182	SURE	1,152
183	SOCIETY	584	183	CLASS	1,141
184	ALWAYS	575	184	B	1,136
185	CENT	569	185	BEFORE	1,134
186	OH	566	186	P	1,120
187	BEFORE	563	187	PROBABLY	1,120
188	KNOWLEDGE	559	188	NEXT	1,101
189	DOES	557	189	MOST	1,100
190	MEANS	551	190	FIND	1,084
191	TALK	546	191	Y	1,084
192	POLITICAL	544	192	TALKING	1,065
193	GIVE	541	193	STUFF	1,054
194	TOO	541	194	R	1,040
195	LAST	534	195	THOUGHT	1,033
196	THROUGH	533	196	H	1,021

197	ALREADY	530	197	WHOLE	1,018
198	E	528	198	OFF	1,013
199	POSSIBLE	522	199	PROBLEM	1,004
200	DOESN'T	518	200	I'VE	1,001

Appendix 3: 50 most frequent keywords in ELFA and MICASE

1. Top 50 KEYWORDS FROM ELFA WITH MICASE AS REFERENCE CORPUS (RC)
(the p value is 0.0000000000 throughout)

N	Keyword	Freq.	%	RC freq.	RC %	Keyness
1	ER	42,390	4.17	40		85,183.64
2	ERM	6,954	0.68	0		13,916.45
3	#	4,826	0.47	258	0.01	7,846.89
4	MHM	6,890	0.68	3,890	0.22	3,249.15
5	HM	2,294	0.23	370	0.02	2,776.76
6	ALSO	3,994	0.39	2,375	0.14	1,749.60
7	YES	2,918	0.29	1,385	0.08	1,695.83
8	FINLAND	808	0.08	3		1,577.06
9	IN	21,767	2.14	26,772	1.54	1,325.64
10	FINNISH	586	0.06	1		1,156.56
11	CENT	569	0.06	5		1,083.63
12	COUNTRIES	836	0.08	129		1,029.22
13	QUITE	1,315	0.13	531	0.03	899.28
14	VERY	4,272	0.42	3,765	0.22	884.39
15	ARE	8,680	0.85	9,671	0.55	841.63
16	RUSSIAN	412	0.04	10		737.40
17	DEVELOPMENT	713	0.07	165		727.17
18	RUSSIA	352	0.03	13		602.69
19	EUROPEAN	460	0.05	60		601.90
20	PER	758	0.07	257	0.01	601.47
21	THE	51,835	5.10	77,672	4.46	584.13
22	TAURINE	287	0.03	0		573.16
23	EDUCATION	600	0.06	159		565.29
24	EU	289	0.03	1		564.73
25	LOCAL	517	0.05	107		559.01
26	COURSE	1,419	0.14	916	0.05	548.23
27	COUNTRY	669	0.07	219	0.01	545.33
28	WHICH	3,941	0.39	4,040	0.23	521.92
29	THERE	5,885	0.58	6,725	0.39	510.28

30	NATIONAL	482	0.05	107		502.70
31	XX	4,853	0.48	5,335	0.31	495.76
32	EXAMPLE	1,433	0.14	994	0.06	490.95
33	SYSTEM	1,016	0.10	588	0.03	461.57
34	DEMOCRACY	264	0.03	12		439.53
35	GOVERNMENT	603	0.06	230	0.01	433.99
36	SECTOR	235	0.02	4		432.32
37	TAMPERE	216	0.02	0		431.36
38	ORGANISATION	213	0.02	0		425.36
39	SOCIAL	742	0.07	358	0.02	422.92
40	POLICY	446	0.04	118		420.58
41	IMPORTANT	1,189	0.12	822	0.05	409.68
42	SOME	3,906	0.38	4,316	0.25	390.49
43	KNOWLEDGE	559	0.05	221	0.01	389.63
44	FOREST	482	0.05	160		388.72
45	BECAUSE	4,093	0.40	4,579	0.26	388.67
46	CENTRE	199	0.02	1		385.73
47	INSTANCE	474	0.05	160		377.36
48	PROGRAMME	186	0.02	0		371.44
49	AND	31,533	3.10	47,110	2.70	363.65
50	OF	26,884	2.64	39,764	2.28	353.68

2. Top 50 KEYWORDS FROM MICASE WITH ELFA AS REFERENCE CORPUS (RC)

N	Keyword	Freq.	%	RC freq.	RC %	Keyness
1	UM	17,819	1.02	0		16,446.11
2	UH	16,675	0.96	179	0.02	13,758.28
3	RIGHT	8,009	0.46	766	0.08	3,701.87
4	GONNA	4,185	0.24	97		3,117.27
5	CUZ	2,192	0.13	0		2,015.83
6	OKAY	10,825	0.62	2,574	0.25	1,987.52
7	KNOW	11,552	0.66	3,039	0.30	1,763.80
8	YOU'RE	4,152	0.24	470	0.05	1,718.09
9	OH	4,157	0.24	566	0.06	1,490.42
10	LIKE	14,159	0.81	4,469	0.44	1,420.46
11	WANNA	1,986	0.11	96		1,239.63
12	WE'RE	2,310	0.13	186	0.02	1,171.78
13	YOU	39,959	2.29	17,553	1.73	1,037.27
14	THAT'S	8,276	0.47	2,431	0.24	993.88
15	JUST	9,404	0.54	2,932	0.29	972.92
16	THEY'RE	2,880	0.17	424	0.04	962.68
17	UP	4,055	0.23	831	0.08	931.97

18	OUT	4,250	0.24	931	0.09	887.26
19	DO	8,893	0.51	2,954	0.29	769.14
20	TWENTY	840	0.05	4		729.44
21	TWO	5,567	0.32	1,631	0.16	671.90
22	ALRIGHT	1,373	0.08	119	0.01	669.85
23	A	37,390	2.14	17,300	1.70	665.74
24	GET	4,765	0.27	1,333	0.13	638.54
25	KINDA	688	0.04	1		619.41
26	N	1,518	0.09	180	0.02	606.91
27	UHUH	655	0.04	0		602.14
28	GUYS	817	0.05	23		586.15
29	C	1,516	0.09	201	0.02	555.32
30	OVER	2,126	0.12	399	0.04	547.67
31	THIRTY	636	0.04	5		536.16
32	ONE	10,485	0.60	4,043	0.40	531.82
33	PERCENT	571	0.03	0		524.91
34	EM	647	0.04	9		517.68
35	HE	4,730	0.27	1,459	0.14	502.28
36	GOT	2,142	0.12	434	0.04	499.66
37	L	941	0.05	69		499.35
38	NINETEEN	541	0.03	1		484.74
39	H	1,021	0.06	93		484.47
40	WHAT	12,902	0.74	5,307	0.52	483.39
41	D	1,420	0.08	221	0.02	449.79
42	THAT	39,075	2.24	18,995	1.87	443.18
43	DOWN	1,496	0.09	250	0.02	440.36
44	STUFF	1,054	0.06	119	0.01	436.50
45	HUNDRED	795	0.05	57		426.25
46	OFF	1,013	0.06	117	0.01	412.78
47	CLASS	1,141	0.07	155	0.02	409.45
48	ME	3,150	0.18	903	0.09	399.47
49	THERE'S	3,785	0.22	1,180	0.12	390.69
50	R	1,040	0.06	138	0.01	380.64

Appendix 4: 25 most frequent three-word sequences in ELFA and MICASE

1. ELFA 3-grams

N	Word	Freq.	Texts
1	I DON'T KNOW	665	104
2	A LOT OF	493	107
3	I THINK THAT	492	94
4	ONE OF THE	487	123
5	AND SO ON	463	89
6	YOU HAVE TO	408	79
7	THERE IS A	389	108
8	I THINK IT'S	365	81
9	THE THE THE	361	75
10	A LITTLE BIT	332	87
11	AND I THINK	327	86
12	AND THIS IS	323	99
13	THIS KIND OF	319	79
14	WOULD LIKE TO	318	94
15	ER I THINK	316	88
16	THIS IS A	316	99
17	IN IN IN	294	73
18	YOU CAN SEE	266	71
19	ER IN THE	264	108
20	IN IN THE	263	96
21	A KIND OF	258	67
22	I WOULD LIKE	257	83
23	THIS IS THE	257	87
24	MHM HM AND	255	43
25	ER ER ER	252	60

2. MICASE 3-grams

N	Word	Freq.	Texts
1	I DON'T KNOW	1,534	133
2	A LOT OF	1,280	139
3	ONE OF THE	803	136
4	A LITTLE BIT	672	134
5	YOU HAVE TO	645	128
6	THIS IS THE	619	129
7	THIS IS A	563	136
8	IN TERMS OF	555	105
9	I DON'T THINK	508	105
10	I THINK THAT	502	93
11	I MEAN I	492	90
12	YOU KNOW WHAT	448	105
13	AND THIS IS	436	119
14	BE ABLE TO	421	119
15	YOU HAVE A	417	115
16	YOU KNOW THE	390	100
17	YOU CAN SEE	375	96
18	PART OF THE	366	110
19	YOU KNOW I	357	94
20	SOME OF THE	356	105
21	I THINK IT'S	353	99
22	SO THIS IS	353	104
23	YOU NEED TO	352	93
24	AND I THINK	348	102
25	AND THEN YOU	336	102

Index